The
Discovery of Childhood
in Puritan England

C. JOHN SOMMERVILLE

The
Discovery of Childhood
in Puritan England

The University of Georgia Press

ATHENS AND LONDON

© 1992 by the University of Georgia Press
Athens, Georgia 30602
All rights reserved

Designed by Kathi L. Dailey
Set in Janson Text by Tseng Information Systems, Inc.
Printed and bound by Thomson-Shore, Inc.
The paper in this book meets the guidelines for
permanence and durability of the Committee on
Production Guidelines for Book Longevity of the
Council on Library Resources.

Printed in the United States of America

96 95 94 93 92   C   5 4 3 2 1

Library of Congress Cataloging in Publication Data

Sommerville, C. John (Charles John), 1938–
The discovery of childhood in Puritan England /
C. John Sommerville.
        p.   cm.
Includes bibliographical references and index.
ISBN 0-8203-1353-X (alk. paper)
1. Children — Great Britain — History — 17th century.
2. Great Britain — Social conditions — 17th century.
I. Title.
HQ792.G7S65   1992
305.23'0942'09032 — dc20   90-23436
                                        CIP

British Library Cataloging in Publication Data available

The illustrations on the title page and chapter opening
pages are from Isaac Watts, *Divine and Moral Songs for
Children: revised and altered so as to render them of General
Use* (1788); courtesy of Rare Book Department,
Free Library of Philadelphia.

FOR EDEN

CONTENTS

Acknowledgments   ix

INTRODUCTION   Children, Historians, and Movements   1

CHAPTER ONE   The Puritan Preoccupation with Children   19

CHAPTER TWO   Puritan Realism in Picturing Children   41

CHAPTER THREE   Childhood in Theory   69

CHAPTER FOUR   Puritan Humor and Entertainment
                  for Children   109

CHAPTER FIVE   Education and Freedom   133

EPILOGUE   Family Feeling versus Puritan Individualism   155

Notes   175

Index   205

ACKNOWLEDGMENTS

I t is a pleasure to remember all those who have offered guidance, encouragement, and support during the long gestation of this project. Aspects of the study were presented at a summer seminar of the William Andrewes Clark Library, the Shelby Collum Davis Center for Historical Studies, the University of Florida President's Scholar Program, and American Historical Association and Southern Historical Association conventions. The author wishes to thank participants at those gatherings for their interest and suggestions, and especially Professors Melvin New, Norman Holland, Herbert Moller, Anthony Grafton, Lawrence Stone, and Stephen Baxter. He is also glad to acknowledge grants from the American Philosophical Society and the University of Florida Humanities Council.

Various journals have kindly given permission to use material that first appeared in their pages. The present chapter 1 is a version of "English Puritans and Children: A Social-Cultural Explanation," *Journal of Psychohistory* 6 (1978): 113–37. Chapter 2 appeared as "Breaking the Icon: The First Real Children in English Books," *History of Education Quarterly* 21 (1981): 51–75. Chapter 4 revises "Puritan Humor, or Entertainment, for Children," *Albion* 21 (1989): 227–47. Chapter 5 first appeared as "The Distinction Between Indoctrination and Education in England, 1549–1719," *Journal of the History of Ideas* 44 (1983): 387–406. The Epilogue reworks material from "The Family Fights Back: Its Struggle with Religious Movements," *Fides et Historia* 15 (1982): 6–23. Thanks are due to the editors as well as to the anonymous readers who frequently offered helpful suggestions.

Like pieces of a puzzle, these studies are more meaningful when seen within the frame of a common argument and gain force by their mutual support. It is very satisfying to see them brought together. The support of Karen Orchard toward this end, and the painstaking work of the University of Georgia Press in preparing the work for publication, has been greatly appreciated.

Children, Historians, and Movements

Children have always been more numerous in relation to the entire population than they are today, but an interest in the subject of childhood did not follow from the mere presence of children; it arose within a particular religious subculture. Sustained interest in children in England began with the Puritans, who were the first to puzzle over their nature and their place in society. The importance of the Puritans to a history of childhood has long been tacitly admitted, but the many books on the subject usually give the impression that Puritans are of interest only because they left the most accessible evidence or because they were such conspicuous advocates of the hard line. This study will gather evidence that the Puritans were more likely than their contemporaries to reflect upon the child's special needs, and it will offer an explanation of that interest which does not invoke their theological proclivities, some economic project, or a shared psychological pathology. Rather, it was the Puritans' future orientation, their existence as a religious "movement," that awakened and sustained their interest in children.

This study is not a history of the family, although it suggests how new concepts of childhood challenged that institution and generated a reaction, nor is the study really about children. It is about that cultural construct "childhood," which expresses our assumptions, hopes, and concerns about the young; it is about adults and their thoughts and feelings. Finally, it is not about Western attitudes generally but about attitudes arising in England.

The failure to distinguish between a social history of children and a cultural history of childhood has often been a source of confusion among historians. Most studies have relied heavily on literary sources, as does the present work, and naturally these literary sources record adult attitudes rather than the child's reality. Adult attitudes are, of course, an important part of the child's actual life, but it takes some sophistication and even guesswork to derive the social history of children from the evidence of adult opinion. Strictly speaking, we cannot know these adults' thoughts, but only such expressions as they were willing to put on paper, and these were most often for the perusal of others. In the present day parents are known to deceive themselves about their own actions,[1] and one can only assume that the same was true in the seventeenth century.

No doubt there had been some concern for children before the early modern period. The least convincing aspect of Philippe Ariès's classic study, *Centuries of Childhood*, is his claim that no concept of childhood existed before the sixteenth century. Other scholars have shown that medieval men and women did make distinctions between children and adults.[2] They may not be the same distinctions that are made today, undoubtedly the reason that Ariès missed them. Historians have also collected evidence of affective involvement with infants and children before Ariès's period.[3] The advent of printing makes following this increase of interest in children possible and points out that it was not widespread through English society but was most obvious among the Puritans.

General treatments of childhood in English and American history typically begin with the Puritans, but the reasons for this emphasis have never been clear. Occasionally historians imply that the seventeenth century was the first period in which evidence on childhood abounds and that Puritans suffered from "extreme loquacity" and a "compelling anxiety to commit their thoughts and beliefs to paper."[4] The views of other groups are presumed to have left few records until they were prompted to write in reaction to the Puritans' moralizing and unsympathetic works. Historians who start from this premise are not impressed with the large number of Puritan works on the subject of childhood and commonly emphasize only the most unattractive aspects of Puritan thought. Of course, it is flattering to modern readers to see a time when things seem so much worse.

When Philippe Ariès attempted to account for the appearance of "the concept of childhood" in France, he admitted some uncertainty as to the causes of this development. He had expected to find that the explanation would be a matter of demographic trends, with the child's status reflecting its scarcity value, but the facts proved otherwise; Ariès concluded that attitudes changed toward the child earlier than the economic or demographic realities and may even have helped to determine the latter. He found the most extensive evidence of the new awareness of childhood in the educational records of the new religious orders and suggested, rather inconclusively, that "the importance accorded to the child's personality was linked with the growing influence of Christianity on life and manners" in this period of religious reformations.[5]

Many scholars are not comfortable, however, with explanations that cast religion in the role of an independent variable. Gordon Rattray Taylor's *The Angel Makers* (1958) typifies an alternative approach that treats the Puritans as a psychological type he terms "sadistic." Their prominence in the history of childhood, as abusers, is therefore only to be regretted. Puritans were drawn to children's vulnerability, a troubling reminder of what these adults had suffered at an early age.

Such a theory has the task of explaining how the physical or psychological abuse began or it will lose itself in a vista of infinite regress. Taylor was not clear as to the origin of the "fear of pleasure," which was, for him, the essence of Puritanism. At times he suggests that this sadism was middle class in origin, remarking that "socio-economic and psychological factors interact in an exceedingly intimate way,"[6] but his class-based explanations are almost lost in a work filled with allusions to religion. Like Max Weber, Taylor treats religion as a causal factor. Theological differences between Calvinism and Methodism, for example, are presented as significant in determining behavior.[7] In assuming the salience of Puritan theology in all areas of their lives, Taylor's work falls into line with most earlier treatments of Puritan domestic relations. What Taylor adds is a translation of this theology into the language of pathology.

Defining Puritanism as a psychological category may sound reasonable when taking a very broad view of history, but it creates intolerable confusion when contemporaries employ the term in a very different sense. Two of Taylor's prime examples are Richard Allestree and Jeremy Taylor, who were, in fact, among the bitterest ecclesiastical opponents of the Puritans or Dissenters and shared neither their theology nor their social circumstances. Historian Taylor cites no seventeenth-century Puritan works except Richard Baxter's *Christian Directory* and his references are usually off target. He describes James Janeway's notorious *A Token for Children*, for instance, as an account of "martyrdoms," although it was something quite different.[8] Exaggerations or misrepresentations of this sort are widespread with reference to the Puritans when they serve as a kind of cultural scapegoat.

Taylor might be dismissed if it were not for other historians who have maintained his thesis and extended it. In a long introduction to a collaborative *History of Childhood* (1974), Lloyd deMause divided all of Western history into psychological stages, presenting childhood experience as a fundamental historical determinant. However, the "psychogenic" dialectic that he offered as an explanation of the shifts in child-rearing practice has not proven convincing to most students of the history of childhood. Even deMause's associates in that compilation largely ignored his stage scheme. It is not clear why a psychodynamic development would result in progress rather than retrogression, a question that had occurred to Taylor.[9] Still, since 1973, a *Journal of Psychohistory* has maintained the hope of creating a recognized discipline that would have particular relevance to a study of childhood (and to groups like the Puritans).

More popular than this psychological explanation of the increase in attention to childhood is a fourth theory that focuses on social structure. Historians who are interested in the structural changes associated with the triumph of capitalism have often commented on the changing place of children in the new scheme of things. They recognize the religious context of an early interest in childhood but tend to view it as a reflection of economic realities. One difficulty with that approach has been in showing that Puritans were, in fact, on the leading edge of economic development. Studies that endeavor to be sensitive to sociological concepts (John Demos's *A Little Commonwealth: Family Life in Plymouth Colony*, 1970) or to anthropological insights (Alan Macfarlane's *The Family Life of Ralph Josselin*, 1970) have not found much about the child's life that they could explain in terms of this modernization. Rather, they emphasize the traditional orientation of their subjects.

The most recent and comprehensive treatments of the child's life have at least tried to be aware of class differences. Lawrence Stone's *The Family, Sex and Marriage in England, 1500–1800* (1977) took the widest possible view of his subject, balancing the effects of class and ideology in a long perspective. Initially he broke child-rearing patterns down by social class, but there was also a need to arrange his family types in a chronological sequence. Though Stone admitted that this "over-simplified and over-schematized" the subject,[10] he wanted to show a linear progression (toward Affective Individualism), and naturally, this cast the earlier period into deep shadow. Once again, the Puritans proved a godsend, for while Stone acknowledged that they gave progress its first, ambiguous push, he could still portray them as retrogressive. There is no doubt of their pioneering introspection but much doubt as to its beneficial effect.

Stone tends to interpret Puritan writers in the most unsympathetic sense possible. At times this leads him beyond his strict evidence, as when he writes that "so far as is known only a handful of children were ever executed" under the New England laws forbidding disobedience to parents; his sources state that there is no record of any such action.[11] By contrast, he presents the attitudes of an anti-Puritan aristocrat, John Evelyn, sympathetically only by omitting that gentleman's chilling words on suppressing his son's pleasures just for the sake of making him stoical.[12] Stone's dismissal of children's literature before the 1740s as "unattractive in tone" suggests impatience with a cultural tradition that he thought unworthy of consideration.[13] The present study seeks to provide just that kind of consideration.

Whatever his feelings about Puritanism, Stone does not suggest that it was simply the expression of social circumstances. He sees a wide range of causes—political, legal, ecclesiastical, educational, economic, and ideological—as helping to bring about a new mentality. He uses the evidence of demography, medicine, dress, school records, family finances, and sewage disposal to assess the impact of environment on the child, but he also never doubts the importance of books in the life of society, and Puritanism—more specifically the doctrine of Original Sin—is frequently presented as an important cause of early modern attitudes.[14]

Philip Greven, in *The Protestant Temperament: Patterns of Child-Rearing, Religious Experience, and the Self in Early America* (1977) specifically subordinated the chronological interest of his subject to a search for consistent and stable patterns. Though not dealing with England, Greven reached a new level of sophistication in describing not "the child" but three different understandings of childhood in colonial America. The fact that he gave one of these a class label ("the Genteel"), one a religious label ("the Evangelicals"), and called the other third "the Moderates" indicates that he was not eager to force the issue of causation. Though his reliance was on literary sources, Greven chose the term "temperament" (rather than "mind") to avoid the suggestion of a strictly intellectual approach.[15]

Finally, Linda Pollock's *Forgotten Children: Parent-Child Relations from 1500 to 1900* (1983) attempted to show what hard evidence there is for the most basic elements of the standard picture—a primordial neglect of children, the absence of any concept of childhood, and nearly universal cruelty toward children—before the eighteenth century. Pollock demonstrates a considerable degree of continuity in the *treatment* of children over that period, despite changes in expressed attitudes and advice. This establishes some empirical foundation for the work of those, like Keith Wrightson, who suspected more continuity and sympathy in child-rearing than other historians had assumed.[16] If correct, her conclusions would confirm the impression given by historians who dealt with individual cases, who usually described more humane treatment than those reporting on the larger picture.

Pollock's energetic and controlled survey of a wide range of personal documents commands respect, but her negative verdict on "progressive" views is stated so categorically that one suspects her evidence, especially autobiographies—the most questionable of all sources on childhood. She is able to show their consistency with parents' diaries from the same period, but diarists are almost as suspect as autobiographers, so she is not convincing in arguing that her extensive reading actually reveals majority practice.[17] Even a minority report, however, is sufficient to deflate the sweeping statements to which historians have been prone.

Pollock does not attempt to explain a rise of affection or interest because she sees no evidence that they have, indeed, risen appreciably in the past several centuries. There was more affection in past times than literary sources have indicated, and there is probably less of it now than we would like to imagine. "Childish" is just as pejorative a term today as it was in Chaucer's day, and "childlike" was just as endearing a term then as now (though before Shakespeare's time the form was "childly"). Ambivalence is apparently a constant feature of attitudes toward children. Values have changed, to be sure, but that does not mean that treatment has improved; it means only that today more guilt is felt about that treatment. This study will make it apparent that it was the Puritans who set us on this road.

There is no getting around the influence of the Puritans. The various theories just described are correct in beginning with them, for they really were exceptional in their early interest in childhood. But the most important aspect of Puritanism in this regard is not to be found in their theology, their psychology, or their class position, where historians have usually looked; rather, it is in the most obvious fact about Puritanism — that it constituted a reform movement. Whatever else the term "Puritan" may mean, by definition it indicates a desire to purify the Church of England and through it other aspects of the nation's life. Puritans were not entirely agreed on what needed to be changed, but a number of them can be found among the supporters of each of the reforming ideas of their day — reform of the law and the judicial system, of the constitution, of marriage, of business practices, of science and education, of language. In an age in which religion was involved in so many aspects of life, it was impossible for religious reformers to avoid a wider radicalism.

After a generation of scholarship that emphasized Puritan radicalism, it is now common to assert their essential traditionalism, noting that they accepted the hierarchical society of their time. Other scholars, such as Margo Todd, see Puritans in terms of a more general, humanist reformism, rather than as radicals.[18] But the unconscious and unintended revolution within family authority was probably as unsettling as the revolution in class relations upon which the historians have become fixated. We shall find indirect evidence that Puritan and Dissenting principles of child nurture encouraged such changes in the family, and evidence of the psychological wrench that this produced. Certainly the Puritans' contemporaries would have been surprised to hear them described as conservatives.

The important point about the Puritans, for purposes of this study, is not their basic ideas or their conscious program, but rather the dynamics of their social organization—first as a movement and then as various sects. Puritanism meets the usual definition of a movement as *any group that organizes to promote change, up to the point at which it becomes institutionalized by community acceptance*.[19] Patrick Collinson has aptly entitled his classic history *The Elizabethan Puritan Movement*. Reform movements provide excellent histories in which to look for an interest in childhood. Because the Elizabethan Church of England resisted the kind of reforms that the Puritans advocated, the movement felt the need to orient itself toward the more distant future. When people organize for change in this way, it is never long before they recognize that the rising generation will be crucial to their enterprise. The reformers will be curious about the younger generation's loyalties and desires, since this group may have to continue the movement. Also, the image of the child will inevitably figure in the movement's ideology, because all such ideologies include a particular understanding of human nature. The movement might also look to children for appreciation, as they will be the principal beneficiaries of the effort. The modern-day continuing interest in childhood might be seen as reflecting our condition of "permanent revolution"—which will end when we despair of efforts to change the world.

In 1660 the Puritan movement was halted by the Restoration of the Stuart monarchy and the traditional church. Although some former Puritans returned to the established church, providing an "Anglican" echo of Puritan initiatives in education, others became "Dissenters" or religious nonconformists, and what had been a *movement* within the church became a *sect*. When Dissenters formed religious sects, they were admitting their inability to lead the nation to higher ground, but they did not give up their orientation toward the future. The children of the sect were the only hope for its survival. A survival-mentality is a harsher matter than the optimism that inspires a movement, and there are hints that Dissent was not as welcoming to children as Puritanism had been. With their decline into pessimism, it would be only natural for Dissenters to express their exasperation toward their children. They maintained an interest in the rising generation, but that interest would have a sour edge. Possibly, the Puritan reputation for harshness with children was actually earned in those later generations.

Readers may wonder whether this characterization of Puritanism makes the essential points, for defining Puritanism has long been a problem for historians. To contemporaries, Puritans were those who made it all too clear that Elizabeth's church was not sufficiently Protestant, or scriptural, for them. Historians, however, have not been happy with this merely negative definition, and some have tried to elaborate an ideology that would set the Puritans apart, a formal theology that guided their efforts at purification. Calvinism by itself, however, did not distinguish the Puritans from their ecclesiastical opponents. Not until the 1620s was there a theological alternative with sufficient standing within the Church of England to warrant notice, so some historians have seen a certain kind of Calvinism—an emphasis on Covenant Theology—as a defining peculiarity of Puritanism.[20]

Other historians protest that this gives Puritanism too intellectualist a cast and prefer definitions more spiritual than theological. Some have taken the experience, or at least the expectation, of a calling or conversion as a more certain mark of Puritanism than any doctrinal formulation.[21] Recent discussions have placed the heart of Puritanism "in the capacity, which the godly claimed, of being able to recognize one another in the midst of a corrupt and unregenerate world." Puritans expected to be able to recognize the elect (by the eye of faith) as those who were in earnest about God's glory. Outsiders might see only the obverse of this devotion to God in the rejection of "worldliness," but those within the circle respected an unsatisfied zeal for God's honor. Such definitions emphasize that the Puritan's "constant struggle to externalize his sense of his own election through a campaign of works directed against Antichrist, the flesh, sin and the world" could broaden into a general reformism, for this is a description not of a position but of a direction.[22]

Among the laity, it might be difficult to categorize individuals by any of these definitions, but there is no problem in identifying the Puritans among our authors; most were clergymen and sufficiently prominent that their desire for church reform was a matter of record. Many were ejected from their positions in the church in 1662 for officially refusing the new *Book of Common Prayer* and thereby making a formal avowal of their nonconformity. By defining as Puritans all those who made their dissatisfaction with the church known, there can be no prejudgment of their attitudes on social issues; that is, the notions they expressed will not be determined by the principle of selection. The present study does not define Puritans as those who were humorless, or sadistic, or believed in infant depravity or predestination. In fact, they allowed considerable latitude in these matters.

Viewing the Puritans as part of a religious movement points up the ways in which its dynamics shaped their attitudes toward children. The necessity of preserving the movement beyond the lives of the founders meant reaching out to the young, trying to impress or appeal to them. Recruitment to the movement proved so difficult, especially after reverses, that it would come to depend on enlisting the children of members, and this would, of course, affect child-rearing practices. Also the failures encountered might be set to the account of young people, who could always be seen as lacking commitment and sometimes as discrediting the effort. Thus the movement's inherent dynamic introduces a measure of social determination into this study.

It might be thought that social change, in itself, would direct attention to children. Movements become likely when change is apparent, when new possibilities are obvious, when disgust with old values becomes overpowering and channels of redress are clogged.[23] The very existence of a movement indicates that something seems wrong, if not in the basic structure of society, at least in the present distribution of status, wealth, or power. This was the case when Puritans did not find their conviction of rectitude reflected in their status and saw their desire for a proper worship frustrated by a worldly church. Still, social change by itself may not be sufficient to generate an interest in childhood; there must also be a vision of the future. Consciousness of change may only lead to a reevaluation of childhood where it is accompanied by movements that conceive and express new views on the subject.

Of course, the very existence of movements is a challenge to a naïve determinism, since they suggest the possibility of being ahead of one's time or at least out of step. A movement's persistence shows the power of human determination, especially if it enjoyed as little apparent success as did Puritanism. Perhaps Puritanism could be defined in such a way as to assert its essential success. By 1800 there were Dissenters who looked back on the history of their tradition and took credit, "more than any other body of men," for England's "political freedom, our religious liberty, and our christian privileges."[24] But this was not the view of those who experienced the collapse of Cromwell's protectorate and its religious projects.

Success would have made Puritanism seem historically inevitable; failure makes it seem like an expression of freedom. After that political failure, however, when Dissent was left with the task of preserving its heritage, it makes more sense to speak of the social determination of attitudes. As a sect, Dissent fell back on the most basic of institutions, the family. Sects are concerned very largely with the problem of sustaining themselves in the face of indifference and disdain. They cannot afford to refuse any support, and compromises are made with such social institutions as the family.

Throughout this study, it will be important to remember that the Puritans were underdogs. In American history it is easy to imagine that there was a time in which no one could withstand them, and their effect on England, too, may have been out of proportion to their numbers. When speaking of the seventeenth century, the term Puritan England is frequently used, but Dissenters were never more than a small fraction of the population, amounting to barely 5 percent in the 1670s.[25] As clergymen, even before the civil wars, they might come under the judgment of the ecclesiastical courts for pushing ahead with reformation; and as laymen, they faced the ostracism and ridicule that any small, sociable community uses to jog its members back into line. Doubtless some Puritans brought this on themselves or might even have imagined some of the slights of relatives and neighbors, but the effect was still real.

If they strayed too far, the sanctions could become brutal. After the Restoration of 1660, Dissenters were legally distinct from their neighbors, unable to teach, to attend the universities, or to hold office at any level of government. Judicial persecution often went beyond the letter of the law, with fines heavier than authorized, the plundering of suspects, denial of basic rights, and imprisonment in jails that resembled sewers. Quakers are the best-known victims of official persecution, partly because they took care to keep records of their sufferings, but others were similarly taunted, beaten, and even lynched.[26] Children were not beyond this persecution. One of the touching stories recounted by the Dissenting biographer, Edmund Calamy, was of a child who asked, as his family fled from a mob that was wrecking its home, whether those were the Philistines.[27]

If Puritans became embittered, it would be understandable. Success might have mellowed them, although it is difficult to imagine their being satisfied with anything short of heaven. Several scholars have noticed, however, how the eighteenth century saw a refinement of techniques for terrorizing children. Gordon Rattray Taylor believed that the more moderate tradition in child-rearing advice disappeared at the end of that century, and E. P. Thompson also dated a general "declension in the social conscience of Dissent" to the years around 1790.[28] They are supported by Pollock's evidence of a noticeably harsher discipline in England in the early nineteenth century.[29] Several American historians observed a similar change somewhat earlier, noticing an increase in the threat of hell-fire to control children in the early 1700s.[30] If the picture of seventeenth-century attitudes presented in the present study is surprising in its mildness, that may be because it stops so shortly after Puritanism changed from a movement into sects.

Even the Toleration Act of 1689 could have served to deepen a sectarian despair. True, it allowed the case for religious reform to be restated in a period of political change, but it also showed that greater freedom did not make England more receptive to Dissenting views. In the high-Tory enthusiasm of Queen Anne's reign (1702–

14), no one could have foreseen the eventual emergence of a liberal England. If Dissenting parents then began to earn the reputation for cruelty that Victorian novelists later fastened upon them, it may have had to do with this disappointment. Their efforts to sway the nation would naturally turn into compulsive action toward the one group entirely within their power—their children. In the history of childhood, things do not necessarily get better with time.

The history of childhood has a particular poignancy, because all humans are so deeply involved with their own childhood years. Given the inescapable moralizing surrounding the subject, Puritans have been especially vulnerable to accusations of cruelty and self-deception, and their disdain for their neighbors has invited psychological reductionism by avenging historians. Were the more sadistic members of society simply being drawn together by a theology whose sourness justified their cruelty? No doubt psychological factors are always involved with attitudes toward children, but the Puritan authors show such marked differences in tone and approach that there is no hint of a common psychological pathology, whatever the predilections of individual authors. In fact, the Puritans' realistic portrayal of children was in contrast with the stereotyped images of childhood found among their contemporaries, and an examination of Puritan humor for children suggests a saner balance in their approach than has been noticed previously.

Childhood, as well as Puritanism, requires definition, since the Puritans and their contemporaries were rather inclusive, not always distinguishing childhood from youth. This was not because they recognized no difference, but because they did not see growth as the discontinuous process described in modern developmental stage schemes. To them childhood was a more gradual and even a longer process. Leaving home for domestic service or apprenticeship did not end childhood; in certain ways it did not end until marriage and household independence. Thus the subject of childhood cannot be limited to the earliest years and still remain true to the historical sources. This may, on the other hand, provide us with new considerations in our own views of the boundaries of childhood.

Puritans were likewise not as sensitive to the status and needs of girls as we may be today. They could not ignore the girls completely, as our survey of child biographies will show, but they were not truly gender inclusive in their interests. In this regard, as in others, we must let the Puritans' own focus guide our interests. While not ignoring our own concerns, we will emphasize what concerned their contemporaries.

Chapter 1 will show how the Puritans emerged as the first group to give attention to children, but other groups followed suit at intervals. Some "Anglicans" had organized themselves as a movement by the end of the seventeenth century, although any such early use of the term Anglican is subject to criticism. Yet we will see the beginnings of a separation between mere "conformists" and those—notably laymen—who were concerned for the reputation of their church and endeavored to give an example of more active and devout churchmanship. Organizations like the Society for Promoting Christian Knowledge, the Society for the Propagation of the Gospel, and the Societies for the Reformation of Manners were organized outside the ecclesiastical establishment to promote more frequent communion, greater moral regulation, foreign missions, libraries, and charity schools. Much of what they did was on the behalf of children.

It makes sense to see this "Anglicanism" as a movement, since these societies were implicitly critical of the hierarchy. They showed an awareness that religion would have to be based on public opinion in the freer circumstances that followed 1689, and some of their members did not even think it desirable to rely on ecclesiastical control through the courts and censorship. As a movement, this Anglicanism discovered its own interest in childhood, and this was colored by its distinctive theology.[31] More secularized intellectuals lagged farther behind, only to emerge in these debates when English "Jacobin" radicalism took on some of the characteristics of a movement in the 1790s.

Chapter 2 reveals a similar sequence while treating a single type of evidence, the image of real children in biography. The contribution of Puritanism to a more realistic portrayal of childhood, and even to literary realism, contrasts sharply with older hagiographical and humanist traditions.

Somewhere we must give a rounded view of the nature and needs of childhood as seen by these pioneers, and this is the subject of Chapter 3. The surprise here is how concern and sympathy for children could overcome the natural tendency to allow the needs and ideology of the movement to determine the writers' views. In the hope of following the proportions of contemporary interests, we have organized the study according to the types of sources employed: books for children, child-rearing manuals, biographies, catechisms, and educational or theological treatises.

Chapter 4 treats efforts to entertain children, not simply to prove that Puritan humor existed, but to show that some Puritans were not lagging behind in such development. There are hints of the importance of social circumstances even in this very subtle change.

There was no lack in the practical application of the new views on the child's nature, and Chapter 5 shows how they were translated into educational prescription. We will see how a closer attention on the part of Puritan teachers fed back into their theory and note the tardiness of Anglicans once again, as education became a contested territory.

An Epilogue will provide a very different perspective on this history of childhood. While the characteristics of any movement encourage individualism, the characteristics of the family work in opposition. Family solidarity is threatened by the loyalty demanded by movements and by the freedom they offer to their adherents. Dissenting families proved to be no different in this regard. In the time of the French Revolution, the English Jacobins, the ideological heirs of the Dissenters, made the implications of a radical individualism so frighteningly clear that there was a general reaction. The eighteenth-century Dissenters were not interested in this extension of their heritage—if they even recognized it as such—and they left the English Jacobins to the mercy of a shocked public.

In the long run, "family" would have its way, as had happened before in church history. Thus the dynamics of the Puritan movement brought unintended consequences, and the instincts born of family life finally marshaled some resistance. In a contest of strength the family would win, for it could draw on deeper resources than the movement; but the family was changed by the struggle and with it the rest of English culture and society as well.

CHAPTER ONE

The Puritan Preoccupation
with Children

A hundred years ago an English clergyman, the Reverend Charles Bardsley, discovered a curious fact in some parish registers surviving from the sixteenth century. In the entries for the 1560s there was a dramatic change in the names that Englishmen were giving their children. Names had not been very important before; there were only a few dozen names in common use in England, so few that they had to be differentiated by a variety of endings and nicknames. There were so many Williams in some villages that they had to take pet-name endings like Wilkin, Wilcock, Wilmot, and Willin. John might be as good as no name at all unless it became Brownjohn, Littlejohn, Micklejohn, Jenning, or Jenkin.

Parents had discovered that names need not be simply labels, they also could have a meaning. Where did they get that idea? From the Bible, of course, and specifically from the Geneva version, which was first published in 1560. In the back of the Geneva Bible was an appendix listing the English meanings of the names in Scripture, and parents could simply name their children by those English equivalents, such as Thankful, Accepted, Sin-Deny, or Safe-on-Highe. And so we have the peculiar Puritan phrase-names that the playwright Ben Jonson had such fun with—Tribulation Wholesome and Zeal-of-the-Land Busy. These are scarcely an exaggeration; the Puritan politician Praise-God Barebones or Barbon had a brother who was christened If-Christ-had-not-died-for-thee-thou-hadst-been-damned Barbon (who, as the black sheep of the family, was often simply called Damned Barbon). It was clear to Jonson and his contemporaries that this was a "Puritan" phenomenon, and as late as the nineteenth century, authors used such names as Ebenezer and Ichabod to suggest religious peculiarity. Bardsley himself was able to establish that it was sometimes a deliberate attempt of Puritan clergy and laity "to separate the truly godly and renewed portion of the community from the world at large." [1]

The new names symbolized the Puritans' sense of a break in history. Many in the first generation of Puritans had broken with their families, and all of them felt some estrangement from the primary institution of English culture—the church. New names indicated a fresh start. The future was to be purified of the superstitions associated with saints' names and from the bondage to family tradition that was represented by the passing of names down through the generations. Puritanism was a reform movement, and while any movement competes with family loyalties, few have chosen such a striking way to symbolize this break. In France, which did not become a Bible-reading nation, the pet-name usages survived, but in England such customs were so far forgotten that they began to pass as surnames.[2]

Not all Englishmen, however, shared this interest in children. This chapter will argue that it was when other movements began to develop that they, too, began to pay greater attention to childhood. In part they were following a Puritan lead, but also they were responding to the dynamic of all movements in this concentration on the rising generation. For instance, the first self-conscious "Anglicans"— those who promoted the charity-school "movement" in the 1690s— began to show an awareness of children at the same time. The threat from Catholic kings and secular Whigs gave them the sense that the nation's values and practices were in jeopardy, and some churchmen saw the advantage of appealing to popular opinion rather than to ecclesiastical control. These early "Anglicans" were the ones who took up the Dissenters' interest in children, even though they regarded it from a different theological perspective. England's more secularized intellectuals discovered an interest in children somewhat later, when radicalism organized itself in the "Jacobin" movement of the late eighteenth century.

Hindsight may make us all too aware of the Puritans' eventual defeat, but we must also remember their initial hopes. A new world was about to be revealed, they thought, filled with a people who had never known the debased religion of a former age. Naturally, the movement felt that these new people should be given new names. Children were no longer simply family elements but had a destiny that would transcend old roles. The parents who gave the new names also felt the need for advice on how to raise their children to realize this promise. Some of these books of advice began, appropriately, with a discussion of naming and its importance in offering a good example and inspiring an interest in scriptural history.[3] For a century the Puritans had a virtual monopoly on books for parents.

The same demonstration of interest and the same social motivation are shown in the Puritans' attempts to create a literature for children. They were the first to write books exclusively for children and the first to show an awareness of the difficulties involved in communicating with them. William Sloane's bibliography of early children's books in English enables us to compare the numbers of such works emanating from Puritan or Dissenting authors with those by more moderate "Anglicans" and still others by authors of a more skeptical bent. (Identification of authors by religious affiliation is easier when it involves clergymen, as nearly all of these authors were. Puritans are those who campaigned for changes in the church; Dissenters those who were cast out of the church after 1662.) Sloane's list was compiled without any regard to religious issues, which eliminates any danger of systematic bias. It lists 261 works published before 1710. Of these, almost 150 were specifically religious, dealing primarily with the young readers' relationship with God. Another 50 struck a closer balance between religious and social or moral concerns. Only about 40 were primarily books of polite conduct, though even they did not escape some religious coloration. The remaining 20 books were devoted to practical instruction, especially how to thrive in trade.[4] If Sloane had included educational literature, the religious emphasis would have been even more striking.

These religious and moral books brought children a new status and recognition in English culture. They may not meet our notions of what children really like, but that is beside the point. Religion was clearly the issue that initiated adult reflection on the nature of childhood. Furthermore, of the authors who can be identified, 104 were Puritans or Dissenters and only 54 were non-Puritans.[5] Given the minority status of Puritan opinion, this ratio is significant. Oddly enough, only two on Sloane's list were by Scottish Presbyterians, who shared the doctrinal outlook of the English reformers.

Outside of these religious circles, there is less evidence that English society had awakened to an interest in children. Louis Wright's survey of Elizabethan literature significantly contained no section of works directed to children, despite its encyclopedic coverage.[6] The few humanist works on pedagogy which have preoccupied historians did not consider whether Latinity was what children needed. Roger Ascham in *The Scholemaster* (1570) thought the issue of childhood — "the good or ill bringing up of children" — important because it "doth as much serve to the good or ill service of God, our Prince, and the whole countrie, as any one thing doth beside." For these humanists the future was not an open one and so childhood was not problematical in the way it would become for Puritans. There was no real need to consult the nature of childhood, since these pedagogues assumed that "ye shall have as ye use a child in his youth."[7] Nor did those seventeenth-century authors who used the child's persona (usually as a focus of cultural nostalgia) create any understanding of real children. As Leah Marcus points out, such authors used the image of the child to refer to *themselves* as children and to the nation's past. She also noticed a contrast with Puritanism: "For seventeenth-century Puritans, their children were the best hope for a better England to come. For conservative Anglicans, childhood was a symbolic link with an idealized England gone by."[8]

There is no theological explanation of the wide difference between the publishing activity of Scottish Presbyterians and English Puritans, but there is a social explanation, namely, that those groups that have no secure institutional basis are most likely to sense the importance of reaching children. The legal establishment of Presbyterian Calvinism in the Church of Scotland made it unnecessary to appeal to the coming generation in this way. Back when the Scots were consolidating their own Reformation, they had struggled against poverty to provide a system of universal public education,[9] but as their movement hardened into a religious establishment, children claimed less of their attention. By contrast, Henry VIII's Reformation was not so much a popular movement as an act of state. Capturing the minds of the young was not seen as crucial until Puritan opinion outran religious politics and turned the Reformation into a movement. This occurred during Elizabeth's reign, when the first of these books appeared — written by Puritans.[10]

Among the Dissenting authors, the tiny sects of Baptists and Quakers were especially active in producing the children's books that appear on Sloane's list. Baptists accounted for most of the children's verse in the seventeenth century (see Chapter 4), and the hard-pressed Quakers were responsible for a fifth of the books we have identified as written by Dissenters. Their vulnerability, their hopes for future vindication, and the decline of their missionary success among adults could explain why Quakers turned toward children in this way. At the other extreme, only four books on Sloane's list were by men who were skeptical or even liberal in religious belief: Sir Walter Raleigh, Francis Osborne, Humphrey Brooke, and George Savile, Marquis of Halifax.

Not only did Puritans and Dissenters write a greater number of works for children, they were also more imaginative than the Anglican authors, who simply adapted the traditional courtesy manuals to a younger audience. Courtesy literature, so popular among the humanists earlier, presupposes static social patterns and deals with "types of human conduct as an expression of class ideals rather than as a subject for metaphysical speculation." [11] Puritans, on the other hand, were apt to introduce just such speculation concerning the ultimate ends of human life. They were suspicious of the manners and values that prevailed in fashionable society. Surely it mattered infinitely more what God thought and what history would reveal about one's character than how polite society might judge one's manners. Puritan books had to warn children against a society in which their brand of religion was unfashionable. By way of insuring commitment to the movement, Puritan authors emphasized doctrinal purity and spiritual inner direction when they addressed young readers. In effect they offered children a base in religious authority from which to challenge a corrupt social authority.

Anglican works for children performed a rather different ideological function. They tended toward greater concentration on youthful vice and submission to authority, an emphasis one would expect from the conservators of culture. Without submitting the literature to a content analysis, a reading of approximately half of the works on Sloane's list shows Edward Burton's *The Father's Legacy* (1649) to be typical of the emphasis of churchmen. Its opening injunction, "First honour God, then thy Prince, thy Parents, and thy Elders," leads to directions appropriate to children who will one day command their inferiors. The promotion of social peace is the first principle of conduct and even the test of religious truth, for that is truest "which makes most for God's glory and man's quiet."[12] Michael Jermin, another religious moderate, likewise directed his own children's duty to God, their superiors, their equals, and finally their inferiors.[13] As with Burton's, the conceptual level of the work suggests that the "children" to whom this advice was addressed had already grown up.

Most of the Anglican works for youth were written after the inroads of Arminian theology in the mid-century. So it is no surprise that they dwell on the sins and follies of youth, for the essence of that piety was a protection of innocence or a purification from passions and lusts.[14] Such a theological emphasis is termed semi-Pelagian, the position that, while God's help or grace is necessary to salvation, men are able and responsible for taking the first step. As a corollary it seemed that if man's will is not the source of all evil, then the flesh must bear a larger share of the blame. There was, therefore, greater concentration on the lusts of the flesh than in Calvinist works. Concern for fleshly sins is also present in Puritan and Dissenting literature, but their emphasis was on a redemptive piety, on spiritual conversion rather than moral repression. The difference is remarkably consistent through the period, along Puritan/Anglican lines.

After 1660 the level of Anglican concern for children began to rise, for with the Restoration of the Stuart monarchy, Anglicans were faced with a situation similar to that which the Puritans had experienced a century earlier. A monarch suspected of Catholic sympathies seemed bent on allowing freedom of worship, so that the position of the Church of England and the religious foundations of society were threatened. Anglican authors also began to take notice of the growing threat of "atheism," recognizing that "the Hopes and Happiness of our Church and State depend upon a sober and Religious rising Generation."[15] The social and political motive of their new concern is clear from Sloane's list, in a surge of Anglican works for children from the time of the Popish Plot (1678) to the

Revolution (1688). This period coincided with the launching of the charity-school movement, which also grew out of Anglican fears for the church, and the fact that Anglicans lagged a generation behind Dissenters in recognizing these cultural changes is to be explained by the institutional security enjoyed by the established church and its consequent insulation from public opinion. Meanwhile, the old-fashioned courtesy literature for the young was maintained principally by gentlemen of a skeptical tendency, such as the Marquis of Halifax and the Earl of Chesterfield.

There is even a difference of style between the two religious groups in writing for children. This can seldom be seen in the sermons that form a part of the literature on either side, but in their other books the Puritans and Dissenters were more obviously concerned with reaching the child's level. Sloane quoted examples from Robert Russell's rare works, in which he limited himself to a child's vocabulary and yet managed to write dramatically.[16] Dissenters offered a variety of ingenious catechisms, some of them intended to be humorous.[17] Despite the Puritan suspicion of the stage, Samuel Shaw wrote plays for his grammar school pupils which make sly allusions to the manners of the day.[18] And John Bunyan was not the only Dissenter to write allegories that might have been read dramatically. There were also biographies and Bible-story books written for little Puritans—enough in the way of entertainment to justify a chapter on the subject.[19]

In comparison to these riches there were very few Anglican works that attempted to speak the child's language. William Jole and William Ronksley produced works that are attractive even by modern standards—verses, riddles, and "catechisms" that allowed children to show off their Bible knowledge.[20] Otherwise, seventeenth-century Anglicans made almost no concessions to the mental limitations of their young audience, for they were slow to recognize the cultural burden that children would have to bear in support of their church.

One might protest that the edifying intention of the Puritans' works shows a fundamental lack of sympathy with the audience. Were not their books written to warn children against themselves? Why should authors go out of their way to berate young readers if their intent was to secure loyalty? We may suspect that they were not as interested in changing children's behavior as in venting their own frustrations. Was not the doctrine of infant depravity an obvious projection of the Puritans' self-hate? And was not their fascination with dying children the sick result of the mortification of their own instincts? In short, we must consider the possibility that there was a psychological motive for the Puritans' greater interest in childhood.

First, it is true that most of what seventeenth-century English Puritans and Dissenters wrote for children was stodgy and preachy. Some of it was clearly unsympathetic. Daniel Williams thought that most men remembered their early years "with a Blush" and he despaired to think that "most of mankind die when young." [21] But the range of tone in these works varied widely, from the disagreeable Williams to the amiable Thomas Brookes and Caleb Trenchfield, and there was the delightfully droll Samuel Shaw to balance the rather frightful Thomas White. Those who were harshest on children, like Williams, also had no use for adults as a group. All agreed that it was sin that aged men and hardened them against God's forgiveness; indeed this is what had suggested children as a more likely audience.

If the subject of original sin and human depravity tended to be associated with youth, so was the subject of conversion. The former suggested despair, but the latter would have raised hope. Authors assumed that conversions would be more frequently experienced in the teen years, whether or not historians can show that they were correct in this assumption. The fact that an author directed his appeal to children, on the face of it, shows respect for their reason and conscience, and there are only a few, like Williams, who belied this respect and sympathy by a despairing rejection. One of the ways in which such despair could have been expressed was through cautionary tales, which were common in contemporary chapbooks. The Puritans, however, disapproved of chapbooks,[22] and it is surprising how very few such tales appear in books written specifically for children in the seventeenth century.[23]

As for the doctrine of original sin and infant depravity, even that doctrine is best understood in its social context. This idea (that the child inherits both the guilt of man's original rebellion and the predisposition to selfishness that resulted) would have to relate to social or psychological circumstances if it were to survive as part of the general culture, but it was the social realities of the Puritan movement that suggest the most obvious explanation. In Puritan theology, the origin of all sin was not fleshly concupiscence but rebellion against God. That is what is meant by terming their piety "Augustinian." Puritans were sensitive on this issue of rebellion, having been forced to oppose the religious and political order of their day in order to be obedient to God. Their position dictated both rebellion and submission, and this conflict was reproduced in their families; as parents, they realized that obedience to God could not be extorted from their children.

It would seem that only Puritan authors reminded their readers that the child's obedience to God overrode that due the parents,[24] and for this reason they expressed inhibitions in all of their child-rearing manuals against the casual brutality toward children which was common in English society. Puritans wanted their children to offer obedience freely, without compulsion. No doubt some parents harbored a lingering temptation toward compulsion, but there is no reason to believe that this amounted to a disciplinarian paranoia. The problem was moral in that it transcended the parents' own emotional needs, for at best they were thinking of how to guide children toward their "true nature." We might conceive this problem differently, but it is one that properly belongs to a discussion of ethics, not psychology. It was an attempt to consider children as ends and not simply in relation to adults' desires.

Perhaps some parents did use the doctrine of infant depravity to excuse the severity of their natures, but there is no evidence that Puritan parents were more severe than their contemporaries. Having edited the diary of Ralph Josselin, Alan Macfarlane remarked that the closer one gets to the Puritans the more sympathetic they seem as parents. Josselin could not remember ever having been whipped by his Puritan parents, and he never recorded disciplining or toilet-training his own children.[25] One cannot infer a lack of sympathy from the Puritan adherence to the doctrine of depravity. The risk of such an inference is obvious in discussing subsequent generations of Puritans and Dissenters, whose beliefs were hand-me-downs. The fact that the writers who mentioned original sin did not show an equal emotional commitment to it suggests what should be obvious—that for most it was not a spontaneous projection of their own guilt but a doctrine adopted for the sake of logical consistency. It could have been just as damaging even so, but it was not uncommon to see the doctrine mentioned in order to increase sympathy for the child since it made parents responsible for the child's state![26] While a few did in fact treat human depravity as a loathsome affliction that made childhood itself nasty, most simply viewed it as a practical difficulty to be faced through discipline during the course of training.

There is other evidence that seemingly harsh doctrinal commitments were softened in practice. The Puritans' Covenant Theology was, in essence, a way of mitigating the effects of depravity in future generations. The covenants were not primarily individual but were guarantees of God's concern over the course of generations, at least in certain families.[27] How does one decide which of these two doctrines—depravity or covenanted grace—was adopted for logical and which for affective reasons? The same dilemma exists in assessing the temper behind ecclesiastical law. Massachusetts and Connecticut dutifully announced that they would enforce the Mosaic law that made disobedience or disrespect to parents a capital offense, but they found ways around actually enforcing that penalty.[28] There seems little doubt as to which of these (the law or the practice) more fully reveals the Puritan heart.

We need to remind ourselves that a belief in the child's innocence is no guarantee of a sunnier childhood; it is possible that the more innocent the child is presumed to be, the more repressive the efforts to preserve that state. All of the attention lavished upon Victorian innocents cannot hide the fact that repressions were building during that period, as the circle of forbidden knowledge was widening to include most adult concerns. Victorian attempts to segregate and sentimentalize childhood may also have resulted from social changes, the frightened reaction to urbanization, utilitarianism, or industrialization. It was thought better that children have a world of their own, so their liberation came in the form of nonsense literature and games. The Puritans did not distrust adulthood as such; they did not show the dread of adulthood that stood behind the sentimentalizing of the child. For the Puritan there was comparatively little forbidden knowledge and less reason for providing a separate culture for children.

With the stories of good children who died young, there might seem to be firmer evidence of the life-denying attempt of authors to revenge their own repressed desires, but those stories also make sense in terms of the Dissenters' social circumstances. Physical persecution of Dissenters had not ceased by the time James Janeway published the first of these in *A Token for Children* (1671)—the first baby-talk book in the language. Partly, the books were a protest against the persecution to which Dissenters were subject after the Restoration. Quaker authors, especially, seemed to draw on their readers' natural sympathy for children as they told of the sufferings inflicted by society. There was nothing fanciful about this suffering: Elizabeth Braythwaite went to jail as soon as she reached the age of legal responsibility (sixteen) and died shortly afterward.[29] Whatever the children died of, the stories usually included some indication of the social difficulties of Dissenting families. One could almost envy those who were beyond the reach of the ostracism that Dissenters faced, but there is no hint that the dying children were envied for escaping adulthood or sexual awakening, which would suggest a psychological explanation.

The most noteworthy feature of these stories is the status they accord to children. If the traditional courtesy literature had taught children how to be adult, these stories showed that life could be lived fully, within its moral and spiritual dimensions, before the end of childhood. To say that the stories make children out to be "little adults" somewhat confuses the issue. Rather, they indicate that Puritans thought that religion was the one area in which children were at no disadvantage as opposed to adults. This emphasis did not help to define childhood as a separate stage of life, but it shows an appreciation of the religious status of children which had scarcely been taken seriously before. Certainly the point of the stories was not God's wrath against the dying children. Quite the contrary; in a supremely awkward way they reinforced the oft-repeated sentiment that youth was the best time of life.[30]

The fact that nearly all of these exemplary youths died may only reveal the author's principle of selection and not an unconscious hostility. Writers felt safer in picking those who could not backslide and in doing so discredit their associates; radical movements have always preferred dead heroes for this reason. Perhaps the number of genuinely serious-minded children could have been multiplied, but only those who were safely out of the way were trusted to public scrutiny.[31] At any rate, we should remember that the stories were true[32] and reflected mortality rates and diseases no longer familiar, so we should not analyze them as we would fictions. Those authors who killed off children gratuitously in their fictional creations were Victorians who believed in childhood innocence. By then the stories served quite a different purpose; it was the authors' way of punishing evil adults. Killing the child preserved the innate goodness before corruption by adult depravity. For seventeenth-century authors there was little need for psychological explanations; social explanations make good sense of the themes and the tone of Puritan literature for children, with little residue to be explained psychologically.[33]

Further evidence of the thoroughly rational motives of Puritan attention can be seen in the collaboration of those authors who were active in producing children's literature or child-rearing advice. The existence of such literary circles indicates a shared interest in these areas and something of the logic behind it. Toward the end of Elizabeth's reign several Puritans began to write for the guidance of parents (a subject that Puritans would virtually monopolize until John Locke's *Some Thoughts Concerning Education* appeared in 1693). Those Elizabethan Puritans were well acquainted with each other and would have known their common interest in the subject of children. The central figure in the group was the Cambridgeshire minister Richard Greenham, who was prominent in changing the direction of the Puritan movement from a primarily political emphasis to a more evangelical one.[34] After Queen Elizabeth triumphed over the Puritans in the 1590s, they apparently decided to influence society from below, through their children.

In the early years of the next century the Puritans' political hopes revived, and this literary activity correspondingly decreased. Such advice as was published on parenting was included then in more general works on domestic relations — most notably William Gouge's

Of Domesticall Duties (1622). But after those political hopes vanished again with Cromwell's death, there was a stream of new works on child-rearing by men who were connected through a London clergyman, Thomas Vincent. Vincent's circle included a number of men who had written for youth or for parents, all of whom were active in London in the 1660s and early 1670s.[35] The disorientation of apprentices and servants new to the city and the temptations of life there undoubtedly awakened these ministers to a specific need. Vincent became something of a celebrity among the young who flocked to his Dissenting congregation — especially to his annual Christmas sermon that was instituted for young people in 1666.[36]

At Stepney, to the east of London, there was another such minister at the center of another group of such authors. Matthew Mead began to deliver annual May Day sermons for the youth of that fast-growing suburb in 1674,[37] and his circle of acquaintances indicates a concerted interest in writing for parents and children. Mead preached the funeral sermon of Timothy Cruso, a schoolmate of Daniel Defoe at the Dissenting Academy at Newington Green. Defoe not only appropriated Cruso's name for his most famous fictional character but he dramatized in part the advice that Cruso had written for youth.[38] This circle of men will reappear in connection with debates over education.[39]

The existence of such groups suggests that the awakening interest in children was largely instrumental and social rather than psychodynamic. Dissenters mounted many concerted campaigns to reach the young and to secure their support for Dissent, and sometimes this took the form of joint recommendations of such works as Jonathan Hanmer's *An Exercitation Upon Confirmation* (1657) and *The Addresse of some Ministers . . . concerning Catechising* (1658). In 1694 the Dissenting ministers of London agreed to preach on the subject of family religion, commissioning George Hamond to publish his discourse on the subject,[40] and in 1720 they did the same, publishing *A Letter to the Protestant Dissenters Relating to the too great Neglect of Family-Worship.* It should be noted that the clergy of New England are notorious for similar efforts to reach youth through their "Jeremiads."

In appealing to the young, these Puritan authors were forced to reflect upon the character of adolescence. Of course their particular interests limited the area of discovery, but it did occur to them that adolescence presented problems related to the cause of religion, and a number of their works appear to agree that the root problem was one of differential development. "The teens" was the time of life in which the senses were the strongest and most powerfully over-balanced reason.[41] Beyond that, it was the time that the young were sufficiently independent to act on their own impulses for the first time. Therefore it was a stage of lawlessness, with youths "submitting to no Government, save that of their own Lusts."[42] The commonest complaints were the pursuit of sensuality—whoring, drunkenness, idleness, and levity. Authors agreed that the young were also rash, untruthful, stubborn, proud, ignorant scoffers, and yet credulous.[43] This was the other side of the coin, the evidence of weak intelligence, and the antidote was to give these young readers a transfusion of wisdom to make up the difference. Hence the grown-up tone of the literature. This is not a sign that the writers had no understanding of adolescence; it meant that they thought it was malleable.

There was less discussion of the special character of the preado-lescent years, but the works produced for young children do show some awareness of how small children's minds worked. In fact, some of the most interesting educational innovations of the mid-century were in catechetical method, in line with the needs of the movement to indoctrinate its members. Puritans were prominent in their atten-tion to catechizing, producing graded series of catechisms in order to begin the process as early as possible.[44] Their unanimity in this matter can be seen in the fact that while the great council of Puri-tan divines in the Westminster Assembly was deadlocked over many of its projects, it did finish its two catechisms. A Puritan educator, Herbert Palmer, advised the Assembly in this effort, taking a major step in catechism reform by phrasing each question and answer as complete statements and independent thoughts, so that they could be learned in any order or number.[45] His ideas on turning catechizing into a reflective educational method is discussed in Chapter 5.

Anglicans became aware of Palmer's innovations in the 1680s and proceeded to produce catechisms that required nothing but true/false answers, though children were probably expected to graduate to more demanding catechisms later.[46] Even in catechisms there was a party difference, with Dissenters concentrating more on doctrine and Anglicans more on moral tenets, following their respective concerns for ideological purity and social rectitude.

In time, Anglicans became even more aggressive than Dissenters in using catechizing to establish social control. In 1685 James II allowed the Jesuits to set up a charity school in London, and suddenly those who had been trying for years to interest Anglicans in educational philanthropy were deluged with money for the purpose.[47] Churchmen had come to realize the threat to their religious culture from a new population of London poor that might be susceptible to Catholic superstition or to a lawless atheism. Charity-school instruction was designed around the catechism to provide an inner check for young people in an increasingly urban and liberal society. The effort to provide charity schools took on the character of a movement—the first time that voluntary societies had managed anything of such proportions.[48] The fact that Anglicans were at least a generation behind the Puritans in their concern to spread education can again be taken as a measure of the greater security of their religious institutions.[49]

Even more surprising is how many of the earliest Anglican champions of children had Dissenting backgrounds. For twenty years after the courtesy literature tradition died away (in the late 1650s), the few Anglican works for children came from Dissenters who had later conformed: Samuel Crossman, Richard Kidder, and Simon Patrick, the last having once been Herbert Palmer's secretary. Kidder was an early proponent of charity schools, in his *Charity Directed; or, the Way to Give Alms to the Greatest Advantage* (1676). The earliest such schools were in Wales, the work of John Tillotson—a Dissenter before he became an archbishop—and his Dissenting friend Thomas Gouge (son of William Gouge). When the attempts to introduce such schools into England finally succeeded, Simon Patrick became the leading figure in raising funds.[50] The leading propagandist for this campaign was Dr. Josiah Woodward, another Anglican cleric with a Dissenting background, whose clergyman father had been an assiduous catechizer and promoter of Puritan educational philanthropies. He had named his son after that youthful model, King Josiah, "in desire of reformation,"[51] but the father's hopes were dashed and he was ejected from his church at the Restoration. Josiah conformed and later held the post of minister at the East India Company docks at Poplar, near Stepney. The man whom he succeeded in this chaplaincy was probably Samuel Peck, still another son of an ejected minister and one of the few Anglicans who wrote works for children.[52] Whether it was from Woodward's father's influence, or Peck's, or Matthew Mead's nearby ministry at Stepney, an interest in children came to dominate Woodward's ministry. If grace did not run in Dissenting families, at least an interest in children did.

The demeaning effect of these charity schools on children has been lamented since Dickens's day, but the point for cultural history is that the schools helped to define childhood and the needs of children. Administrators wanted to monopolize children during those years when they were most susceptible to moral influences, in line with the Anglican emphasis on social and moral preservation. They frankly stated their goal of boarding as many children as possible in order to get them away from evil influences, for the schools were designed to remove children from slum families that could only train them in begging, thieving, and prostitution. Indeed, the more the parents were blamed, the more the children were regarded as innocent.[53]

While such charity education was minimal, the techniques used in this moral enterprise showed an increasing sensitivity to the nature of the child. Pamphlets on pedagogy resulted from various schools' experience, and James Talbott's *The Christian School-Master* (1707) describes their graded curriculum. Teachers were encouraged to work toward a balance between unorganized play and organized competition. Unfortunately the trustees' plans for teacher-training institutes came to nothing, for they surely would have stimulated new ideas on the methods of education. In the meantime teachers were advised to observe older masters and consult with them on questions of technique.[54]

There might have been more headway in education and more discoveries of the child's development if children had been less a part of the growing cultural struggle, for education became an issue between Anglicans and Dissenters during Queen Anne's reign. This struggle, described in Chapter 5, became central to the development of party politics in that troubled period. Then, at last, the free-thinkers were heard from on the subject of education. In 1723 Bernard Mandeville reissued his shockingly radical *Fable of the Bees* that contained an appendix scoring the motives and results of the charity schools. Mandeville had no confidence in attempts to change human nature. He saw childhood as something that one could not mold to one's ideal and believed that efforts to improve society's moral tone would always be futile. Educational philanthropists simply wished to dominate, and Mandeville thought they were amply rewarded by the applause of society females with their "petty Reverence for the Poor." The only result would be to produce more literate minds than England could employ, and these would turn to organizing footmen for higher wages. Behind all of this mischief stood the clergy, who were anxious to bolster their own sagging status. But if religion were to maintain its usefulness as a soporific, he slyly warned, it must not be mixed with reading and writing.[55]

John Trenchard, the radical journalist, joined the attack in the pages of *Cato's Letters* in that same year. It was clear to him that the church hoped to end "free Government" by imposing clerical authority on the poor. At best, such beggar children could only be made into the dreariest pedants or devotees of "chimeras and airy Notions." At worst, they would upset the order of society, and "What benefit can accrue to the Publick by taking the Dregs of the People out of the Kennels, and throwing their Betters into them?"[56]

One wonders whether these free-thinkers were angered primarily by ecclesiastical pretension and only used these economic arguments to gain adherents, or whether they were as socially conservative as they appear. They certainly put the charity-school apologists on the defensive, and the latter explained over and over that the intention of the schools was not to overturn society. Modern students are inclined to treat these assurances as evidence of the reactionary origin of the movement, not realizing the nature of the attack from the "liberal" flank.[57] Mandeville and Trenchard saw more clearly than some historians the subversive possibilities of a minimal education, and while they might be philosophically liberal, they were not socially radical. It was obvious to them that barely literate minds might be open to more extreme ideas ("airy Notions") than the children who had been steeped in classical culture in the grammar schools. Indeed, it is arguable that the grammar schools, with their decadent humanism, did more to turn Englishmen toward the past and dull their appetite for learning than the charity schools did. Even the philosophers David Hume and John Gay admitted that the liberals' classical education might stand in the way of new ideas.[58] But they did not therefore press for educational reforms that would transform childhood and society. Social radicalism continued to be largely religious in character.

Secularized intellectuals had long been suspicious of educational expansion. In the seventeenth century Francis Bacon and Francis Osborne, a friend of Thomas Hobbes, had objected to the proliferation of schools, and the profane Lord Kames was still repeating Mandeville's objections in the 1770s.[59] In France, Voltaire and La Chalotais used the same arguments, reserving their more contemptuous statements about mass education for their private correspondence. Even Locke and Rousseau felt differently about schools for the poor than their treatises on the education of elites might suggest. When, in 1697, Locke submitted his ideas on poor-law reform as a member of the Board of Trade, he suggested that children on relief be sent to a "working school" from age three, in order to free parents for full-time employment while the children were kept in order and became inured to work. Reading was not mentioned, and as for educational content Locke suggested that the children be taken to church on Sunday to be "brought into some sense of religion."[60] If he had meant *knowledge* of religion, he probably would have said so.

Education for everyone still required the kind of faith that only the religiously minded could muster. In England certain Puritans were the first to attempt to translate Comenius's educational reforms into reality and to enlist the state's aid in educational expansion. Likewise, the pioneering efforts of La Salle in France and Francke in Germany to expand educational opportunity were religiously motivated.[61] Philippe Ariès associated the changes he describes, both in

education and attitudes toward children, with the religious movement of Jansenism and the Jesuit order.[62] However self-serving the
interest of religious reformers may have been, it is in sharp contrast
to the neglect of children by the more philosophical spirits of the day.

Culturally, if not psychologically, it was natural that free-thinkers
should have neglected childhood, for they were only too eager to
escape the long "childhood" to which medieval religious authority
had subjected Western man. Enlightenment, they often said, is man's
emergence from a self-imposed childhood. As yet, these philosophers
could only conceive childhood in negative terms—dependence and
ignorance. Religion reminded man of his dependence, but Enlightenment represented his coming-of-age. It is interesting to speculate
on how Lord Chesterfield or perhaps Edward Gibbon would have
looked upon baby-talk books or the products of charity education—
Chesterfield, who constantly threatened to withdraw his love if his
son did not prove worthy of his advice, and Gibbon, who turned
his *Memoir* into an attack on the cult of the child by chronicling
the delusions of his youth.[63] Along with the Romantics, one wonders
whether those Enlightened notions of adulthood and independence
were themselves an impoverishment of the human spirit.

Eventually the English Enlightenment would become a movement
in the radical political societies of Thomas Paine's time, a time in
which hope for earthly progress overcame a static social perspective.
Only then did radicals recognize the importance of education and
child care for man's future happiness. Apparently it was Paine—a
former Quaker and former Methodist—who was the first secularized
radical to advocate universal education.[64] Until then the history of
childhood was religious in flavor.

By Paine's time, Dissent would have had ample time to sour in
defeat. If it is true that Dissenting literature took a crueler edge
in the eighteenth century, it was only to be expected. The tension
between authority and autonomy, which was always implicit in the
Puritans' reform agitation and their doctrine of the rebellious spirit,
lost its political and social reference when Puritanism became a sect.
This tension could only descend to an interpersonal and psychological level.

Nevertheless, some permanent gains had been made. The social motive behind the Puritans' interest did not blind them to certain realizations about children, and they began to pay closer attention to the variety of childhood, breaking the literary icon of innocent simplicity. The Puritans were the first to encourage inner direction by disparaging "worldly" values and to design reflective educational techniques as part of their early realization of the distinction between education and indoctrination. This respect for intellectual autonomy would be joined with a commitment to the child's moral autonomy. One hardly expects to discover such attitudes within Puritanism, and perhaps they hardly expected it themselves. But the peculiarity of their societal position and the demands of their Text had forced them to a new understanding of these strange new beings in their midst.

CHAPTER TWO

Puritan Realism
in Picturing Children

The beginning of literary realism in the treatment of childhood marks a notable advance in the history of the human consciousness. Childhood is, after all, the most difficult of all subjects for us to face in an objective way, as our vision passes through a filter of memories of ourselves at that stage, including our unresolved conflicts and unfulfilled wishes. Insofar as we remain immature, our notion of childhood will remain a projection—of self-pity, self-righteousness, or self-hate. "The child" can also serve as a cultural icon for an entire society—an image of perfection or of some power or virtue which adults seem to have lost.

There are, however, other times when writers have broken through to more realistic perceptions of the child's life and have forced these views on their culture. One such period in England's history was during the seventeenth century, when Puritan and Dissenting authors focused a new attention on children. The most striking feature of this literature is that one stereotype of childhood did not simply replace another and the needs of a pessimistic Puritan theology did not dictate that descriptions of childhood innocence give way to tales of childhood depravity. Rather, Puritan authors created a much greater variety in their treatment of childhood than other biographers had. Given the difficult social circumstances with which their children were coping, there is nothing in the stories to strain our belief, however repellent they may be. It would not even be true to say that the Puritans put forward a new view of childhood; rather, they presented several different views. This variety itself amounted to a greater realism, and it was the taste for individualized detail which was later to be exploited in the realistic novel.

The more realistic appraisal of childhood may have been jarring to others who thought that the "realism" profaned something that was considered holy. A certain horror at sacrilege would have been perfectly natural, given the importance that the icon of holy simplicity had assumed in English literature. The high point of a regressive devotion to image over reality may well have occurred in the High Middle Ages, when the image of the young ran heavily to such prodigious youngsters as Bevis of Southampton. More regularly, however, children in medieval folklore and literature were presented pathetically, as the victims of adult misconduct, abandoned by their parents and buffeted by the world.[1] Of course, this view of childhood still persists in our fairy tales. The principal difference is that in medieval literature there was no alternative image of actual children, even in books that purported to be factual.

The *Golden Legend* is such a book. This thirteenth-century compilation became the standard version of the saints' lives, and it touched on the early years of more than a tenth of its subjects. Several patterns of early piety are established in that hagiography which strain our belief to various degrees. There are girls who refuse marriage to lustful Roman officials and, as a consequence, are ripped apart in the most awful martyrdom. There are boys who run away to monasteries or elsewhere to escape their parents' worldly ambitions for them. There are also children whose mothers had dreams or experienced other omens of their future greatness and whose earliest years confirmed their exceptional characters, and there are a few whose exploits as infants were miraculous in themselves. St. Nicholas was said to have stood up the day he was born and to have fasted by taking the breast only once on Wednesdays and Fridays. St. Quiricus, at age three, attacked his mother's persecutors and was inspired to speak the words of the Holy Spirit against them. This sort of thing also might happen to ordinary children; for example, St. Brixius had to clear himself of a fornication charge by getting a month-old bastard to declare in court that Brixius was not his father.[2]

In general, the alleged deeds of these saints as infants indicated that their character was not their own but that the saints themselves were God's gifts to the church. Youthful saints were not practical examples of holy living so much as objects of devotion, and as such, the farther removed they were from everyday life, the better they served their purpose. Hagiography is distinguished from biography by its use more than by its form.

The influence of the *Golden Legend* in England was extensive.[3] Translated by William Caxton and others, it went through at least eight printed editions by 1527, but Renaissance humanists scorned such fabulous tales. Literary historians have remarked on the fact that the humanists found little use for child characters of any sort, devoted as they were to "the cultivation of the highest human physical and mental powers. . . . When [fictional] children do appear in sixteenth-century literature, they are, more often than not, aristocratic revivals of the classical ideal of the *puer senex*," the child who is old before his time.[4] One sees it in Shakespeare's child characters, who are praised for their precocity or thrust upon the stage as figures of mute pathos.

John Foxe, who at one time was called a Puritan but is now termed an Erasmian or moderate, offers an example of this humanist attitude whenever he touches upon the biographies of some actual children.[5] His *Acts and Monuments* of the English martyrs was published before the advent of Puritanism and was generally popular in Protestant circles, but he concerned himself with childhood only when forced to do so, as in the cases of Edward VI and Lady Jane Grey who did not live beyond youth. These unfortunates were praised for their precocious maturity and were, in any event, expected to be exceptional because of their high birth. Edward was said to have had a "sage and mature ripeness in wit and all princely ornaments," including clemency, gravity, and devotion. He was considered remarkable for his "knowledge of tongues, and other sciences, where-unto he seemed rather born, than brought up." It was conceded that his knowledge of navigation, genealogy, and finance were not inborn but rather the result of application, and he is pictured as laboriously taking notes in a Greek cipher on sermons and on "things that pertained to princely affairs." Lamenting his early death, Foxe implies that England was undeserving of such a king, as it proved by relapsing into popery so soon after his death. Quoting an old saw, Foxe concluded: "Things that be exceeding excellent, be not commonly long permanent."[6]

Lady Jane had been, if anything, even less childlike. As a girl her mastery of languages was astonishing, and at sixteen or seventeen she had written with erudition to a backsliding chaplain on the errors of Catholicism. When death came she was not a stranger to it, having grown up, as she put it, in "woful days." Children, and especially the highly placed, were close to death in those dangerous days. Her parting advice to a younger sister was, "Live still to die, that you by death may purchase eternal life. And trust not that the tenderness of your age shall lengthen your life; for as soon (if God call) goeth the young as the old: and labour always to learn to die."[7]

Foxe's highest praise was that a child was prematurely old. On the other hand, he had heard of foolish children who "detected" their Protestant parents to the authorities and were then forced to light their parents' execution fires. This, he termed the most unnatural order in all of history, since it flouted the most sacred authority on earth, that of parents over their children. Foxe derived some hope from hearing that other children had encouraged one of the martyrs in the flames by crying, "Lord, strengthen thy servant, and keep thy promise," which he saw as mainly a commendation of their parents.[8]

Anglican biography developed in this humanist tradition of respect for youthful paragons, and the purpose of the many biographical collections of the day was to describe the heroes of the English church and state in an edifying light. Anglican authors apparently did not think that mentioning their subjects' childhood years was necessary; for example, Izaak Walton's lives of English divines almost ignored the time before their university years. He only remarked on Richard Hooker's uncommon gravity and slowness of speech as a child, and on Robert Sanderson's diligence and mild disposition, qualities that made them seem more mature. The general impression is that these pillars of the church spent childhood "in a sweet content."[9]

Two royalist martyrologies that commemorated those who had suffered under Puritan rule also contained nothing on the subjects' lives before their university, legal, or military training.[10] Several other Anglican biographical collections sometimes mentioned precocious intellectual attainments by way of explaining an early appearance at the universities, but the subject of childhood did not arise otherwise. One biography gave a noblewoman the character of early piety; because she was a girl, there was presumably no educational record to report.[11] Thomas Fuller's *History of the Worthies of England* was typical in beginning his subjects' lives with the college, inn of court, or the religious order in which they were "bred up."[12] One feels that the dignity of his subjects would have suffered by the inclusion of their puerilities and that Anglicans were sensitive to such breaches of decorum. The point in terming these biographers Anglicans at this early date is that their works had not only a didactic but a sectarian purpose; the church's dignity was bound up with that of its "worthies."

David Lloyd was unique among Anglican biographers in his interest in the curiosities surrounding the birth and early years of his subjects. Naturally, he was dependent on many informants, and must have been preserving a tradition in English culture which other writers had chosen to ignore. He noticed, for instance, that a twelfth child often proved remarkable, and he frequently used astrological metaphors, though rarely an actual horoscope, in accounting for his subjects. Although astrology may have seemed a bit exotic to his readers, metempsychosis — the transfer of souls — apparently did not. It struck Lloyd that Sir John Finch was born the same night that another jurist, Edmund Plowden, died, and that the Catholic controversialist Thomas Stapleton was born on the same day that Sir Thomas More died. Judge Sir Francis Crawley was said to have been born the very hour that Plowden died, and his father is said to have recommended the law to him for that reason.[13] Spencer Compton, Earl of Northampton, was thought to have been born the same hour and near the spot where the Gunpowder Plotters were captured, an omen of the rebellion which he would die fighting. Compton's devotion to the royalist cause dated from his first step, which was to reach for the king's picture, and his first word was "king." (In fact, young Compton was born in 1601, before England acquired a king.) Lloyd recorded similar presages in the lives of Archbishop Laud, whose strange dreams marked him for greatness, and of Robert Bertie, Earl of Lindsay, whose first word was "sword" and who chose the sword when Sir Walter Raleigh offered him the classic choice of sword or toy. Readers are left to make what they will of the tale that when Prince Henry clapped an archbishop's hat on the head of young Charles I the latter tore it off and trampled on it.[14]

These prophetic, premonitory stories were a common form of the denial of the free development of character or history. Historian Keith Thomas has recently remarked on the oddity of predictions that were fabricated after the event. Apparently they stemmed from a desire to justify events as preordained and to soften the impact of radical change. It gave history the providential legitimation it needed in a traditional society.[15] To such a mentality, outstanding figures could best be explained or justified by uncanny circumstances.

Lloyd was aware that such tales were being discounted when he was writing in the 1660s. While recording that Sir Thomas Trevor entered life smiling rather than crying, he felt it necessary to make light of the similar Catholic account of St. Rumbald,[16] but he is like the Catholic hagiographers in implying the predetermination of childhood and of character. In Lloyd's case this was probably not a considered theological position; his predilection for these stories may amount only to a delight in curiosities, similar to those found in John Aubrey's biographical notes. All of Lloyd's children were prodigious, from Sir John Suckling, who was born two months late and spoke Latin at five ("being so soon a man, that like Adam, we would think he was born so") to Ralph Hopton, who had memorized six hundred Latin and Greek words, with their genders and declensions, by four and a half.[17] The comparison of Lloyd's *Memoirs* with the writings of other Anglican biographers makes their reticence concerning childhood that much more apparent.

Meanwhile, Catholic hagiography maintained its older traditions, implicitly rejecting any "normal" character development in the lives of the saints. As late as 1745 the Catholic coadjutor bishop Richard Challoner's *Britannia Sancta* presented the childhoods of Britain's own saints in an almost medieval light. When he mentioned childhood there was no sense of development within those years, only an intimation that the subject "pass'd his youth in an innocent simplicity."[18] This implied a denial of conflict or growth, in effect a denial of childhood itself—as a stage of life separated from adulthood. The saints are usually represented as having maintained the same character throughout life; indeed, many are said to have given evidence of their blessedness even before birth, by portents or dreams experienced by their mothers. In his entire list there were only two who were reported to have fallen into sin during their youthful years.[19] For others, whose conversions came later in life, childhood seemed irrelevant, as in the case of St. Ulrick, who was made a priest as a mere boy but lived the life of a rich worldling until a religious awakening. The faults of his youth are passed over as mere heedlessness, like those that the *Golden Legend* mentioned in alluding to the boyhood of St. Francis of Assisi.[20]

When Challoner wrote the *Memoirs of Missionary Priests*, which commemorated the Catholics martyred in England from the reign of Elizabeth until the Popish Plot, he used more modern sources and the stories have a more realistic cast, but only half a dozen of the lives include any mention of the subjects' early years. Even when these heroes were converted to the Catholic church when young, it is pallidly explained as a "misliking" of the schismatical English church, and there is no hint of a moral or intellectual crisis. Challoner's only lively tale was that of George Gervase, who was kidnapped to "the Indies" as a boy. There he "quite Lost his Religion" before making his way back to England twelve years later, at which time he was converted or reconverted by his brother. Another of Challoner's subjects saw a vision of coming persecutions while still a child and growing up a Protestant.[21] The rest are simply described as having pious or sweet dispositions.[22] The only development one can see in this hagiography was a decline in attention to youth.

When one turns to Puritan and Dissenting literature, one steps into a different world where childhood is presented as real and important. In preserving the stories of children who had left a godly testimony before dying young and the accounts of the early years of those who had lived to become leaders, Dissenters did not present only the stories that reflected credit on the subject. Some of these accounts verged on cautionary anecdotes, and others magnified God's mercy, but none of them strain our belief in the way that the other traditions do, although we would interpret many of the stories quite differently. Above all, they show a variety in treatment that suggests a greater realism.

To my knowledge, the first account of a real child of ordinary social rank, from William Sloane's bibliography of children's books or other sources, is the Presbyterian John Bryan's funeral sermon for twelve-year-old Cicely Puckering, which was delivered in 1636. It is typical of several later works. Cicely had been a model of patience and of "gracious" discourse. It was recalled, to her credit, that she had once reproved a nurse for grieving for her own dead child, seeing that God's will was always accomplished in all events. Cicely was, indeed, a grave child, having smiled only twice during her last illness, both times at the mention of death. Though she grieved over her sin, she did enjoy assurance of salvation and looked forward to union with Christ. Bryan presented Cicely's example for the instruction of adults more than for children, reminding them of the Savior's warning, "Except ye be converted, and become as little children, ye shall not enter into the kingdom of heaven."[23] Already, the child could be seen as a model for adults.

Two years later an Anglican clergyman, Charles Croke, tried his hand at the same genre. His publication differs in two respects from Bryan's work and the later Dissenting tradition in that he dealt with a child of the upper gentry and simply characterized him (as obedient, sensitive, serious, kind, and clever) rather than telling stories that would have demonstrated these traits.[24] Other Anglican biographers did not follow up this work with a tradition of more realistic description. Perhaps their desire to deal with figures of rank ran counter to the impulse to offer an uninhibited portrait.

In 1636 a cautionary tale was published that actually named the child, the first such mentioned in Sloane's bibliography. Cautionary stories were already common in chapbooks and ballads, but there is seldom any assurance that they were true. Only a few such works were taken so seriously that their authors were willing to put their own names to them. But in this case Robert Abbot, a Puritan parson, took some pains to describe the sad life of a young parishioner, William Rogers, who had fallen into vain company, which led to very early alcoholism, sickness, despair, and death. Abbot hoped to reclaim others who might be entering just such a course, for it is not suggested that Rogers was unusually wicked. He had been a civil and virtuous youth before he began to neglect religion, and it was not indicated that God had intervened to cut him down in his wayward course. To Abbot, the effects of sins of the flesh were quite sufficient to explain the young man's decline, and there is nothing supernatural about the story. In fact, its very realism shows that the author intended it to serve as a practical warning rather than as sensationalistic entertainment in the manner typical of the chapbooks. Abbot does not even seem vindictive. He had offered Rogers assurance of God's forgiveness and could not account for Rogers's persistence in the view that he was damned.[25] He did not suggest that the doctrine of predestination would offer a sufficient explanation.

A more serious indictment of youth was published anonymously in 1641, possibly by a Puritan minister, purporting to be the actual confession of an apothecary's apprentice who had poisoned his master.[26] But Puritan authors in general were not given to such writings, and the only other cautionary tale that Sloane lists among his seventeenth-century children's books appeared in 1668, the story of sixteen-year-old Thomas Savage who had been enticed by his girl friend to steal from his master. The theft had resulted in the murder of a housemaid, for which the boy was eventually executed. The short book was not primarily an account of the crime or of punishment, providential or otherwise, but was rather a description of Tom's conversion while in Newgate Gaol. The six Puritan ministers who visited him and who published the story of his conversion left it, as far as possible, in his own words. They did not conceal his subsequent lapses into drunkenness or his temptations to escape, for they could also show growing signs of the authenticity of his conversion — his love for God's people, his increasing horror of sin, and his appreciation of God's condescension in the offer of grace.[27] This is the only account of a real youngster which became really popular in the seventeenth century, though some like Janeway's *Token for Children* were to attain popularity later. Savage's story went through approximately twelve editions in the first year alone and numerous reprintings on into the eighteenth century.

Far more typical of the Puritan or Dissenting interests were the stories of pious children. Their purpose was not simply to excite wonder or admiration, in the manner of the medieval tales, but to encourage emulation. Medieval authors had offered the lives of the saints as a guide to life, but only as the stars serve as a guide to sailors; the reader was not expected to reach that level. One did not simply choose sainthood in the medieval understanding of the word. It might be supposed that the doctrine of predestination formed a similar barrier against spiritual ambition among Puritans, but clearly the stories are meant to inspire action. In fact, these books may have served as a means by which the Puritan clergy counteracted the fatalism implied in the doctrine of predestination.

The very titles of these works make clear that the lives described are meant as practical examples, as is evident in a 1661 account entitled *The Virgins Pattern: in the exemplary life and lamented death of Mrs. Susanna Perwich . . . for the use and benefit of others*. Susanna, however, does not quite meet our expectations. She had a sweet disposition and was accomplished in music, dancing, penmanship, and poetry; but shortly before her death, at the age of twenty-one, she experienced a heightened sense of the reality of sin and of Christ's mercy. The author terms it a conversion and describes how it changed her character, making her more constant in religious duties and more censorious. Apparently this did not turn her friends against her; upon her death they contributed elegies, acrostic rhymes, and anagrams upon her name, all of which became traditional in these accounts.[28]

Similarly, in 1666 a Baptist, John Vernon, published the life of his son for the encouragement of children who were facing religious persecution during the Restoration. Little Caleb had been an obedient and precocious child, begging to read the Bible at four years old, but the seriousness of life had borne down on him at age seven when his father was jailed for nonconformity. Some of the boy's letters are included in the account to show his state of mind at this time and perhaps to serve as models for young readers. The father described how by age ten Caleb had relaxed sufficiently among his schoolmates that he had sometimes been "frothy" or silly, but Caleb was at least aware of his faults and gave suitable answers to those who were to judge his candidacy for baptism. This interrogation is included at some length. Baptism came a bit earlier than Baptists were accustomed to administer that sacrament since at twelve Caleb was obviously dying of consumption. It was he who insisted on immersion, though he had to be carried to the service, and he died shortly afterwards. Again, his schoolmates contributed verses and anagrams, which are presented in the account, much as great poets and scholars would have done for prominent figures.[29]

Baptists faced more severe persecution than most of the other Dissenters, and another of their ministers, Henry Jessey, offered the stories of two pious girls by way of influencing other children. In neither case were the girls presented as flawless in virtue, but they were serious-minded. Mary Warren worried about the lack of such seriousness in others and about her own pride. Her recorded adages relate to her final pains and God's provision, and others are as intimate as her worries over whether her father truly loved her mother. The other girl was eleven when she fell sick and found that she lacked the assurance of true faith, but after her father tried to offer her comfort from Scripture she did discover a firm belief within her soul. Recovery was something of an anticlimax.[30] The fact that she was still alive was probably responsible for the fact that she was never identified by name. There must always have been some fear in such cases that children might grow up to discredit their early testimony.

Use of the children's own words and the presence of realistic detail testify to the authors' belief that these child biographies represented real possibilities for young readers. The audience that learned to expect this treatment of real subjects was being prepared for the later, novelistic realism. Adults were more open in describing children than they were in describing adults, and the details of a child's life were necessarily more humble. Child subjects, therefore, have fewer secrets than any group of adults in seventeenth-century literature. This would be especially true of the dying children, who were the most defenseless of subjects.

One particular work from this period seems to defy our characterization of child biographies as edifying and instructional rather than hagiographical. That is the account of Martha Hatfield, which appeared in 1653. Martha had lost her sight and hearing at age eleven, and she suffered convulsions and occasional paralysis. The case baffled all who saw her, but there was obviously a religious dimension to her illness since her ravings concerned the things of God and her fits involved ecstatic visions. The girl had not shown remarkable religious interest before, though she had always been a sad girl, hiding and weeping for long periods. It is hard to know how much pretense may have been involved, for while her mouth might be paralyzed for months and unable to take solid food, at other times she would suddenly rebuke those who wondered aloud about the possibility of satanic influence and attacked Quakers who claimed similar revelations. Observers claimed that she never spoke nonsense and that she sometimes even corrected herself while under the prophetic impulse, but it seemed uncanny that she could break out teeth with her gnashing and go several weeks without food and half an hour without apparent breath. All of these factors give depth to her banal and repetitive speeches on the sweetness of Christ and her fears of Satan, that subtle serpent. Having no reason to suspect a sexual basis for her disturbances, observers could make nothing of her uncontrollable giggling after saying "Come, my people, enter into my Tabernacle" or of her following depression over Satan's temptations and her announced desire that all Christians may become pure virgins.

Some explanation was needed and it was found in the millenarian expectations of the 1650s. Martha's Puritan vicar admitted that God generally governed the world through uniform laws, but to overcome unbelief He might use extraordinary interventions, "especially in these last Ages of the World." Martha, then, was part of God's call for a national repentance. She had made no original prophecies, much to the disappointment of some onlookers, but the fact that she had recovered after the community began monthly days of prayer and "humiliation" provided the moral of the episode. Martha recovered and claimed to know nothing of what she had said during her long ordeal. Indeed, she felt so ordinary that she expressed the fear of living in such a way as to bring shame on her earlier testimony.[31]

Of course, Martha's experience could not be emulated by other children, nor did it fit the Puritans' eschatological expectations as closely as they might have wished. There are incoherent elements that the author allows to stand for, like so many of the pious scientists of his day, he tried to honor God by scrupulous accuracy in describing this phenomena. The compatibility of the Puritan mentality, literary realism, and empirical philosophy is evident in these accounts,[32] and that, not the demands of Calvinist theology, seems to have offered the perspective for these works.

Another Puritan work published in 1653 might suggest the same sort of millenarian explanation as that used in Martha's case. John Eliot, in reporting the progress of his work among the Indians in Massachusetts, included descriptions of two Indian children under three who had surprised their respective families by expressing their submission to God's will even as they were succumbing to plague.[33] Eliot thought that this was remarkable in children so young, but he did not suggest that this missionary success augured the coming of New Heavens and New Earth in the New World. Ethnic prejudice might account for the failure to make this connection.

The Restoration of the Stuarts seemed to mock the millenarian dreams of the Puritans. Children would later revive these same hopes among Quakers and even Anglicans, but in the meantime Dissenting child biography fell back into the old pattern of an exemplary piety.[34] The most notorious of all such works appeared in 1671: James Janeway's *A Token for Children: Being An Exact Account of the Conversion, Holy and Exemplary Lives and Joyful Deaths of several Young Children.*[35] Janeway's subjects were seven boys and six girls, only two of whom could have lived beyond twelve. He had studied young children closely enough to list their characteristic failings: lying, profanity, truancy, and playing on the Sabbath. His pious examples are not simply the reverse of this image, however, and the children's spiritual development did not follow an invariable pattern. In short, these are true stories. Some are fragmentary, but Janeway did not flesh them out with stock virtues; in fact, he shows a certain independence from theological prejudice. He left the theologians to make what they could of the fact that one of the girls was notably pious from the time she could speak, "as if she were Sanctified from the very womb." On the other hand, one beggar boy had acquired such bad habits by the age of eight that people were amazed at his later change. In half of the stories there is no record of a dramatic awakening to religious concerns, and where he reports that children showed a love for family prayers or a conscientious obedience by age two or three, he comes close to denying the necessity for conversion.

So often criticized but so seldom read, it seems necessary to recount just one of the stories from Janeway's collection to give the flavor of the work. The one that strained belief even then, according to Janeway's preface to the second edition, was the account of a boy who, before he was two or could "speak plain, would be crying after God, and was greatly desirous to be taught good things." He objected whenever his parents tried to put him to bed without a time of family devotions and would shame them into fulfilling this duty. Not satisfied with that, he would sometimes be found kneeling by himself in prayer. As he began to grow up, he enjoyed going to church and to school, and he would often tell his mother, "I have had a sweet lesson today: will you please to give me leave to fetch my book that you may hear it?" He sometimes broke into "tears and sobs" while reading the Scriptures and grieved over the general corruption of his nature even when he had no specific sins to repent of. It is a relief to find that he did sometimes play with other children. But Janeway was more impressed with the fact that he could often be found praying by himself instead and that he made it a point to concentrate on his Bible or catechism on the Sabbath. Playing with others must have been a trial since the boy so dreaded hearing profanity or "filthy words." At times, they "would even make him tremble, and ready to go home and weep." At age six, when he learned that he was dying, he expressed some fear as to his eternal destiny, but when friends reminded him of his prayers for forgiveness and a sincere conversion, he brightened up. The doctrine of the resurrection of the body struck him as strange, but he allowed that "nothing was impossible to God." [36]

It is not an attractive picture but it is probably sufficiently accurate to suggest some of the strains that such children faced. The censoriousness, self-sufficiency, bookishness, and emotionalism that characterize Janeway's subjects are deplorable in children so young, but an overdeveloped inner life and imagination were no doubt necessary if they were to live as Dissenting strangers in a hostile world. Evidence that children did identify with these paragons appears in some unlikely places. Benjamin Franklin thought enough of Janeway's work to print an edition of it in 1749, and William Godwin (1756–1836), the famous free-thinker, remembered the work as a major inspiration to him to accomplish some great thing in his own life.[37]

Not everyone believed Janeway's stories, however, and in subsequent editions he had to offer the names and addresses of witnesses to stop the "atheistical objections, scoffs and jeers" of his detractors. Others who observed the commercial success of the work did not emulate his devotion to truthfulness. For example, Benjamin Harris, the interloping publisher, tried to pass off *A Token for Youth* as by "J. J.," using at least six of Janeway's children along with twelve others for whom he was unwilling to give names and who are described in less circumstantial detail. Others do not seem to have caught Janeway's point. Cotton Mather compiled *A Token, for the Children of New England* (1700), but its theme is not so much early piety as early death. The only ages given are the subjects' ages at death, but nothing is said of conversions. Rather, the children are blandly presented as models of Christian virtue. Essentially, it was an expression of regional pride, Mather adding this material to the first American edition of Janeway's book to show that New England was not without youthful models of its own.[38]

Closer to Janeway's work, and almost as unpopular among historians of children's literature, is Thomas White's *A Little Book for Little Children* (1674).[39] White retrieved some grisly tales of child martyrs from Josephus and the Books of Maccabees. To these less-than-realistic stories he added a long account of one intellectually precocious child and another story about the premonition of an early death experienced by two children. Two other cases are more ordinary and present the very words of the children, taken from letters and conversations. White claimed to have collected other examples that he was forebearing to mention. Perhaps these children were still alive and might yet discredit their associates.

The fact that most of these pious children died has led some historians to presume that Dissenters thought that the only good child was a dead one, but in a separate literary genre the Dissenters collected what evidence they could of the childhoods of those who lived to become prominent. Naturally, these accounts contained less vivid detail on the figures who had survived, since childhood was far in the past by the time anyone thought to make a record. Also, childhood is only a small part of the biographies of notable Dissenters, but from the first, their realism contrasted sharply with Catholic hagiography and with the lack of concern among humanists or Anglicans.

The fact that Dissenters made an effort to recover the earliest history of their heroes can probably be attributed to the fact that the Puritan movement was a reforming venture. However traditional the Puritans or Dissenters might be in certain respects, they did not think it was sufficient to fill social roles in the old manner. Biographers wanted to see how their early leaders had found a new path and how they had stood up against social pressures. They sensed that even childhood could not be ignored. Of course, their explanations of character change often fell back on God's inexplicable intervention, but they were not certain how much might still be explained in natural terms, and they strove for realism in their descriptions.

The Dissenting writer Samuel Clarke published the largest number of these biographies, but his dependence on others who composed and preserved the accounts resulted in an obvious diversity in the reports. The first of Clarke's collections (1650) included continental reformers going as far back as Calvin, who was remembered as "a severe reproover of his School-fellows faults." The Englishman Bernard Gilpin had likewise reproved a friar's hypocrisy in youth.[40] But not all of Clarke's heroes were so exemplary. Puritan theologian William Perkins was admittedly "very wilde" in his university years, and the Frenchman Francis Junius had given himself up to "vile pleasures" for a year as a student before he was reclaimed for religion. Clarke commented obliquely of another subject that "the Lord in mercie forgave the vanities and ignorances of his youth, and preserved him from such falls, as might have made him a shame to the Saints."[41] Obviously he was sensitive to the charge that the Dissenting movement could not control its own children. The Anglican minister Thomas Fuller had similarly answered the Catholic charge that the children of England's clergy turned out badly—an argument of divine judgment on clerical marriage. Fuller pointed out that Anglican clergymen were usually old when they did marry and therefore tended to dote on their children or that they died before seeing them grow up. Then too, as a son of the manse, he knew that more was expected of the children of the clergy and that an unforgiving public watched them more closely than others.[42] Still, there is a difference between Puritan and Anglican authors; only Puritans seemed to think that the behavior of the children, even of the laity, might bring the adequacy of their movement into question.

In *The Lives of Thirty-Two English Divines* (1677) Clarke continued his mixed reports of a later group of Puritan leaders for whom there was more recent record. Paul Baynes had led an "irregular" life at Cambridge, and he, John Cotton, and John Dod were only converted while students there.[43] Mrs. Jane Ratcliffe had been frivolous in youth before her conversion. Others were exemplary, like Julines Herring who used to organize his schoolfellows to pray and repeat the catechism, and Herbert Palmer who even at four or five would ask "that he might hear somewhat of God." Palmer, who later became a reformer of catechetical method, had always professed to want to be a clergyman while other children were being asked whether they would prefer "to be a Lawyer, a Courtier, a Countrey Gentleman."[44] Still others had been converted as young as ten, before conversion could be represented as a dramatic break in the course of their lives.[45]

The number of allusions to childhood increased with each new work by Clarke, from seven to eleven and to sixteen in *Lives of Sundry Eminent Persons* (1683). There is even greater variety in this last work, as it includes Clarke's own autobiographical sketch, in which he admits having "degenerated from the Principles of my first Education" after age thirteen. Lady Mary, Countess of Warwick, and Mrs. Margaret Baxter had admitted at least to youthful vanity,[46] and others had experienced some guilt that had led them to a conversion crisis—the theft of flowers or fruit, the encouraging of cockfights, or a dandified extravagance.[47] For some, conversion did not enter the picture, either for lack of record or because it was not such an invariable pattern of spiritual experience among Dissenters as it became in the Methodism and Evangelicalism of later centuries. There were others who seem to have had an easier passage, perhaps an experience referred to as conversion but without indication of spiritual conflict.[48]

Nowhere is the contrast between Anglican and Dissenting treatment of childhood shown more clearly than in Clarke's pictures of Sir Philip Sidney and Lady Elizabeth Langham. For Sidney, Clarke relied on the Elizabethan memorial by Sir Fulke Greville: "I knew him from a Child, yet I never knew him other than a Man: With such a staidness of mind, lovely and familiar gravity, as carried grace and reverence above greater years."[49] Such a testimonial seems old-fashioned and unrealistic in the context of Dissenting biography, where there was already some suspicion of youthful piety, and this suspicion appears most notably in Clarke's account of young Elizabeth. Her mother, the Countess of Huntington, had brought her up "secured from the knowledge of Vice" and "from the very News of those evils which were acted abroad," as was possible in the isolation of a wealthy rural household. The countess's success in this case was alarming, for Elizabeth grew up to be such a model child in her modesty, prudence, and charity that her mother began to fear that the girl had become too scrupulous. The countess felt the need to tell her that "sundry things, which she had spoken to her, were never intended as peremptory Commands, but only as Advices and Counsels, which, in things of Indifference, must not be overcharged." Fearing that Elizabeth would "overstrain the Bow," her mother told her that "if she intended to hold on that course, she was not fit to live in this World." The daughter did not change her demeanor, however, and the biographer admits some surprise that her devotion "had not the Fate that usually befalls such *Precosious* Flowers, to be blasted and fall off before it come to maturity."[50] In short, Calvinists had discovered that children could be too good to be true.

In the generation after Clarke, Edmund Calamy III took up the task of collecting the records of Dissenting biography (published in 1702 and 1713), showing the same interest in childhood and the same variety of description. Some figures, such as both of John Wesley's grandfathers, were simply remembered as pious youths, their piety apparently proof against temptation.[51] John Bailey had been instrumental in the conversion of his licentious father, who was struck to the heart after hearing his son pray with the family at the request of the boy's mother. Calamy also apparently approved of another subject who was said to have hid under hedges to pray while other children played and in later life was severe with children caught playing on the Sabbath.[52] But there were also less edifying examples. Richard Baxter was censorious as a child and had to be converted from this pharisaism, while other subjects had resisted God's calling. It took a bout with smallpox to break down Nathaniel Bradshaw's youthful resistance and two remarkable deliverances, including a near drowning, in Edmund Staunton's case.[53] Some were even worse advertisements for the Dissenting movement, being prey to the vanities and dissipations common to youth, reading obscene books, and becoming "addicted to expensive and forbidden sports."[54]

Most surprising of all are those subjects who, in late adolescence, skated on the edge of the abyss, beginning to doubt the very "foundations" of religion. Such was the case of Nicholas Thoroughgood, who spent some time in the skeptical atmosphere of the University of Padua but eventually became so convinced of the reality of spiritual things that he left for Cambridge and the ministry. Richard Hawes had, to all appearances, been converted at nine but lost this "deep sense of religion" while studying for the ministry. After he was disinherited by a father who was indifferent to religion, Richard began to drink heavily and even considered suicide, but thanks to a providential preservation during the Civil Wars his faith was restored. Even this did not mean an immediate release from serious doubt and temptation.[55] Thomas Browning, who had been "designed by his parents for the ministry," saw his early piety wear off at Oxford where he became "hardened" toward religion. It was only after his marriage that he was induced to attend services again and was struck by spiritual truths. A remarkable candor is shown in the admission that Thomas Rowe's early seriousness in religion apparently brought on a melancholy that lasted through his adult ministry.[56] A similar account was published separately in the life and death of young John Draper, who had been tempted to blasphemy and unbelief. He confessed to snickering at sermons and even to tearing up his Bible in a rebellious fit at age seven.[57]

These were the spiritual skeletons in the closet of Dissent, just as the neuroses of a movement's heroes might be today. Even the revelation of youthful lusts was not as damaging to the Puritan cause as bouts with unbelief. While it might be embarrassing to allude to the grosser sins of a church's leaders, these failings do not call the church's ministrations into doubt. By contrast, the admission of a debilitating melancholy, suicidal despair, disbelief, and blasphemous impulses strike at the heart of a faith, calling the ideological adequacy of the movement into question.

Dissenters were frank in their treatment of such episodes. They could afford to be, since by God's grace the subjects had triumphed over their temptations to doubt. Indeed, Calamy may have included the stories to encourage those young readers who had faced such doubts and emptiness. Movements can survive the taunts of moral hypocrisy and the lapses of sensual youth, but they could not endure if the faith of the rising generation were to fail. The need for a conscious commitment is more obvious to the adherents of a movement than to those whose views are buttressed by the social and cultural institutions of their day.

One notable feature in this literature, then, is the very uncertain place of conversion in the accounts. It seems that the biographers were looking for such an experience but often did not find it. They never apologized for the omission, however, and some accounts implicitly denied the necessity of a crisis experience. Like Janeway, writers left readers to make what they would of children who were always simply good. On the other hand, it seems that conversions were expected in childhood rather than later in life.

Quaker works make something of a contrast in the matter of conversion. It hardly enters the picture where the usual expectation is unspotted innocence. The thing that makes the Quakers' child biographies so poignant is the juxtaposition of the ostracism and persecution that children suffered with the childhood innocence that they proclaimed. This assertion of innocence makes Quaker works less diverse and less realistic than other Puritan accounts and more like the image of the child which was to prevail in Victorian fiction.

The tone of their accounts can be seen in the first of the Quaker memorials, published in 1675. Eleven-year-old Joseph Briggins had never resisted his parents' instructions or been sullen. Mary Whiting, too, was said to have been sober and tractable from her childhood, always more apt to weep than laugh, and she lamented the dancing and sports of her village neighbors. In writing the story, her brother was so bold as to say that she lived her entire life unspotted from "any defilement whatsoever," in that "purity and innocency" to which most persons must be restored by grace.[58] Jonah Lawson's innocence supported him against the temptations of a "mixed school," where he stood against quarrelling, lying, and swearing. The parents of eight-year-old Sarah Camme testified that they had never heard her utter an "unsavory word," and even in her dying delirium her expressions were "Harmless and Innocent."[59] Little Sarah knew well what life could bring; she matter-of-factly braced her sister for a martyrdom by burning or drowning, as she imagined. Elizabeth Braythwaite had already been jailed for her religious profession when she died at age seventeen, and God had prepared her for that ordeal by visions of heaven.[60]

Given this birthright innocence, there was little possibility of development even had these children lived, but other Quaker children were not so lucky and needed the kind of visitation of the Spirit which was reported in 1679. This revival raised the same apocalyptic hopes as those inspired by Martha Hatfield in the 1650s. A collection of eyewitness accounts of the events at Waltham Abbey, Essex, was published in December, 1679, when the revival was already six months old. At first, only a few girls had been affected, but the stirring then spread to more than forty children, especially to some "who had been more stubborn" before. Some girls as young as eight were involved, and the testimonies of six children are recorded, presumably in their own words, for, as the editors make clear, Quakers took seriously the notion that God proclaims His truth from "the mouths of babes and sucklings." The contributors of these accounts hoped that publication might prompt the revival to spread to other lands.[61]

These hopes were realized in 1689 when reports of the "French Prophets" began to appear. It was said that the movement began with a sixteen-year-old French shepherdess, Isabeau Vincent, who first prophesied in 1688, and the strength of the revival for the next six months was among children even younger than she.[62] At first this news was welcomed in England, as it was reported that these young prophets had predicted William III's victory over James II at a time when the rumors in France were to the contrary.[63] But when "Camisards" showed up in England in 1706, the English took a much less favorable view of this wild revivalism. Children were still prominent in the movement in France and one of the earliest English prophets was a sixteen-year-old girl, Betty Gray.[64]

This less favorable view of the movement did not keep some Anglicans from hoping for a similar religious revival led by or encouraged by youth. They recognized that their church could only maintain its position in a freer society by taking on some of the characteristics of a movement, with the latter's inevitable orientation toward the future and therefore toward youth. It is apparent that discussion of such revivals was responsible for some of the earliest Anglican descriptions of real children. In 1708 Joseph Downing, the official printer to the Anglican charity-school movement, published an account of a group of children in Silesia who had begun to meet several times a day for prayer. The revival spread from these children, none older than fifteen, through the Lutheran population of that province, and soon separate groups of girls and boys, some as young as six, were meeting to pray that the Austrian emperor would stop harassing their churches. It was recorded to their credit that these children did not turn to fanaticism, although the families represented were clearly a part of the Pietist movement, roughly equivalent to English Dissent. The children were faithful to their Lutheran hymnals and prayer books, and adults were pleased to note that they were more willing than ever to go to school. The revival had greatly influenced adults also, and it was reported that a young Jewess had been converted — which at that time had an apocalyptic significance.[65]

The following year, Downing published a life of Christlieb Leberecht von Exter, a prodigy who had written several hymns and twelve chapters of a projected book on the revival of New Testament Christianity by the time of his death at age ten. At eight he had begun to have experiences of "an exaltation" — which the writer found inexplicable except in religious terms — that alternated with periods of depression that the author interpreted as humility. Towards the end, young Christlieb suffered weeks of continual headaches that prevented him from completing the book. It is clear that his father, physician to the Prince of Anhalt, had pushed him into the lime-light, but the author did not seem suspicious of a piety that was constantly praised in the child's hearing and that consisted so largely of censoriousness.[66]

In 1710 there was no fresh news of a worldwide revival of religion among children, but Downing kept up this interest by publishing an account of "the Good Armelle" who had died in 1671. Armelle Nicolas was not a child but a simple, illiterate maid in a distinguished French household. Her "childlike, hearty and confident conversing with God" had suggested a nun's vocation, but she did not care for the convent when allowed to try it and returned to domestic service, where she offered a radiant example.[67]

In 1715 came some real news. Three Jewish sisters, ages eight to twelve, had approached a Lutheran minister in Berlin to ask for religious instruction and for protection from their parents. The minister was afraid of involving himself until the King of Prussia sent a commission of privy councillors and ministers to look into the case. The children expressed a willingness to return if their parents also converted, and they were forced to face the parents in the presence of the commissioners. No reconciliation had been possible, however, and the king was now maintaining the girls at his own expense while their instruction went forward. They had already learned the Lord's Prayer and several other texts from Christian playmates, and they claimed that there were other Jewish children with similar intentions who were being kept "close at home . . . but they would find means to escape."[68]

Downing, in his capacity as printer to the Anglican charity-school movement, had worked closely with the Reverend Josiah Woodward, who probably prepared these accounts for the press. As early as 1706 Woodward, son of a Dissenting minister, had expressed his hopes for such stirrings of youthful piety. Thinking of the young members of the Societies for the Reformation of Manners, he wondered "what suitable Praise can we offer to God, the Giver of all Good, when we behold Youth punishing Lust, and giving Examples of Piety to Age?" Surely this "gives a seasonable Demonstration to this Epicurean Age, that there are vaster Pleasures to be reap'd from the blessed Entertainments of Religion, than from the utmost Indulgence of sensual Vanities."[69]

So even some Anglicans were now looking to childhood as a religiously significant period of life. Those Anglicans who were concerned over the secularizing trends of English society joined Woodward in the Society for Promoting Christian Knowledge in an effort to promote Anglican piety through education and persuasion, especially among the younger generation. It was natural for them to want to read of eminent examples of youthful piety, but other churchmen, whose loyalty was more institutional than ideological, remained aloof. When John Walker answered Calamy's record of the sufferings of Dissenters with *An Attempt Towards Recovering an Account of the Numbers and Sufferings of the Church of England* in 1714, he included nothing of the childhood years of these ministers. Nathaniel Salmon's *The Lives of the English Bishops from the Restauration to the Revolution* (1733) likewise began the biographies with the university affiliations, as though reference to childhood could only have been an embarrassment to the memory of such eminent men. Anglicans were more likely to choose gentlemen and aristocrats as subjects, whereas Dissenters included a greater number from the middling groups in society. This was partly a matter of choice, for Anglicans could have been more "democratic" in their choice of religious heroes, and their concentration on upper-class subjects may have inhibited them from including the least dignified years of those subjects' lives. Dissenters had fewer such qualms.

Historians of childhood rarely find evidence that can serve as a check on their literary sources, since diaries, letters, and court records reveal only adult perspectives on childhood. Autobiography is even more problematical, being the most subjective of sources, but the evidence from autobiography tends to confirm the distinction observed between Anglican and Dissenting biographies. Studies of seventeenth-century autobiography remark on the novelty of the Dissenters' approach. The literary scholar William Matthews views John Bunyan's *Grace Abounding to the Chief of Sinners* as "traditional" in its threefold structure of "early sinfulness, conversion, calling and ministry," but he admits that the time Bunyan spent describing his conversion was not typical. Despite "a certain repetitiousness and limited scope in these lives," Matthews thinks that Dissenters did get closer to the real lives of common people than earlier writers had done. In general, he found that few autobiographers recognized the importance of the childhood years, that, on the whole, they "paid more attention to their ancestors than to their own childhoods." [70] One suspects that these might be especially his Anglican authors. Paul Delany supports this point by observing that "secular" autobiographies were more concerned with social origins than with character development.[71] Owen Watkins, in a study devoted specifically to Dissenting autobiographies, was surprised to find that troubled childhood consciences did not appear as frequently as he had expected.[72] In short, there was variety among Dissenters in this regard, as well as a consistent difference between Dissenting autobiographies and those written by others—just as in the biographies.

At the dawn of the age of reform, John Foxe had seen the state itself establish a new religious order. Merc youths had played a role in these changes, but only when dynastic accident had raised them to power above their elders. It must have comforted Foxe to think that Providence had insured that the children who had inherited power were as exceptional as Prince Edward and Lady Jane. Later Anglican churchmen were not concerned as much with change as with preservation and looked to the state to conserve the Reformation. But for Puritans and Dissenters the Reformation had stopped short of its goal, and they feared that their ideal might disappear for another thousand years if it were not secured in the minds and affections of the young. To a large extent, their descriptions of real and godly children were meant for an audience of children, as is obvious from the forms in which these works were published.

In these writings, Dissenters revealed that they saw more in children than they had been conditioned to see. The early lives of religious leaders and of those godly youths who died before making their mark demonstrated that there was no formula for spiritual development. Some children had a natural gravity, a very few received supernatural signs that confirmed an inclination toward the min-

istry or that warned them of impending death. Some experienced
conversion before it could have been associated with any particular
tension or guilt, and others fell into sin and despair even after conversion. This variety and individuation set Dissenting biographies
apart. Their genuine curiosity about childhood overcame even the
temptation to glorify the lives of their leaders. For just as Oliver
Cromwell thought that his portrait should show "warts and all," his
Puritan supporters were not repelled by pimples on the image of
childhood.

Puritan empiricism and literary realism did not achieve the kind
of objectivity that Darwin and his fellow biologists demonstrated
in their attempts to keep developmental diaries on their offspring,
but in a sense the Puritans did more. They broke through not just
an earlier model of childhood but an icon. The medieval tradition
of childhood perfection had reached such heights that it bore no
relation to the lives of real children. If the child saints were used
as examples, it could only mean the repression of real children. Of
course, those saints were not examples so much as cultic figures, their
merits being imputed to their worshippers. In the medieval period, it
would have been possible to indulge real children precisely because
the ideal of childhood was so impossibly elevated. Puritans looked
at children more closely, however, and may well have become more
demanding. It was their eagerness to do the right thing, and their
clearer view of some of the realities, that suggested the need for new
theories of childhood.

CHAPTER THREE

Childhood in Theory

One cannot approach Puritan writings without preconceptions; their characteristic doctrines are sufficiently familiar that one is alert to their expression in the text. With reference to childhood, for example, we imagine Puritans to be so obsessed with eternal salvation that everything they mention will be related to this end. We hardly expect them to pay attention to educational performance, socialization, family harmony, or ordinary politeness for their own sakes. What is unexpected in this literature is the degree to which Puritan theology was bent to accommodate the actual experience of children. As we look at several kinds of literature — theological treatises, children's books, and child-rearing advice — we must be prepared to have authors defeat our expectations and mitigate the central beliefs of English Calvinism. Children left a mark at every stage in the development of Puritan doctrine, from Covenant corporatism through evangelical conversionism to an individualistic moralism.

THE "OFFICIAL" CHARACTERIZATION of childhood among such religiously oriented authors will, of course, be in their theological writings, so it is surprising to find that sympathy for children (and parents) caused Puritan theologians to lapse into an uncharacteristic inconsistency and uncertainty.

The problem began with baptism. If nothing else, Protestantism stood for the need for a personal, unmediated relation between the soul and God. Consistency seemed to require that baptism and membership await an adult decision and there were some who accepted just this position, whatever it might mean for the status of the child. Baptists denied that sacrament to their children until they could choose for themselves, but the great majority of Protestants felt uncomfortable with this radical individualism and began to search for some other justification of the earlier practice of baptizing infants. Even Baptists found themselves holding child-dedication services, which their neighbors sardonically termed "dry baptism." Infants were entered in their records as "the Children of the Church."[1]

Other Puritans and Dissenters were also hard-pressed to be consistent when they included children within the sacramental embrace of the church. Their most widely accepted justification lay in the covenant theology that was central to Puritan thought. Some scholars have emphasized the voluntaristic aspect of the covenant concept, supposing that it mitigated the deterministic tendency within Calvinism. Certainly there was some fruitful ambiguity within the doctrine on that point, but for most of those who organized their theology around God's covenants, the more immediate use was to offer a rationale for infant baptism, so as to cover the child's nakedness.

John Calvin was not the sole source of Puritan theology, but he remained a respected figure and was widely read. While the covenants were not central to his thought, his treatment did set the tone for much of what Englishmen were to write on baptism and the Covenant of Grace, and that tone is remarkably sympathetic. Calvin did not bother to explain the normal conditions by which men entered God's covenant for the disappointingly simple reason that he thought people were born into it. The very formula of the New Covenant, he claimed, was that "I shall be your God, and the God of your descendants after you" (quoting Genesis 17:7). In other words, the Covenant of Grace was analogous to the Old Covenant with the nation of Israel, and the practice of baptism corresponded to circumcision. Surely God would not mean to do less for the children of Christians than He did for the children of Israel. If the Jews found circumcision to be a meaningful rite, surely God would provide something just as good for His church—which was, of course, baptism.[2]

Calvin was consciously arguing against the Anabaptists of his day. Feeling the force of their individualist logic, he searched for arguments for those who found his typology insufficient. Christ himself had instructed his disciples to bring the little children to him, "for of such is the Kingdom of Heaven." But "If the Kingdom of Heaven belongs to them, why is the sign denied which, so to speak, opens to them a door into the church, that adopted into it, they may be enrolled among the heirs of the Kingdom of Heaven? How unjust of us to drive away those whom Christ calls to himself!" Calvin knew that parents would be glad to hear this, for the baptism of their children "floods godly hearts with uncommon happiness, which quickens men to a deeper love of their kind Father, as they see His concern on their behalf for their posterity."[3] The fact that Calvin could assume such parental concern speaks well for the emotional climate of the families that he knew. His eagerness to reassure the parents, even if it meant using shaky arguments, indicates his emotional commitment in favor of the child.

There were still those, however, who could not get around the fact that infants were incapable of religious faith. Should these be denied the sacraments of the more spiritual covenant? "To silence such gainsayers, God provided a proof in John the Baptist, whom He sanctified in his mother's womb—something He could do in others."[4] So it must not be necessary that children understand God's word of redemption: "He has certainly used another way in calling many, giving them true knowledge of Himself by inward means, that is, by the illumination of the Spirit apart from the medium of preaching." For those who shut the door against children, "Let them only tell me, I ask, what the danger is if infants be said to receive now some part of that grace which in a little while they shall enjoy to the full? For if fullness of life consists in the perfect knowledge of God, when some of them, whom death snatches away in their very first infancy, pass over into eternal life, they are surely received to the contemplation of God in his very presence." To Calvin anything less was too unpleasant to contemplate: "To sum up, this objection can be solved without difficulty: infants are baptized into future repentance and faith, and even though these have not yet been formed in them, the seed of both lies hidden within them by the secret working of the Spirit."[5]

Calvin's logic might be questionable but his enthusiasm for this conclusion is unmistakable. Not all of his English followers were so warm in their expression of these doctrines, but we need not assume that this was due to a degenerating psychological climate brought on by predestinarian rigor. Calvin's followers were working against a developing individualism that made it increasingly difficult to maintain his religious corporatism.

To complicate matters, they faced a problem that we are likely to forget—that childhood was all the life that many persons experienced at a time of such short life-expectancy. Recognition of this melancholy fact is revealed when Calvin alludes to children who "happen to grow to an age at which they can be taught the truth of baptism."[6] Deciding the child's status was the only religious doctrine at issue in many human lives, so it is no wonder that theologians gave it their attention; an interest so realistic need not be thought of as intrusive.

The other major continental source of English covenant theology was Professor Zacharias Ursinus of Heidelberg University, whose *Summe of Christian Religion* went through six editions in England between 1585 and 1595 and an additional five by 1645. Like Calvin and Zwingli before him, Ursinus depended on the idea of the covenants to secure infant baptism against the doubts of the Baptists. Perhaps because he came from a generation later than Calvin, Ursinus felt more deeply the necessity of a personal religion, and he hedged on the efficacy of baptism unless it was followed by an adult life that bore the fruits of the Spirit: "Infants beleeve by an inclination to faith, and therefore are to be baptised," he suggested. The sacrament does not "bestow" grace but rather "promises" it to those who experience "faith and conversion." Still, he saw no real problem, for when he imagined those who were entirely outside God's care, he thought primarily of infidels and hypocrites, much as Calvin had thought of "the Turks and other profane nations."[7] Apparently Ursinus's ethnocentricism mitigated his individualism and worked in the child's favor.

The first English theologian to develop this covenant tradition was a Puritan, Dudley Fenner, writing in the 1580s. Like Ursinus, Fenner displayed the same uneasiness about the place of infant baptism: "Only in children remaineth some shew of doubt, but seeing the Apostle saith, they are holy; that is, within the covenant of God, *I am thy God, and the God of thy seed*, Christ and his benefits in this covenant of grace doth belong unto them, that living, by faith it may be applied, or dying, the Spirit of the grace of God may worke in them, as he knoweth how, and hath not revealed." Apparently Fenner accepted the word of Scripture for God's promise of grace to children but lacked an enthusiastic conviction of the doctrine.

Still, like Ursinus and Calvin, Fenner presumed that only "papists, prophane and wicked persons" were ineligible for admission to the further sacrament of the Lord's Supper, for nothing short of the parents' "idolatry" would "disannul" this covenant. Otherwise its very purpose would have been defeated, for this purpose was, after all, to offer reassurance to children and their parents.[8]

Cambridge theologian William Perkins's reputation is evidenced by the enormous popularity of his writings, which encouraged the growing Puritan emphasis on evangelical conversion. When Perkins was writing, in the 1590s, the theme of God's covenants was so well established that he could hardly ignore it. But one senses that he was grudging in his acceptance of infant baptism, feeling the need to assure readers that, while the faith of the parents brings the baptized child into the covenant, it did "not applie the benefits of Christ's death . . . for this the beleever doth onely unto himself."[9] The fact that Perkins insists on this qualification may indicate the confidence that parents were placing in the covenant membership of their children. In effect, he was warning readers not to presume upon the election of their children.

Other prominent Puritan writers showed more confidence in the covenant. William Ames, whose works were nearly as popular as the treatises by Perkins and Ursinus, thought his audience was obsessed by conversion and asserted that "Faith and repentance do no more make the covenant of God now then in the time of Abraham . . . therefore the want of those acts ought no more to hinder baptism from infants now, then it did forbid circumcision then."[10] Richard Sibbes likewise saw a danger from "Anabaptistical spirits [who] would not have children baptized if they believe not." For the covenant was for the very purpose of assuring that "the promise is made to you and your children."[11] Covenant corporatism was obviously being challenged by evangelical conversionism.

This doctrinal debate took on a real urgency in the 1640s when the ecclesiastical government of England was crumbling. Infant baptism was, after all, the cornerstone of a state church and religious compulsion, for birthright membership allowed the ecclesiastical authorities to treat everyone as religiously committed. Church and state had a decision to make in this area. Baptist spokesmen like Christopher Blackwood and John Tombes could count on their readers' commitment to a spiritual, conversionist piety when they attacked sacramentalism, but mainstream Puritans like Thomas Blake could count on sympathy for children as well as on covenant theology in securing infant baptism. Blackwood pointed out that the children of the visibly "elect" were frequently visibly wicked, but Blake could counter by threatening: "Deny infants Christ [in baptism] and God is alike pleased with them as with the brood of cockatrices, and seed of serpents."[12] Obviously Blake did not think that pious parents would accept that kind of talk about their children, whatever became possible in Jonathan Edwards's day, and they did not. The matter was not settled on the basis of argument, in which the Baptists gave as good as they got. Debate simply faded away; after the Restoration the Dissenters continued administering baptism to their infant children.

New England theologians wrestled with the logic of infant baptism a little longer. Thomas Cobbett, who traveled with the first colonists, joined in attacking Blackwood and any others who would deny children baptism with the "Arke-like succour thereof in drowning times." To exclude children from baptism was "to exclude them from any ordinary state and way of salvation," Cobbett thought, ignoring the implications of predestinating election. He could not simply ignore conversion and tried to make a distinction: Experience showed that not all participants in covenant membership gave later evidence of election, so there must be an external as well as an internal covenant, one in which the children of believers were "Federally and Ecclesiastically holy" though not "inherently" holy. What use was a covenant that did not save? Cobbett answered that the covenant was the seed of conversion itself, enabling the child to take part in the "privileges" or "ordinances" of the church which would make his calling clearer, easier, or more likely. Otherwise God would be forced to seek "extraordinary" methods to convey grace, such as He was presumed to use with "Pagans, or Turkes," or "Indians and Blackamores."[13]

Cobbett was not willing to give up either sacramentalism or conversionism, but he sensed that he was in a difficult position. In his exasperation with Anabaptist conversionists, he demanded "Were they Gods to know the secret guile of hearts?" He thought it was "Better that 99 who happily [i.e., happen to] have not so peculiar a title thereto, bee folded up in the Church, then that one of such Lambes bee left out in the wide Wildernesse."[14] That is, children were to benefit from a presumption in their favor, a rule of charity implied in the covenant. John Cotton, the most respected minister of that generation of transplanted Englishmen in New England, wrote voluminously on the covenant and revealed the same confusion and sympathies that Cobbett had demonstrated.[15]

By mid-century the tide was running against a confidence in God's grace and in favor of a greater emphasis on human responsibility. In Connecticut, Thomas Hooker wrote books on the covenant primarily in order to undermine the doctrine, declaring that "covenant grace is one thing, and saving grace is another." He accepted infant baptism, but only because he understood it as the infant's promise to obey God's commands. All of God's ordinances "presuppose in the right use of them, *Faith in the receiver*." Hooker allowed that God might as easily "powre faith into the heart of infants" as into an adult,[16] but he could not say this with the conviction that Calvin had shown a century earlier. Having seen a new generation of children exhibit some all-too-human traits may have sapped confidence in the covenant.

In New England, where conditions had been more nearly ideal than in England, each passing generation brought deeper disappointment over the failure of covenant membership to insure a godly society. When conversions were slow in coming the idea of the covenant invited the use of "Jeremiads," which scolded those who had a relationship with the God of their fathers whether they liked it or not. Thus children now had the worst of both approaches, being pressed to choose something that had already been chosen for them.

Of course it was the response of children (or their lack of response) that demonstrated that the covenant, which had been adopted for their benefit, was an unrealistic concept. As a result, children were open to Wesleyan evangelicals who tried to force their consciences. In the eighteenth century even Dissenting theologians were emotionally committed to the doctrine of human responsibility and the individuality of childhood, and their arguments shifted off the old, Calvinistic foundation. Historian Joseph Haroutunian has traced how the eighteenth-century debate on the nature of man declined in logical rigor as affective commitments came to dominate theological discourse.[17] One suspects that an interest in children was behind this psychologizing of theology.

Children do not necessarily benefit from increased attention. Covenant doctrine had long preserved an earlier corporatism and sheltered children from an intrusive interest in their individual state, but concern over the future of Puritanism and the frontier communities appears to have opened the doctrine to voluntarism and moralism. The child's position would not be as comfortable as in Calvin's more evangelical doctrine of grace, and pressures would grow with each passing generation.

IF THEOLOGIANS FOUND themselves adjusting to the realities of childhood, this was even truer of the writers of the first books addressed to children. Puritan authors are often thought of as uncompromising and uncomprehending where young readers are concerned, but their Calvinist piety was bent by the effort to appeal to the older children and to make sense to the younger ones. They found that there were some things in their theological vocabulary that they simply could not express to these groups. Even the doctrines of depravity and predestination were made compatible with a respect for the child's freedom and moral value. Though this literature for children is not to our taste, at least it shows a sincere sympathy. In short, the Puritans' respect for the truth, as they saw it, was no more than their respect for the child.

Puritan writers were slow to separate the smallest children from the usual audience of young people. Like their contemporaries, they used the term "childhood" to describe the entire period of social and economic dependence. Age discrimination was not of interest to any writers until the Puritans' evangelical and educational efforts matured, leading them to address even the smallest children. At that time the Puritans began talking down to their audience. The literature for that age group contains more fright, more humor, and more stories than for the teens. This is, naturally, a realistic assessment of developmental differences. Even today, small children get, and indeed demand, a measure of fright in their nursery tales, comics, and animations, sensing of course that the terror will be resolved. The children of the Puritans also knew that the theological terrors would be resolved, for no Calvinist author ever left his readers dangling over an abyss. Whatever we may imagine the implications of predestinarian determinism to have been, the works were always designed to offer hope. It was, after all, a didactic literature, meant to guide and encourage.

By proceeding through William Sloane's inclusive bibliography of the earliest works published for children, one can get some sense of how remarkable Puritan and Dissenting authors were for their time. The first book on his list, aside from chapbooks that preserved earlier oral lore for young and old, was a courtesy or conduct manual adapted for younger readers. While courtesy books are normally associated with the humanists, Francis Seager's *The Schoole of Vertue and Book of Good Nourture* (1557) has enough of a religious flavor that it was long attributed to a Puritan, Robert Crowley.[18] Like the rest of the genre, however, its goal was to fit the child into static patterns of behavior and belief. The second on Sloane's list was more original because it mentioned the burdens to be thrust upon a rising generation in a time of change, which became a characteristically Puritan theme. That work, *The Exhortation that a Father Gave to His Children Which he Wrot a Few Dayes Before His Burning* (1559), was written by a Protestant martyr, Robert Smith, and was often reprinted (in the *New England Primer* for instance). Amid the conventional admonitions to uprightness and charity, the implicit theme was the rejection of a corrupt society, which would have been entirely out of place in a courtesy manual.

Puritans consistently maintained this distinctive tradition, in counterpoint to the courtesy literature of Elizabeth's reign. James Canceller's *The Alphabet of Prayers* (1564) was likewise written out of the fear of judgment on a heedless nation, hoping to stir both young and old toward a national repentance,[19] and Sloane's fifth work, by the famous Puritan preacher Henry Smith, suggested that England was relying on youth to begin such a revival of piety. Smith took it as a commonplace "that none but young men do heare our doctrine," and he pictured their elders as drowsy and drunken, actually encouraging wickedness in the young "least the childe should proove better than his father." In fact, he had heard "an olde Father of this Citie say . . . that if there were any good to bee done in these dayes, it is the yong men that must doe it, for the olde men are out of date." The young would need, however, to give up the notion, apparently widespread, that it was their "privilege to bee lascivious and vain."[20]

There was scant relationship between these works and the conduct manuals for the young by such men as Lord Burghley and Sir Walter Raleigh. Burghley's precepts were not far from the parody that Shakespeare composed for Polonius.[21] Even that was more attractive than the cynical advice that a disillusioned Raleigh left to his son: Befriend only your betters. Resist your lust for beauty lest it stand in the way of advancement, but prey on this lust in others, if only to marry off your daughters cheaply. Be careful not to love your wife more than she loves you, or risk becoming an object of ridicule, and so on.[22] Nothing could have been better calculated to horrify Puritans, to whom even good manners smacked somewhat of hypocrisy.

Curiously enough, this courtesy tradition lived on in Puritan literature for girls, showing the Puritans' conventionality in this area. Only those by women authors — Dorothy Leigh's *The Mother's Blessing* (1616) and Elizabeth Joceline's *The Mother's Legacy* (1624) — were truly courtesy books, and they are directed primarily to a female audience.[23] Thus, Puritans made a distinction with regard to females, emphasizing humility, modesty, charity, and a general inoffensiveness when addressing the female audience. These had been the characteristics recommended by humanists to young courtiers, but they were not those needed by male reformers.

In relation to girls, Puritans shared the tendency of all contemporary authors to see virtue primarily in negative terms. Mrs. Leigh subsumed all female virtues under chastity; goodness was less a matter of acting virtuously than of preserving and defending one's virtue.

Thus female virtue was like a moral deposit that a girl might squander or that a heartless world could steal. The passivity of such a role was ratified in Mrs. Joceline's disparagement of learning in women, which seems incongruous in view of the literary grace of both these works. They were, apparently, the most popular of the earlier works for children, Leigh's claiming fourteen editions by 1629.[24]

In the 1590s another secular approach to childhood appeared in the literature of youthful nationalism, which rivaled the Puritan and courtesy works. England's wars with Spain had created an emphasis on the martial and patriotic apprentice and even brought this character to the dramatic stage. The resulting plays and ballads developed two emphases not shared by Puritan authors—a prudential ethic dependent on adult rewards and a fabulous tone. Chapman, Jonson, and Marston's *Eastward Ho!* (1605), for example, was the first play that concentrated attention on young characters. The outline of the plot is familiar because of Hogarth's etchings on "Industry and Idleness," which were directly inspired by that play more than a century later.[25] Its prudential theme centers on a brace of daughters who show the rewards of modesty and of haughtiness, respectively. All this would have made no sense except against a background of adult rewards, quite unlike the Puritan stories of children who died without any worldly recognition. The traditions of romance encouraged the fabulous exaggerations of other plays and ballads, as when Thomas Heywood's characters in the *Foure Apprentices of London* (1600?) go off to win the crusades once and for all.

Puritan works for children, like Puritan biographies, were markedly realistic by comparison. In 1626 John Wilson reviewed the history of England's Reformation in verse for young readers, perhaps having noticed the popularity of Foxe's *Book of Martyrs*.[26] Wilson seems even more serious than the playwrights about actually depicting heroism during these difficult years of Charles I. Likewise, the few Puritan ventures into the field of cautionary literature have a more realistic tone than the ballad tales. Robert Abbot's *The Young-mans warning-peece* (1636) was the most clear-cut Puritan contribution to this genre. The story, already recounted in Chapter 2, involved a young parishioner who had lapsed into sin and unconquerable despair, persisting in the belief that he would be damned despite Abbot's assurance of forgiveness, but the reader misses the tone of triumph or vindication which is so characteristic of chapbook morality. Even in an anonymous broadside ballad version, "Youth's Warning-peice," this makes a very different impression than such standard chapbook fare as "A Warning to Youth" (1603). The latter was the tale of a rich merchant's heir who, once launched on a career of whoring and drunkeness, seduced a good girl who then took her own life. It was his misfortune that the poor girl's mother was a widow, since widow's curses are especially potent. Thus, it was only to be expected that he would simply rot away under her wrath. By contrast, Abbot was satisfied simply to warn the young not to presume on the privilege to "sow their wilde Oats." He went on to lament the new fashions of "nakedness," beauty spots, and powdered hair. He feared that these only encouraged the lusts characteristic of youth at a time when the senses were most acute.[27]

The subject of the particular strengths and weaknesses of youth occupied a number of the Puritan authors who were concerned with reaching the young audience, and such considerations amounted to a rudimentary definition of adolescence. Thomas Brookes, one of the more sympathetic of the Puritans and a very popular author, was quite explicit in listing the weaknesses of youth: First, "Pride of heart, pride of apparel, pride of parts; young men are apt to be proud of health, strength, friends, relations, wit, wisdom." "The second evil that youth is subject to, is sensual pleasures and delights." Then "rashness," followed by "mocking and scoffing at religious men and religious things," and finally "lustfulness and wantonness." His fifth point, therefore, is a repetition of his second, indicating that he thought this weakness could use added emphasis.[28]

Brookes only listed these weaknesses after praising youth as "the choicest and fittest time for service. Now your parts are lively, senses fresh, memory strong, and nature vigorous; the days of your youth are the spring and morning of your time." Indeed his catalogue of failings only represents perversions of these same qualities. Nor was Brookes simply praising the *possibilities* of youth, contrasting them with the sorry performance of the children he had known. He believed that most who were ever converted were converted when young: "It is rare, very rare, that God sows and reaps in old age; usually God sows the seed of grace in youth that yields the harvest of joy in old age. Though true repentance be never too late, yet late repentance is seldom true." "It is ten to one, nay an hundred to one, if ever they are converted, if they are not converted when they are young." [29]

Some Puritan authors were less generous than Brookes in addressing young readers. John Chishull agreed that adolescence was the time when affections were at their strongest, when one experienced the extremities of love, joy, zeal, desire, and hope, but it could only be considered the best time of life if it were spent in God's service. Chishull's premise was that youth was distinguished from maturity by a lack of consideration for the future. Unfortunately, this concern for an eternal future was precisely the beginning of religious consciousness. His forlorn conclusion was that it will always be a rare youth who devotes himself to godliness. It sounds as though Chishull had reversed the famous text to read, "Except you become as little adults, you shall not enter the kingdom of heaven," but in fact, he was even more pessimistic about adults, who were usually too set in their ways to repent or change. "Men have seldome above one chusing time," this Calvinist asserted, and Scripture associates that time with youth.[30]

John Maynard appealed to young readers on the basis of their strengths, arguing that religion gave ample scope for their wit, memory, affections, strength, courage, health, and even mirth and high spirits. The Bible was full of examples of young men chosen for God's special missions. While youth may lack a necessary measure of thoughtfulness, it is still "the choice age of a Man's life." In fact, this Puritan thought it was sin that aged men,[31] where humanists would have taught that wisdom enjoyed that distinction.

The emotional tone among Puritan authors varied too widely to suggest a common psychological basis. To the contrary, their differences were associated with theological variance. For example, London Dissenter Thomas Vincent minimized the doctrine of infant depravity: "Your hearts as yet in a great measure are a *rasa tabula*, like a fair table, or white sheet of Paper in which little is written; Do not furrow the Table with Conscience-wounding sins; do not blot and besmear the Paper with the defilements of Lust: But get the Law of God engraven upon the Table of your hearts." Such a suggestion, that children might really avoid blotting their copy-books, shows Vincent's theology shading off into the semi-Pelagian piety of Anglicanism. As in Anglican devotional literature for adults, Vincent was inclined to see depravity in terms of the concupiscent flesh rather than the rebellious will. He was especially concerned with fornication, which he termed a pollution, borrowing language that was more characteristic of Anglicans. Like them, his stress was more on protecting the young from sin than on converting them to righteousness. He even showed an unexpected appreciation of the beauty of childish devotion—seeing it as being like early blossoms, more striking and poignant than adult piety.[32]

Vincent's pathos in describing an early piety seems to envision a very young group and reveals an obvious sentimentality. He treated religion as something of an intrusion on the perfection of the early stage of life. Infantile piety added a measure of maturity that was jarring to his sensibilities, as though growing up was too painful. Vincent was not alone among Dissenters in his sentimentality: James Janeway admitted being especially touched at seeing children weep over their sins, and Thomas White thought that "pretty little hands lifted up in prayer, are very beautiful in the Eyes of God."[33]

Sentimentality of this kind is not expected among Puritans but neither is it a healthy sign, since it indicates an unresolved self-pity that is rooted in childhood memories. We should note that these semi-Pelagian works books were as likely as any to refer to the possibility of damnation.

At the other extreme in temperamental tone, John Ryther was overwhelmed by a sense of the profaneness of "these giddy reeling times" and depressed to hear men say that "they see no difference betwixt the posterity of the Godly and the Ungodly." Make no mistake, he warned, hell burns more fiercely for the children of religious parents, because they have sinned against a greater measure of truth.[34] It is doubtful that this sentiment implied any genuine sympathy for the children of the less religious parents. Many authors, despite a basic sympathy, seem to have been irked by youth's lack of restraint, and their commonest complaint was of the pursuit of sensuality.

Adults might well have been more aware of youthful lusts than we are today for the reason that the lives of the young were so much more open to observation at that time. Where could the apprentice go to meet his friends and commit his follies? Perhaps it was only in the street and the public house that he could be himself. To be fully adult was to be master or mistress of a house and therefore out of public view, so youth and visible lust would have been nearly synonymous. This circumstance may help clarify the frequent concern with Sabbath-breaking, which now seems merely quaint, as Sunday was the only time of the week that many young persons were able to choose their own companions and activities. Admonitions concerning Sabbath-keeping were commonly coupled with warnings against bad company, and no doubt many youths were introduced to loose or even criminal behavior on that of all days. So it was actually realistic, rather than ridiculous, when authors mentioned Sabbath-breaking in connection with the young criminals executed at Tyburn. Many writers were struck by the extreme youth of those they had seen hung there, but this does not seem to have been a matter of satisfaction to clerical authors, whatever it was to the readers of chapbooks.[35]

Dissenting authors were not apologetic in mentioning the depravity from original sin in their works directed to children; neither did they dwell on the subject as though they found it congenial. In fact, they often sought some new way of expressing the doctrine, perhaps treating it politically, as rebellion against one's "sovereign and Rightful Lord." For one author it meant that "the best of us have a disposition to the vilest sins," as if there were a meaningful distinction in the word "best."[36] Another author euphemistically wrote, "All men come into this world with their backs turned upon God." Edward Lawrence, smarting over the rebellion of some of his own children, spelled it out most uncompromisingly: children are by nature atheists, haters of God, whoremongers, liars, thieves, and murderers.[37] Other authors put it more elegantly: "We are all born Epicures, are naturally Devotees to Bacchus and Venus . . . poor slaves to our Appetites!"[38]

Practically speaking, the doctrine meant that the young could not be weaned from sin by a surfeit of it. Sin was addictive, so there was no use indulging the young in the hope of a positive reaction. Experience verified the doctrine; why would profane company be more attractive to the young than godly company except that human bias runs in that direction? The powerful influence of dissolute peers shows clearly that sin is more contagious than righteousness.[39] This view was at variance with the common notion that the young would outgrow their early tendencies, a view expressed in such proverbs as "Young Saint, Old Devil" and "soon ripe, soon rotten." Puritan authors pointed out that men do not train their horses or dogs according to any such principle. Although they were not so fond of the analogy between child-rearing and horse-breaking as were the gentlemen authors of courtesy literature, they were frequently reminded of Zophar's words to Job, "Man is born like a wild ass's colt," which came to the same thing.[40]

To imagine the young as wild, undomesticated animals is evidence of a fundamental lack of affinity, the most brutal expression of which appeared late in the century. "Thou by nature art brutish and devilish," the Presbyterian scholar Daniel Williams began and proceeded to remind young readers of the children who were torn apart by she-bears for mocking Elisha. Idiots were more likely to be saved than ordinary children, he thought, because they had less to answer for. Williams was an unusually bilious individual, and his disgust was not confined to children; if anything he was harder on their elders: "Oh, it's ill dealing with old sinners! They are conceited, full of prejudices, and immersed in worldly cares; the calls and threatenings of God are grown familiar to them, and their souls stupid and void of affection." [41]

Such an attitude was not universal or even common among those Puritans or Dissenters who wrote for children. Williams may represent a generation of Dissenters that had soured on the failure of the movement and blamed the young for their lack of interest. Earlier criticism and threats had been accents within a wider context of reason and hope, and writers had not indulged their hostility by repeating cautionary tales of God's revenge on swaggering young sinners—or at least they did not publish such sentiments in signed, religious works. One author did remember a profane lad who was afflicted with a canker on his tongue and mentioned it as ironically appropriate,[42] but compared with the mass of such stories in contemporary ballads and chapbooks, to say nothing of the theater of retribution, religious authors dealt gently with the young. Even when preaching the funerals of wayward youths, ministers were reticent about the details of their misadventures.[43]

If Dissenters despaired of the situation in Restoration England, they did not blame youth or even human nature as much as they blamed society. Williams thought he could detect an actual campaign "to debauch young people in their manners, to prejudice them against holiness and sobriety," and he believed that it was part of James II's plan to reduce the nation to "slavery and popery."[44] There was a generation of young wits who ridiculed religion as the fancy of a "melancholy imagination" and formed "Atheistical Clubs" in which they boasted of having extinguished conscience and proved it by carousing.[45] None of this could be blamed on the young, for divines recognized the idealism of adolescence and repeatedly said that if men were ever to be truly devoted to religion they must begin in youth, the springtime of life, "the flower, cream, and quintessence of our time."[46]

Where in all this discussion did the doctrine of predestination fit? Would not an individual calling rule out the hopes for entire groups such as "youth"? Inconsistency at this point suggests that an interest in children worked against theological abstractions, even among Calvinists. Writers commonly remarked that vices seemed less rooted in the young because they had not yet blossomed into acts.[47] Sin had not yet become habitual in children, so lusts could be stifled at their inception and correct habits fixed for life.[48] Of course, correct habits were not sufficient without an inner change, but Dissenters did not write as though men were entirely passive in this regard. Even those who did mention God's sovereignty in conversion saw an advantage in youth, associating it with "the accepted time, the day of salvation" of 2 Corinthians 6:2. Beyond that, experience had shown that God was most likely to extend the offer of grace in one's early years, presumably so that the whole of life could

be spent in His service. A number of writers appeared to limit God's
arbitrary determination to the *time* of His offer of grace, and readers
were free to infer that every man received a call and that failure to
respond exonerated God of responsibility.[49] Even Daniel Williams
agreed that "there is not a child of six years old under the gospel-
means [i.e. evangelical preaching], but the Spirit of God has been
striving with," though he managed to make this seem a threatening
rather than an encouraging notion.[50]

A few authors were so determined to reach even the smallest child
that they introduced a more general simplification, not to say corruption, of Reformed doctrine. Robert Russell's attempts to translate Calvin into baby-talk appear to promise heaven to all children
who obeyed their parents, avoided lies and profanity, studied hard,
prayed every day, and shunned naughty playmates and Sunday play.
Similarly, the children who heard Thomas White threaten hell for
children who swore, lied, or broke the Sabbath may have inferred
that avoiding these things would satisfy an indulgent God.[51] If so,
they would grow up fortified against evangelical religion.

These authors sensed that a simple moralism was all that children could understand of their birthright religion. There was no
use in attempting to teach an evangelical doctrine of grace which
would call all this into question. For while children have a feeling for
retribution, they can hardly understand the demands of charity (as
distinguished from simple generosity). Thus, the attempt to reach
children at a very young age made its small contribution to the erosion of Augustinian piety and the triumph of semi-Pelagianism in
the eighteenth century.

Such a simplification of Puritan moral doctrine was not a necessary or logical development but the result of an understandable desire
to include even very small children within the movement, nor was
the mitigation of predestination a dialectical inevitability. It reflects
the natural desire of parents to encourage their children to reach
out for God's hand. All of this, however, helped change Calvinism
from a theological perspective, which looked down from the heights
of heaven, to a human perspective that would make the Creator's
justice a burning issue.

Hope for children was not the result of a theological liberalization as historians have tended to assume; rather, it preceded and helped cause that liberalization. Respect for children had always characterized such Calvinists as Timothy Cruso, who alluded to "the vast variety of mercies which attend us throughout our Infancy and Childhood," implying God's special love for the young. In the midst of much sour commentary, Edward Lawrence counseled children to "Put a true value on your own Beings, for ye cannot love God and Christ, if ye do not love your selves." Oliver Heywood wanted young readers to study their own characters to see which traits might be developed to best advantage. Matthew Mead reminded the young of how much of the Scripture was specifically addressed to them, mentioning the teachings of Solomon and of Jesus and the Epistles of John.[52]

One might almost become suspicious of the Puritan preoccupation with children except for the likelihood of early death. Writers believed that "most of mankind die when young, heaven and hell arc fuller of young people, than of such as are arrived to a greater age," and for this reason they were impatient with the common excuse that religion could be left to later life when it might be more congenial. Mead quipped that the dying thief had stolen away many procrastinators who reasoned that, if he could be saved in his last agony, they could as well.[53] The common objection that young saints become old sinners was irrelevant. Youth was not only the best but for many the only time of life. Anxiety on this score was only realistic in a century when life expectancy at birth could fall as low as 28.5 years (in 1681).[54]

Puritans had the field of children's literature to themselves until late in the century when Anglicans also became alarmed at the growing threat of "atheism." They had, at length, recognized that "the Hopes and Happiness of our Church and State depend upon a sober and Religious rising generation" and even that the "Future Good of the Universe depends upon the Sobriety of Youth."[55] Some of the Anglican writers sounded like the most insensitive of the Dissenters, warning the young reader that he was "by nature a Child of Wrath" and that he hung over the Burning Lake by "a brittle thread." One complained that the doctrine of original sin was being unjustly despised in a prevailing atmosphere of pride and self-righteousness.[56]

Still, differences in theology could create differences in approach. Some Anglicans were quite consciously seeking to undermine the doctrine of evangelical conversion, having adopted a semi-Pelagianism that emphasized moral duties as the very basis of religion. As an example of this moralistic doctrine, Thomas Ken emphasized that by the creation of good habits "your duty will grow natural to you." While he could not simply ignore the idea of a spiritual calling, he neutralized it by paraphrasing St. Paul's paradox from Philippians 2:12–13: "Though 'tis God that works in you to will and to do of his good pleasure, yet God also commands you, to work out your own salvation your self."[57] Simon Patrick thought that instruction could keep a child free from "pride, ambition, desire of riches, . . . as little children naturally are, till the seeds of those vices be stirred up in them by others."[58] There were "seeds" of sin within, to be sure, but they were not expected to sprout unaided.

Anglican moralistic piety suggests a defensive concept of virtue, as the hope of keeping oneself "undefiled" recurs in Patrick's prayers for young readers. William Smythies thought that "there are many (and I pray God encrease the number of them) who *Fear God from their Youth*, as Obadiah did, who never were converted from a Sinful and Ungodly Life. . . . The care of their Parents to bring them up in the *nurture and Admonition of the Lord:* Their early listnings *to the voice of their Teachers*, and taking their Council, hath prevented the necessity of Repentance." Richard Kidder saw conversion as only a means toward a holy life and not as an end in itself, hoping that it could happen without crisis and from the simple attraction of holiness.[59]

Given this view of the child's moral condition, suppression rather than transformation became the theme of Anglican literature. Semi-Pelagian moralism lacked a dynamic doctrine of conversion that might encourage children who were already conscious of guilt; rather, writers prescribed the continual privation of the senses to cause the passions to wither and temptations to cease.[60] The idea that the passions could be sublimated into a holy zeal would have been rejected by these moralists as Puritan "enthusiasm." This did not make matters easier for their children, however, who must have been discouraged to have Anglican authors present Christ as their moral example, since he had effortlessly triumphed "over all the vain delights of youth; and woulds't choose no place but the Temple to reside in," subjecting himself to his parents and delighting in the conversation of the learned.[61]

There were, to be sure, earthly rewards for youthful diligence. In fact, Anglicans were more likely than Dissenters to refer to prudential considerations. Josiah Woodward twisted the story of the prodigal son into a tale of youthful mistakes rather than of forgiveness, presenting an image of youthful piety strongly resembling that of the resentful elder brother.[62] Smythies drew the prudential conclusion to this view: "The young man that bears the Yoke, may be sure from the Promises of God, that he shall be Rich and great in the World, if it be good for him and others, that he should be so." Who did not know that diligent apprentices were likely to marry their masters' heiresses? [63] If Dissenters shared such dreams, they did not express them in such bald terms.

Given the Anglican emphasis on avoiding sin rather than on redemption from it, their greater attention to fasting and self-denial is only to be expected. Similarly, they were more outspoken than Dissenters in alluding to such matters as the "unclean thoughts" that occur to boys at bedtime. A greater emphasis on sorrow for sin was part of their idea of the individual's initiative in atonement; penance became a way for the soul to take revenge upon itself.[64] In short, a moralistic doctrine of free will was no easier on children than the Calvinist doctrine of grace.

The Quakers have not played an important part in this account thus far because their movement was forced into sectarianism so quickly and so brutally that they turned to their children with desperation rather than hope. The result was a repressiveness even more pronounced than that contemplated by Anglicans.

Quaker authors were the most unequivocal in asserting the innocence of children. They liked to speak of themselves as Children of Truth, Children of Light, or Children of God, and such childlike traits as tenderness and sensitivity to correction were the virtues they prized most highly. More than any other group they took seriously Jesus' association of the humility of childhood with the coming of God's Kingdom. On the other hand, they could not fail to observe that the children of outsiders did not exhibit these qualities, calling them "Dogs, Swine, Goats, Ravening Wolves, Vipers, Foxes and Serpents."[65] Some of their own children also were criticized for "sitting down at ease in the Flesh," which "makes a Stink, and brings infamy upon the blessed Truth which you profess." Despite an innocent start, it seemed that all children shared a taste for the world's vanities,[66] and that was, of course, the reason for the many prohibitions that Quakers and their children observed.

The preservation of a presumed, but rather fragile, innocence required that Quaker authors emphasize obedience to parents, since they could not accept so many of society's customs. Also, since parents would soon be gone (life-expectancy being what it was), Quakers seemed more insistent on the restraining fear of God than did other Dissenters.[67] Despite this circumspection, Quakers wanted to think of their way of life as natural. Their notion of humanity's most instinctive behavior did not include sin, so William Penn could encourage children to "Be natural," but it was soon obvious that this did not give much leeway to the child. The innocence of Christ was offered as a practical guide: "As he is like God, we must be like him." Essentially, the example was "one continued great Act of Self-Denial."[68]

What the Quakers feared most was the sophistication and the deceptions of the society around them. What they wanted most was to retain the intensity, freshness, and gentleness of childhood. Their works reveal the final reversal of time-honored attitudes, for where the courtesy literature had cautioned against spontaneity, singularity, and frankness, treating them as faults, the Quakers viewed these as virtues. Like others since them, however, the early Quakers had to ignore real children in order to sustain an iconic vision of childhood innocence.

PUBLISHED ADVICE to parents followed the same pattern of development that had dominated early children's literature, beginning with a Renaissance tradition that recycled the advice of the ancients. This was soon absorbed in a Puritan stream of reformist writing that Anglicans later emended.

The initial transformation began in such works as Bartholomew Batty's *The Christian Mans Closet* (1581). Bartholomaeus Battus was a Fleming from Alost whose work had been published in Latin; William Louth's translation brought it to an English market that he thought would welcome it. The work follows the pattern of the humanist dialogue, collecting the wisdom of the ancients along with biblical injunctions, and there is little of a practical nature to go with the classical adages. Swaddling, for example, is only introduced as an analogy for the care that must be taken that the child's character not be allowed to develop deformities. Batty did warn against spoiling or "cockering" children, but he expressed the hope that parents would strive for moderation in discipline. The time-honored method of beating about the head with the fists or staves had produced deaf, "blockish" children. Far better to restrict oneself to the rod used on the backside where it cannot cause permanent damage. Also, parents should not threaten or taunt their children but should instruct them sweetly and allow them suitable recreations. A Protestant tone emerges in his directions for parental instruction against lying, fornication, drunkeness, and Sabbath-breaking.[69]

Thomas Becon, writing in the 1540s and 1550s, was too early to be termed a Puritan, but he anticipated several of their emphases. Becon was somewhat apologetic about citing the classics, and he thought that teachers should try to counteract the questionable tendencies of Greek and Latin authors. Most significantly, he advised children to obey God rather than parents in any case of clear conflict. This notion of the child's autonomy marks more of a break with the past than the humanists would have found possible and showed the revolutionary challenge that religion posed to family authority. While there is no reason to suppose that this advice gave children the confidence to assert themselves, it may have given parents some pause. Otherwise, Becon's advice was much like that of Batty: mothers should nurse their children, education should begin early, and parents should lead children by their example. In discipline, one should use simple admonitions wherever possible, and schoolmasters should stop their habit of beating like "frantic men." In the humanist tradition, Becon hoped that children would be taught manners appropriate to family life, church, and street, but this advice soon dropped out of Puritan manuals as they came to show less regard for the good opinion of society. In other respects, Becon also provided transitional sentiments. Later writers would have been too realistic to put an erudite doctrinal dialogue into the mouth of a five-year-old as Becon did, nor would they have quoted the apocryphal Jesus of Sirach, who forbade laughing, smiling, or playing with one's children.[70]

Richard Greenham's works (of the 1580s) were more influential in Puritan circles, setting the tone for the later child-rearing manuals of the Puritans. Greenham recognized a developmental aspect in the childhood years, telling parents not to lose heart if children resisted instruction since many who rejected it at first would later embrace it. Of course, it was also true that some who seemed to receive doctrine at first showed no profit from it later. Despite these possibilities, Greenham favored the direct approach: "Though pleasure bee good" in itself, he admitted, "yet pleasure in youth is not good," for if it becomes rooted too early it grows into a wantonness that cannot be bridled. So "correction" should begin early, tempered by the realization that the fault was likely to be the result of the parent's bad example. This should not keep one from the necessary discipline, however, but should make it wiser, more loving, and more prayerful.[71]

All histories of Puritan attitudes toward children refer to this program as "breaking the will," but actual citations of the phrase come from the eighteenth century rather than the seventeenth, when doctrinal and social patterns had changed.[72] At any rate, it should be observed that Greenham's object was not to destroy the will, at least in boys, but to train it toward approved goals. Authors did not promote a permanent dependency but a self-mastery that would allow purposeful action. A "disciplined" will would be a better description. The deeper wish of the Puritans was that young people could convert some of their enthusiasm into religious affections; they wanted to see energy and spontaneity in their children, but only if it could be channeled in the right direction. They knew they could force their children to keep rules, but their many invocations of the beauties of righteousness and the love of God indicated that there was something beyond discipline.

By Greenham's time the contrast between this Puritan view and the more traditional views would have been glaring. Sir Thomas Elyot's *The Governour* (1531) is the best-known humanist statement of advice, mirroring an aristocratic society in which boys were being raised to rule others rather than themselves. So as not to break his spirit, the aristocratic child was to be sequestered from any unsavory example until well into his teens so that no bad habits would surface and no discipline would be necessary. Not only was the child not to be forced or beaten by his governess or tutor, but he was not to be fatigued at his lessons; music and art could be introduced as diversions when he grew restless. The upper-class child was to retain his "courage" and his "gentle wit," meaning his aristocratic willfulness and high spirits, and some degree of self-assertion might even be induced by rigged competitions. Elyot suggested that noble children should be pitted against socially inferior companions who had been instructed to let themselves be worsted every now and then.[73]

Sir Thomas More came closer to the Puritan position in wanting to eliminate this aristocratic pride and to promote more egalitarian virtues, but his methods toward this end, as described in *Utopia* (1516), were quite different from theirs. More depended very little on self-discipline, relying instead on the close supervision of the community to shape the child's mind and behavior. Not only children, but the entire society, was isolated from evil example. The submission of children was unambiguous; in the absence of a servant class, children took that position, waiting on tables while their elders ate. This continued until they were of marriageable age—eighteen for women, twenty-two for men. Even after marriage, the son's family remained in his father's house. Thus, total social control allowed More to ignore the question of the child's discipline.[74]

The Puritans promoted a much different program, seeking to produce free-standing individuals who could operate in any circumstances with only the guidance of a religious conscience. It was this

problem of training without crushing the will that made discipline
the central feature of the child-rearing manuals. Historians have
sometimes taken the amount of space devoted to discipline to indicate a pathological ferocity among the Puritans when in fact it
represented only their awareness of the need for balance.

A godly form of household government (1598) was the most frequently
reprinted guide for parents in the early seventeenth century (seven
editions had been printed by mid-century). It is a work of collective
authorship that goes under the name of Robert Cleaver and shows
how early the Puritan movement began to reflect on the area of
child-rearing. Cleaver begins by reminding parents that "the ende in
correcting, must not bee to wrecke and revenge thine anger, or malice" but "to reclaime him from such evill, as bringeth danger to him,
and make [him] more careful of his dutie afterwards." If a "gentle
admonition" will accomplish this it would be a mistake to go further,
for physical punishment is always resisted by our stubborn natures.
Cleaver obviously did not have any appetite for frontal assault. The
child will only be hardened in rebellion if he feels the correction to
be unjust or unreasonably severe, for "though his bodie be but small,
yet he hath a great heart."

Obviously, Cleaver hoped to work with the child's nature rather
than against it, so talk of "breaking the will" would be misleading.
Correction (spanking) should not be administered in anger or without allowing the offender to speak in his own defense. One should
"never reproach the offender, by reviling, or taunting him with the
fault, but minister correction in love, and desire to have his sore
cured and his credit salved." Shame is also a potent force but should
be used sparingly; being disgraced constantly will cause the child to
lose that very sense of shame.[75]

All of this anticipates John Locke's position of a century later.
Like Locke, Cleaver's intent in discipline was to get it all behind
one as early as possible so that later conflicts could be avoided. At
an early stage there was hope of correcting waywardness by "education," whereas later a stronger arm was necessary. Unfortunately, in
Cleaver's view, a parent's natural affection might stand in the way of
consistency, for he recognized that children are man's greatest joy

in life next to the enjoyment of God Himself: "Such is the fond and too much cockering affection of some parents towards their children, that there is more neede in these daies, to teach and admonish them not to love them too much then to perswade them to love them." Other authors were to echo this concern for the "over-loving of your childe; for that is an ordinary fault even in the best Parents." One writer expressed the thought that this might be why God takes some children to Himself.[76]

The Puritans' complaint that some parents were too fond of their children is the primary evidence that they were more cruel than their neighbors, but it is ambiguous evidence. For one thing, Cleaver did not think that this "fondness" (i.e., foolishness) showed a concern for the child's welfare but that it was a self-indulgence of parents who were too busy to be bothered and who later found they could not stand the children they had spoiled.[77] Also, it is not clear whether Cleaver was complaining about over-fondness among outsiders or among the Puritans themselves. Finally, were his readers influenced either to moderate their discipline or to moderate their affection? Perhaps some parents found justification for their severity and forgot Cleaver's cautions in the heat of the moment, but others might well have begun to wonder what feelings they were venting in punishing their children.

Discipline was not Cleaver's only subject, of course. He also encouraged mothers to nurse their own children, for the use of wet-nurses was against natural order and Scripture's implied command, and it was a threat to the child's physical and mental health. The encouragement of maternal wet-nursing was, of course, a humanist concern of long standing. Cleaver also agreed with humanists on the importance of good manners in speech and gesture. Education, he thought, was the best patrimony that parents could leave to their children—sons or daughters—for it could never be lost. As for a daughter, her virtue should be her modesty or "shamefastnesse." She is not expected to be eloquent, witty, or wise, he adds generously. Like Becon, Cleaver ends by warning children that their duty to God must override even parental demands.[78]

Cleaver's most obvious omission was any discussion of predestination or election. Like Greenham, he brushed off the doctrine as a source of confusion: "Wherefore, not speaking of election, or reprobation, which we leave onely to the Lord, to make good or bad: we exhort parents to use the ordinary meanes to bring up their children." Parents had done their duty when they had taught the laws of God and had offered an example of conscientious conduct, for children learn more from glances and gestures than "by any rule, doctrine or precept whatsoever."[79]

Cleaver's moderate advice set the tone and the agenda for later works such as William Gouge's popular *Of Domesticall Duties* (1622). Gouge, a father of thirteen, avoided practical advice on such things as swaddling, since "what the particulars be, women better know then I can expresse." He took time to refute a multitude of objections to the nursing of infants, which women may have devised in response to humanist and Puritan pressure. Avoiding nursing was the one vestige of liberation that many mothers enjoyed, preferring to work for the half-crown per week it took to hire a wet nurse. Gouge worried that they were risking the child's health and even forfeiting its love. Like Cleaver, he also cautioned those who abused their power over children, parents who were too sour and austere, reviling and threatening their children, beating them severely and allowing them too little "libertie."[80] Gouge's attitude was fundamentally the modern one in which child-rearing is viewed as a trial of parental self-control, the process being as much a test of the parent's character as a way of shaping the child.

Gouge and other Puritan authors expected parents to be impelled by affection for their children, quite aside from motives of duty, and they reminded parents of how they grieved over sick, wayward, and unhappy children.[81] Some parents had stifled this natural affection by covetousness, and one complaint was of parents who neglected children even while they were busy amassing an inheritance for them. Still, "Though some are without this *natural affection*, yet this affection is *natural*."[82] Excessive severity toward children was widely taken as evidence of "distempered" emotions, for many faults were so innocent that punishment would only make matters worse.[83] One writer warned of a number of harmful results that might come of beating children—fits, cursing, running away, death. He recommended many levels of discipline short of physical violence: parents could rebuke piercingly, pathetically, scripturally, tenderly, or even sweetly, depending on circumstances.[84] But there was nothing in the advice to parents to match Daniel Williams's outburst at his young readers: "*Correction* is become unfashionable. The Lord pity us! . . . Let me tell you once for all, Sirs, youth is chiefly governed by *fear*." [85] Most Puritan authors preferred citing the biblical injunction, "Provoke not your children to wrath, but bring them up in the fear and admonition of the Lord" (Ephesians 6:4) to the more notorious Proverb (13:24), "He that spareth his rod hateth his son: but he that loveth him chasteneth him betimes."

Sympathy tempered the law as well. In New England, where Puritans could choose which laws they thought most agreeable with God's Word, it was declared that the punishment for a child who smote or cursed his parents was death, as prescribed in Exodus 21, but they found ways around this penalty. The only record of a court's considering the enforcement of this law was in the case of a twenty-nine-year-old who had been threatening his father.[86] Among English Dissenters, Richard Baxter dismissed the commandment altogether, on the grounds that it was meant for the special circumstances of the Jewish nation during the Exodus. He proposed an institutional approach to incorrigible children which would involve "houses of correction" in each county. If not "humbled and subdued" by a stay there, parents might refuse the child any further maintenance rather than put up with his disruptive behavior or support his vices. Another small indication that the balance was not weighted against the child is the fact that the church book of Bunyan Meeting includes two admonitions for unkindness to children but only one for disrespect to parents.[87]

When it came to discussing the child's innate rebelliousness, there was the same diversity in child-rearing manuals as in children's books. Some writers pointedly rejected Aristotle's image of a tabula rasa: "The soul of every childe is as a book blurred and blotted, all the faculties are like mis-printed leaves; so that much must be rased out before any thing be written in." [88] For others, the metaphor was more ambiguous: the child was "a paper less blotted" than was an adult. Several wrote hopefully that parents might write at will on these "blank papers" if they were reached before Satan printed "his own image on them."[89] In other words, a number of Dissenters shared Locke's later faith in the power of education. At least one Dissenter viewed it, literally, as a means of grace: "Though their hearts be exceeding sinful, as we have heard before; yet if we instruct them in the knowledge, and train them up in the obedience of the Word of God, this will be a means to purifie and sanctifie their hearts, and to reform their lives: for the word of God hath a sanctifying vertue in it."[90] The subject of education appears in all of their child-rearing books, but there are no instructions on how to force the kind of conversion crisis that became a regular feature of eighteenth-century evangelicalism.

Mothers were mentioned only perfunctorily in relation to child-rearing, even though the training of children was "the most eminent service that women can do in the world." Through their children "they may become chief instruments of the reformation and welfare of churches and kingdoms, and of the world." Mothers were to share in discipline and to lead the family's worship in the absence of the father, but as historian Kenneth Charlton has demonstrated, "One has to look very hard indeed to find 'mothers' and their role as educators" in the literature of the time.[91]

Child-rearing books were directed primarily to fathers, for essentially their subject was authority. This is not to say that the works were primarily about discipline, since instruction, example, and concern were also part of the proper exercise of authority. Nor did ultimate authority rest in the father; Puritans and Dissenters were unique in stating that a parent's authority was forfeit if it was not exercised legitimately and that children first had to obey God.[92] After all, parents as well as children were under authority, and the books gave orders to parents, not children. Writers did not assume that the exercise of authority would create a tense relationship: "Do you also sometimes hearken to the good advice, which even your children do seasonably, and in a suitable manner give to you?" asked one.[93] True, fathers should be sober, discreet, and even aloof, and some writers forbade their playing or jesting with their children. But parents could still be cheerful, candid, sweet, and loving with them. "Study to make your Children *love you*, and then everything you enjoyn them will be easie." [94]

Anglican rejection of the most uncompromising views of human depravity did not mean a brighter tone in their child-rearing advice. Jeremy Taylor expressed the semi-Pelagian sentimentalism associated with the Victorian novel: considering children who die fortunate in not knowing evil or trouble, secure in their innocence.[95] This was a far cry from the accounts of dying children collected by Janeway and others who did not consider early deaths to be fortunate. To be sure, Taylor was not representative of Anglicans generally, some of whom expected the child's "tabula" already to be badly scrawled over.[96] Though often bitterly anti-Puritan, Richard Allestree, in *The Whole Duty of Man*, agreed with them that too many parents neglected the discipline of their children, "nay, perhaps please themselves to see the witty shifts of the child, and think it matters not what they do while they are little." Like the Puritans, he cautioned that correction must not be given in rage but must be proportioned to the fault and to the child's "tenderness." [97]

Coming upon John Locke's classic *Some Thoughts Concerning Education* (1693), one is struck by how close his tone is to that of the more sympathetic Puritan and Dissenting authors. His work was also in the humanistic tradition, but it offered the more rounded treatment of child-rearing that humanist pedagogues had failed to produce. The novelty of his approach is that he does not argue from Scripture or from classical authors but relies on his disciplined powers of observation. Also, he is much more thorough, commenting on matters of dress, exercise, diet, and health which earlier authors had avoided. Essentially, however, Locke was only adding emphasis to the advice that earlier books had given and that may well have been followed by his own parents. His motive in writing was that "the early corruption of Youth is now become so general a Complaint."

Locke had in mind especially the failures of his aristocratic patrons. He thought that the indulgent atmosphere that spoiled so many promising children of this class had more to do with the parents' own vicarious desires than with any real sympathy for the child. He treated their "fondness" with sarcasm: "The Fondling must be taught to strike, and call Names; must have what he Cries for, and do what he pleases," but "When they are now too big to be dandled, and their Parents can no longer make use of them as Play-things, then they complain, that the Brats are untoward and perverse." Rewards and punishments were equally ill chosen, leading the child to suppose that the goals of education were sugarplums and the avoidance of whipping. The beatings that parents allowed — and even expected — from schoolmasters were mindless; this discipline was never employed in the teaching of the newer subjects like French or Italian but only in Latin and Greek. The truth was that physical punishment was never effective unless it was reinforced by a sense of shame, for the child must believe that his parents were not only bigger than he but were also right. Like Puritan authors, Locke thought there were often better ways to teach this than by spanking, which might only harden the child in rebellion. Sad to say, the aristocrats of his acquaintance had better success in training their dogs and horses.[98]

Subduing the will was a different matter in children than it was in horses, and Locke paid even closer attention to this problem than had the Puritans. For him, the primary goal of education was fostering the ability to deny one's immediate desires so that one could follow reason rather than appetite. More evangelical writers had hoped for the transformation of desires into religious affections rather than seeing them extinguished in this way. Locke trusted to willpower and conditioning and dismissed infant depravity along with other innate traits, commenting off-handedly that "Few of Adam's Children are so happy, as not to be born with some Byass in their natural Temper which it is the Business of Education either to take off, or counter-balance."[99] It all seemed to be a natural rather than a spiritual problem, and the solution was simply a matter of training.

One soon sees the disadvantage of this more liberal view of the child's nature, for taking the child's freedom seriously made it possible for Locke to be more demanding. Like the Puritans, he thought that parents were erring on the side of permissiveness. If they required only what reason demanded, then "if you command and he refuses, you must be sure to carry it, whatever Blows it costs if a Nod or Words will not prevail, unless, for ever after, you intend to live in obedience to your Son." The hope was to have as little beating and as few such "Contests for Mastery" as possible, and Locke cited an example in which one mother, in a single memorable morning, undid all the damage done by an indulgent nurse: "A prudent and kind Mother of my Acquaintance, was, on such an occasion, forced to whip her little Daughter, at her first coming home from Nurse, eight times successively the same Morning, before she could master her *Stubbornness*, and obtain a compliance in a very easy and indifferent matter. If she had left off sooner, and stop'd at the seventh Whiping, she had spoiled the Child for ever. . . . As this was the first time, so I think, it was the last too she ever struck her." [100] More religious authors did not express quite the same satisfaction in their severe treatment of willfulness until early in the eighteenth century. At that time "Arminian" evangelicals agreed with Lockean liberals in holding children more accountable for their failings. John Wesley's mother is frequently cited along these lines and treated as sufficiently "Puritan" for the historian's purpose, but it should be remembered that, in reaction against her Dissenting background, Susannah Wesley had become a high-church Anglican and Jacobite, with the theological enthusiasm of a convert. Her notorious advice that allowed no crying after correction may have come from reading Locke, who considered this a last "declaration of their Insolence, or Obstinacy." On the other hand, Locke saw the positive value of play, was the first to speak of encouraging the child's curiosity, and encouraged a real familiarity between parents and child, so that there was gain as well as loss in his advice. [101]

Locke did not expect much help from God in the task of child-rearing and this may be responsible for the greater weight of his program. On the other hand, he believed that the child's nature would reinforce parental efforts, for while he did not accept innate principles of "sympathy" or "benevolence" in mankind, as did the Platonist philosophers of his day, he did postulate a "Principle of Aversion." [102] By this he meant that children would eventually react against an excess of any sort, even of play or idleness. Such a principle contradicted the Puritan doctrine that mankind never had a surfeit of sin. Locke denied, for example, that the pleasure that children took in inflicting pain could "be any other than a foreign and introduced Disposition, an habit borrowed from Custom and Conversation." After all, the books of entertainment and history which adults foisted on children were full of "nothing almost but Fighting and Killing." [103]

This fundamental difference between Locke and his Dissenting contemporaries is no more striking than their agreement, especially when his advice to the aristocracy is compared with that of earlier humanists. His goal of self-control is diametrically opposed to Elyot's hope of encouraging the child's willful spirit. Locke's work is constantly critical of a class that saw children only in terms of family ambition, as symbolized in the use of surnames or patronymics as given names. Like the Puritans, Locke dismissed the manners that meant so much to the aristocracy: "so Children do nothing out of Obstinacy, Pride, and Ill-Nature, 'tis no great matter how they put off their Hats, or make Legs." [104]

The ideal of a self-reliant personality was the Puritan legacy to Locke. His Principle of Aversion was where they parted company, but even he stopped short of the indulgent naturalism of Rousseau. Locke and the Puritans maintained the older assumption that human instincts were stronger than moral restraints and would break through if the latter were not reinforced by social institutions. Rousseau stood on the other side of a great divide, thinking that children's fragile natural instincts would be crushed by civilization unless space was cleared for them to grow. Since Rousseau the burden of proof has shifted to those, like the Puritans, who assume that "if the bridle were let loose" children would rush headlong to destruction. [105]

Historians have wondered whether children raised under the Puritan emphasis on discipline could have achieved a balance of "self-control without loss of self-esteem," of autonomy without a paralyzing shame or doubt. There is some cause for this concern, because Puritan authors did have early childhood in mind, and the ages of two to four have been identified as crucial in the development of autonomy. [106] As far as practice is concerned, there is no evidence that would allow confident generalizations. Of course, the Dissenters' long reputation for courage in their convictions and independent conduct suggests that autonomy was often achieved. Perhaps Jessie Bedford has had the last word in remarking that Puritan discipline undoubtedly crushed some children and made others into prideful prigs.[107] There is no way of knowing how many fell somewhere between those extremes. Even with harder evidence, no description of child-rearing practices can be understood outside its personal, emotional context. That climate was described by one Dissenter as "our longing for [children] before we have them, our joy and contentment afterward, the inestimable value we set upon them, our industrious care to keep them, our extreme griefe when we lose them, our *Sympathizing* with them in all conditions." [108]

There is just as little evidence of the practice of contemporary Anglicans, but John Evelyn — liberal churchman, naturalist, scholar, politician, philanthropist — was sufficiently proud of his own practice to offer it as an example. He thought that education was so important in the development of character that some thinkers had quite reasonably "taken education for religion it selfe." Accordingly, in a short-lived educational experiment, he had crammed his son with eight hundred Latin and Greek words by age five — when the boy died of an ague. The child had also been learning French, the catechism and prayers, and the organ. What time he had left for play was constantly interrupted by Evelyn for no other reason than "that I might thereby render him the more indifferent to all things." He was rewarded by hearing the boy complain of "being weary of this troublesome world," a sentiment that Evelyn applauded.[109] If any Calvinist parent made this equation of education and religion, or self-denial and salvation, he had not learned it from his Puritan books.

Daniel Defoe, who abandoned his Dissenting background, showed what could happen when the spirit went out of Puritan theology. In *The Family Instructor* (1715) he attempted to translate child-rearing advice into fiction, an effort often repeated for eighteenth-century readers. What is missing in this volume is the Puritans' sense of the divine presence within life. The "conversion" of the parents in the story amounts to a sudden and rather inexplicable determination at

"reformation." They are struck by the necessity of being more serious, regular, and pious, but not by any new sense of God's grace that
might have inspired gratitude. Their new-found piety shows itself
entirely in negative terms—a rejection of novels(!), plays, ballads,
profanity, and Sabbath-breaking. In the words of the mother to her
bewildered children, "we must be angry now at what we were pleased
at before; and pleased now with what we were angry at before. What
we laughed at and made a jest of in our children before, we must
now mourn over, and correct them for. What we not only allowed to
be done, but even did ourselves before, we must forbid now. What
we accounted pleasant before, must be frightful now; and what we
delighted in before, must be dreadful to us now." [110]

These, then, are the rules for avoiding hell, and they seem completely arbitrary except on the basis of some rejection of the physical
creation. This could only be taken as Puritanism by those who define
the term negatively rather than historically.

John Wesley gives another indication of the direction of the future
by combining the worst of his parents' Anglicanism and his grand-
parents' Dissent in his own consideration of childhood. It has already
been noted that his mother took advantage of a theological conviction—that infants "turned a year old (and some before)" were free
moral beings—to begin a discipline that did not allow even crying
under punishment. In one paragraph describing her program, she
used the word "conquer" four times, as well as "subjecting," "subduing," "governing," and "breaking," to characterize her assault on
the child's will. Her Dissenting father, Samuel Annesley, would have
exhibited more restraint, having once published the sentiment that
"Parental power is not absolute." [111]

Wesley had no children of his own, or he might not have been
so fond of the phrase "breaking the will," but his design for Kings-
wood School gave him an opportunity to carry his mother's program to new heights. The regimen there—no play, no vacations, no
drinking between meals—can only be described as tyrannical, despite the plausible explanations he could always provide. Even in that
day Wesley could not find masters who would enforce such rules.
His hope was that such strictness would preserve something of the

child's baptismal innocence, a particular emphasis he had acquired from his clergyman father.[112] But this belief was at cross-purposes with the evangelist's realism, for Wesley could not help seeing that boys had lost their purity by the time they arrived at his school. So on top of the (already useless) restrictions, he added a spiritual pressure designed to induce conversion.[113]

Either a franker acceptance of the spiritual limitations of the un-regenerate, in the tradition of Reformed doctrine, or a firmer belief in the church's sacraments might have been easier on children. The mingling of traditions created too great an ambiguity, which allowed psychological factors to determine theory to a greater extent in the eighteenth century. Until that time, a sense of God's sovereignty had limited the freedom of parents. It was this degree of respect for the child's autonomy which made Puritans more thoughtful, if not better, parents.

There are many subjects that were passed over almost entirely by these authors. Puritans and Dissenters showed scarcely any interest in physical care or occupational preparation, for their concentration was on moral and spiritual development. The relationships that mattered were with parents and with God; there was hardly a mention of siblings, much less of neighbors. The authors' worst fears did not relate to status decline or spinsterhood but to a spiritual rebellion that would cut man off from his true nature and from the company of the faithful. Locke's originality was in looking into a host of these mundane matters, rather than in what he had to say about training techniques.

In brief, Puritan and Dissenting writers were moved to include children within the circle of God's grace, regardless of whatever adjustments were required in their theology. Their long head start in writing to children meant that they were early in distinguishing between young people and small children, and they realized the need to allow some autonomy if their movement was to enjoy the heartfelt adherence of a rising generation. None of this necessarily made the child's life any sunnier, nor would a more voluntaristic theology decrease the pressure, but it does show that the Puritans were learning as much from children as they taught them.

CHAPTER FOUR

Puritan Humor and Entertainment for Children

Although Puritan works of entertainment and humor for children were not many, some of the emblem books, allegories, plays, and verses were extremely popular, and they offer some insight into the Puritan response to children. Of course, the surprise is that there were any such works at all; the concept of Puritan humor is virtually a self-contradiction. And yet, among the many "Earnest Exhortations to the Rising Generation" and "Solemn Advices to the Children of Godly Parents," there are some relatively light-hearted works that are in danger of being ignored because they do not fit our expectations of the Puritans. In them Puritan writers, without stepping out of their didactic roles, attempted to work around the resistance they may have sensed in their children.

The literary scholar Stuart Tave has noticed a general shift from the crude and somewhat cruel ridicule of the sixteenth century to the more amiable "characters" of the eighteenth century. Essentially, it was the shift from "laughing at" to "laughing with," showing some sympathy toward the foibles that the writer has recognized in himself. Tave is willing to believe, with contemporary commentators, that this development was peculiar to England and that it was related to the freedom of English society and the indulgence of individuality.[1] Politically, the Puritans had a hand in creating this freedom, and they were also the most frequent examples of those who indulged eccentric "humours." Puritans had begun serving as the favorite butt of satire in Ben Jonson's day, when they were pictured as hypocritical and affected in their singularity, but by the end of the century they were sometimes pictured rather poignantly, as sincere in their slightly mad enthusiasms.[2] Of course, Puritans need not be considered pioneers in the history of English humor just for being ridiculous, but several apparently welcomed the role of clown. Thus they contributed to the more humane humor that Tave describes and did so partly in an effort to get closer to children. Though we should not make more of the evidence than it will justify, clearly the Puritans did not lag behind others in their attempts at providing humor for children. Beyond that, one can venture an explanation of the introverted, self-mocking character of this humor, prompted by the Puritans' rather uncomfortable social and psychological circumstances.

The most famous example of Puritan humor, the Marprelate satires of 1588–89, were not for children, but they do indicate the form of humor that certain Puritans would ultimately be able to offer to children — the figure of the clown. One could hardly have expected this. Wit can be biting, and the Puritan party was never lacking for satirists who could flay the opposition,[3] but Martin Marprelate (the pseudonymous author) is different. The author created a persona that is nearly as droll as Tristram Shandy. In fact, there is more than enough humor for one character, and as Martin capers around his hapless victims, he seems to multiply before our eyes. Marginal notes appear, in which Martin comments upon and encourages himself. As things get out of hand, he finds it necessary to rebuke this commentator, adding new confusion to his rollicking attack. In a later tract his son, Martin Junior, sets about publishing some of his father's unfinished manuscripts, and he threatens that "though I bee but young, yet I beginne prettily well to followe my father steppes; for I promise you, I am deceived, unlesse I have a prety smattering gift in this [E]Pistle-making, and I feare in a while I shall take a pride in it."[4] At times the debate threatens to become a circus as Martin Senior engages his opponents, the reader, and interested bystanders, putting words into their mouths.

It is the element of self-mockery that is most remarkable in the tracts. The devastating parody of the bishops is not blunted, but one is aware of a greater self-consciousness in the author than is usual in satirists. This is doubtless related to the Puritan's sense of being an outsider and again suggests the importance of social factors, for it was figures on the sectarian fringe of the Puritan movement — Independents and Baptists — who ventured farthest into this strange territory. The clown has often been used in religious and Christian expression to personify the limits on man's pride and the promise of God's acceptance of our most childish nature.[5] This is an inversion of the world's wisdom, little more than "foolishness" in the eyes of adults, but several Puritan and Dissenting authors and preachers would deliberately accept something of this clownishness for the sake of reaching children.

Psychological theories of humor would seem promising in accounting for Puritan efforts. Such theories generally manage to rob the subject of all enjoyment, making one uneasy because of the aggression, malice, and apprehension that seem to lie at the bottom of humor. Freud differentiated humor, strictly defined, from comedy in that one sees oneself in the comic situation. Freud made a three-fold division within his subject that theorists still find useful. Simple *jokes* short-circuit a rational process with a connection suggested by an unconscious process; *comedy* and satire find amusement in the actions of others; but "humor" finds pleasure defensively, in a situation that is personally painful. Humor is "the ego's victorious assertion of its own invulnerability. It [the self] refuses to be hurt by the arrows of reality or to be compelled to suffer. It insists that it is impervious to wounds dealt by the outside world, in fact that these are merely occasions for affording it pleasure." In the words of one commentator, "in humor the superego makes the problem, big to the ego, seem suddenly very small. In a humorous attitude toward others or toward oneself, the superego takes the role of an exalted but comforting parent." Freud associated this process with childhood memories so that it translates as, "I am [now] too big to be distressed by these things." [6] In short, humor is distinguished from comedy or satire in that, rather than directing aggression toward others, it is directed toward one's childhood self.

Puritans and Dissenters certainly felt an abundance of pain in their lives, pain imposed by magistrates, neighbors, and their own very active superegos. Particularly after the Restoration, their outcast status and powerlessness often did not accord with their economic standing or their feelings of rectitude. One result was the acute self-consciousness and convoluted humor that Freud described, and it is clear from biography, educational technique, and children's literature that some Puritans were attuned to the child's viewpoint. Apparently, childhood experience was more accessible to them than to most of their contemporaries, so they were particularly in need of minimizing threats and building confidence through humor, which, when all is said and done, is a very complicated approach to pleasure for people who find pleasure elusive.

In his discussion of seventeenth-century humor, historian Keith

Thomas reminds us that satire—in fact all comedy—has the conservative function of enforcing social standards through shame and ridicule. As reformers, Puritan satirists had a more difficult time appealing to their readers' sense of the fitness of things, of the "self-evident" nature of their position, than did the conservatives. The more respectable of these reformers did not give up the hope of convincing their society, and the fear of being discredited made them critical of Martin Marprelate and of the clownishness of the Ranters and other sects. Also, a number of Puritans opposed humor out of principle; as Thomas Granger put it, if one could "but dive to the ground of his laughter," it would be found to be at someone else's expense. Being able to identify with victims spoiled some of the fun. So it is touching rather than ridiculous to learn that a group of Baptists resolved in 1655 not to joke any more and that the Fifth Monarchists debated whether laughter was always sinful or only under certain circumstances.[7]

Not all Puritans took such a severe view. The Geneva Bible (1560), long the Puritans' favorite translation, included marginal notes assuring its readers that Jesus' warning (in Luke 6:25), "Wo be to you that now laugh: for ye shal waile and wepe," was only "signifying them that live at ease and after the pleasures of the flesh." Likewise, St. Paul's prohibition of "foolish talking, neither jesting, which are things not comelie" (Ephesians 5:4) could only mean to ban talk "which is either vaine, or els by example and evil speaking may hurt your neighbour: for otherwise there be divers examples in the Scriptures of pleasant talke, which is also godlie."

Puritan reflections on the subject showed some awkwardness, however, as when Lewis Bayly (c. 1610) hobbled humor with his qualifications: "If thou be disposed to be merry, have a speciall care to three things: First, that thy mirth bee not against *Religion*. Secondly, that it be not against *Charity*. Thirdly, that it bee not against *Chastity*, and then bee as *merry* as thou canst, *only* in the Lord."[8] In time, however, some Puritans began to see that humor was not only permitted but even healthy. The Dissenter Edward Reyner (1656) asserted that mirth is useful in "sober and honest delight, for recreation of the minde, and refocillation of the spirits, to make them quick and nimble, when they are dull and heavie, and us fitter and fresher for the duties of our callings."[9]

Among the Puritans, there were some who thought that even children needed a measure of this "refocillation," and their attention to children encouraged the more genial humor that Tave noticed. Parents who did not want to see their children suffer from the ridicule of outsiders, or to join in ridiculing anyone else, may have wanted to offer something different for their amusement. So while others were only republishing the traditional chapbook lore for children, Puritans were composing books for their entertainment and edification. What is more, they put their names to these works as though they did not think this activity to be beneath their dignity. These works are the first attempts to offer something new by way of amusement.

At first glance, the works do not seem very promising. For example, *Apples of Gold for Young Men and Women* (1657), by the Independent minister Thomas Brookes, might seem all too typical of a Puritan emphasis on avoiding damnation. The effect of this work on a child of today (or even an adult), who had never before heard anyone seriously mention eternal punishment, would be incalculable, but one must remember that the children of Puritans were accustomed to threats of this kind. Having heard it all before, it must have taken on a sing-song familiarity for many young people. At least that is what preachers complained of, as the depreciation of their rhetorical currency forced them to raise their threats to ever higher levels. The first thing to be noted about Brookes's work is that it became one of the most popular works of Restoration England, going through seventeen or more editions by the end of the century— the equivalent, in number of copies per household, to three million copies in the United States today.[10] It cannot be dismissed as only another way that Puritan parents found of torturing their children; there is an account of one Puritan girl who discovered the book at age fifteen, loved it, and recommended it to all her friends,[11] even though much of the work seems to have been directed to an even younger age group. Such popularity is enough to make one look more closely at its contents.

The book is not exactly funny, but it does give a similar kind of pleasure by generating a good-natured acceptance of the world. In a recent study of humor, Professor Norman Holland has noted that a playful atmosphere is a necessary precondition of laughter.[12] Brookes achieved some such playfulness despite his purpose of calling children and young people to a seriousness regarding eternal matters. He avoided the boilerplate theological vocabulary of his day by terming this "being good betimes." And rather than threaten the children who had grown blasé, he tried to coax them into the kingdom by a thousand and one stories, anecdotes, and illustrations, gathered from classical, biblical, and other literary sources. Folklore is notably absent, for he was addressing a literate generation and disdained the chapbook stories that they were outgrowing.

Brookes entertained children with "emblems" — the fashion among the poets of the day in symbolizing moral and spiritual lessons. "The whole world is circular, the heart of a man triangular, and we know a circle cannot fill a triangle: yea, if it be not filled with the three persons in the Trinity, it will be filled with the world, the flesh and the devil." Without pausing for the reader to digest that, he plunged ahead: "The world may be resembled to the fruit that undid us all; which was fair to the sight, smooth in handling, sweet in taste, but deadly in effect and operation. Ah, young men, have none of you found it so?"[13] Such comparisons tumble out on top of one another: "They say of the crocodile that when he hath killed a man, he will weep over him, as if he were sorry, and did repent for what he had done; the application is easy." "Some say that when the serpent Scitale cannot overtake the flying passengers, she doth, with her beautiful colours, so astonish and amaze them, that they have no power to pass away till she hath stung them." One can imagine children losing the thread of his discourse amid the luxuriance of these illustrations, for he loved the exotic: "Pliny writes of the crocodile, that she grows to her last day; so aged saints, they grow rich in spiritual experience to the last."[14] Interspersed with these illustrations are anecdotes: "The flatterers told Caesar, that the freckles of his face were like stars in the firmament." The anecdotes come to mind so fast that he can hardly get them down on paper: "Augustus died in a compliment, Galba with a sentence, Vespasian with a jest; Xerxes died laughing at the picture of an old woman, which he drew with his own hand; Sophocles was choked with a stone in a grape; Diodorus, the logician, died for shame that he could not answer a jocular question propounded at the table by Stilpo." [15] Such illustrations certainly were not necessary to explain or enforce his points. In fact, they probably were distracting since they are not always highly pertinent. One must conclude that Brookes simply enjoyed such anecdotes and thought that children would also.

The bouyancy of the work can be attributed to the fact that it does not really picture the world as threatening. Given Brookes's subject — taking care of eternal concerns since temporal life is fleeting — this may seem dubious. The basis for such a characterization is that he draws his illustrations from so wide a compass. He finds no tradition really alien since all seem to support his points; he likes to quote the Talmud and the teachings of such Catholics as Cardinal Bellarmine. Classical authors are as important to him as Scripture: "The heathen have long since observed that in nothing man came nearer to the glory and perfection of God himself, than in goodness and clemency." The pagans were not only wise but also good: "Caesar would not search Pompey's cabinet lest he should find new matter of revenge." [16]

The many lessons Brookes drew from creation meant that nature was man's moral home, whatever he might be implying of the joys of heaven. Beyond that, he hints that some of his illustrations were fabulous ("they say," "some say"), implying that the realm of the imagination was not alien to him either. Only occasionally did Brookes draw the line at something truly outlandish. "The Ethiopians paint angels black, and devils white, in favour of their own complexion . . . and thus they flatter and delude themselves." Also, "The great Cham [Khan] is said to have a tree full of pearls hanging by clusters; but what is the great Cham's tree to Christ our tree of life, who hath all variety and plenty of all fruit upon him?" [17] The almost comic tone of these examples suggests that even these worlds were embraced within his sympathies. So Brookes's book contributed to a feeling of belonging, which is necessary for all children and more particularly to those who face ostracism.

There were those among the Dissenters who did not fully appreciate the work. Edmund Calamy III remarked, "Though he [Brookes] used many homely phrases and sometimes too familiar resemblances, which to nice [strict] critics might appear ridiculous, he did more good to souls than many who deliver the most exact composures. And let the wits of the age pass what censures they please, 'He that winneth Souls is wise.' " [18] Still, even the most well-disposed reader must have found something slightly ridiculous in some of Brookes's outbursts: "That is a sad word of the prophet 'Cursed be the deceiver that hath in his flock a male, and yet offereth to the Lord a corrupt thing.' Ah! young men and women, who are like the almond tree, you have many males in the flock: your strength is a male in the flock, your time is a male in the flock, your reason is a male in the flock, your parts [abilities] are a male in the flock, and your gifts are a male in the flock." Brookes could not resist stretching even his most serious points, as in the story of the young man who had been warned of the evil of his ways but who rejected such admonitions: "I will do well enough, for when death comes, I will speak but three words which will help all: and so he went on still in his sinful ways, but in the end coming to a bridge on horseback, to go over a deep water, the horse stumbling and he labouring to recover his horse, but could not, at last he lets go the bridle and gives up himself and horse to the waters, and was heard to say these three words, Devil take all." [19] Apparently such illustrations embarrassed Calamy and other Dissenters who would have liked to avoid the ridicule of their neighbors, but Brookes did not seem to mind adopting the role of clown, since it was in a good cause.

The Independent minister Hugh Peters was another such, becoming something like the court jester to Cromwell's regime. His reputation was so widespread that two books of his "jests" were published immediately after his execution (for regicide) in 1660. [20] They were the stuff of which chapbooks were made, but many of the stories contained circumstantial detail and reveal a consistent character. Sometimes, when his sermon was nearing its end and people were making for the doors, Peters would hold their attention by starting a story. It seems there was a group going on pilgrimage—a man, a swallow, and an eel. They were all tiring of the trip and so, coming to a wood, the swallow gave the others the slip. When they reached a brook, the eel did likewise. The man, going on, came upon a bundle of switches: "Now beloved, what think you these rods were for; I'le tell you, they were to whip such men as will make haste from a Sermon, and return to hear a tale. So much for this time."[21]

This was only one of the many jokes that originated in the pulpit. Once, to the dismay of his audience, Peters turned over the hourglass *again*, saying that they should have another glass before they parted. It was sometimes his practice to knock on the lectern as if on the door to heaven and then to open the pulpit door as if to let the phantom in. At times he would dive down out of sight in the pulpit and then pop up again to report that he had been to heaven (or hell) and to tell who he had found there. To see if one country congregation was awake he told them to beware of the three W's—wine, women, and tobacco. Seeming to come to himself amid the murmers of the audience, he added, Well, it's a weed, isn't it?[22]

No subject was too sacred for comedy to the irrepressible Peters. While attacking organ music in worship, he told one congregation that they should sometimes vary their confession and say, "Lord have mercy upon us miserable singers." To the argument that the revolutionary Parliament was acting without precedent, he responded, "What think you of the Virgin Mary, was there ever any precedent that a Virgin should conceive?"[23]

What is of interest is the reaction to all of this. Not all Puritans thought Peters equally delightful and, in fact, some definitely disapproved, but this did not stop him from becoming chaplain to the Council of State and one of the most popular preachers at Cromwell's court. Puritan wags called him Oliver's Archbishop of Canterbury. Peters even became wealthy enough to excite the jealousy of laymen, and according to one story, he was confronted at the Stock Exchange by someone who told him, "Mr. Peters, you are a knave, or else you had never gain'd so much wealth as you have. Say you so, said he, marry if you were not a fool, you would be a Knave too."[24] Cromwell, who was known for somewhat coarse practical jokes, apparently was not offended by Peters's brand of wit.[25]

Peters's humor was not particularly directed to young people, but there was a connection. He was the principal force behind the founding of Harvard College for training the youth of New England, and when he returned to England, he attempted to promote the founding of three more regional colleges there, to serve students younger than colleges accept today.[26] At least, one can say that children were not shielded from his humor or that of numerous other Dissenting ministers who were known for a sense of fun. In collecting the biographies of Dissenting ministers, Calamy describes many of them as "chearful" and a surprising number as "facetious."

Matthew Pool was "very facetious in his conversation" and in evening gatherings "would be exceedingly but innocently merry, very much diverting himself and his company." William Yeo was said to be "well respected by the neighbouring gentry, being a genteel man, and very facetious in conversation," and several others were likewise "much valued by some persons of rank" for their wit. Calamy also cited as facetious such leaders of the Puritan movement as John Howe and Jeremiah White, who were likewise chaplains to Cromwell.[27]

Some of these ministers even produced plays for children, despite the Puritans' well-known hostility to the London theaters. Samuel Shaw, who lost his pastorate at the Restoration, wrote plays for his grammar school students to perform, and at least three of these were published. Shaw's plays constituted an ingenious teaching device. One of them, *Grammar*, shows the parts of speech getting into various difficulties with King Syntaxis, but a sophisticated student would have noticed that these conflicts were analogous to the ecclesiastical and political conflicts of the day. *Rhetoric* presents the figures of speech and the princes Ellogus (rhetoric) and Eclogus (pronunciation) involved in disputes that would have been of interest to students of the classical curriculum.

Even today, Shaw's preface shows why Calamy described him as "ready at repartees and innocent jests":

As for the Reasons for publishing (if you must needs know) I am not infallibly certain that it was done either to gratifie importunate Friends, or

prevent surreptitious Copies, nor will I make Affidavit that the Author
writ it all in three days and a half, or in the hurry of a World of other
business and Avocations. For I have observ'd several Friends of mine
have very solemnly made such excuses, and yet the World has not be-
liev'd a word on't, or at least concluded them Fools for Writing when
they had no better Leisure and no body compell'd them to it. But to
speak the whole Truth, I verily think that our Author wrote this small
piece (as poor folk get Children) for his pleasure, and though he has no
Cause to be asham'd on't, yet like Batchellors, by their pretty Babes at
other folks fires, did not much care to own it [Shaw published anony-
mously], so that 'tis now Printed meerly for the Booksellers profit and
the Readers Diversion.

Shaw's method of teaching is described as "winning and easy." [28]

The preface to the third of his plays, *The Different Humours of Men
represented at an Interlude in a Country School* (1692), freely admits
that it was meant to prompt a laugh and asks its audience to put on
its "holiday humour." This play has nothing to do with the esoteric
aspects of Latin instruction, but the jokes still fall flat because there
is no plot structure to create a truly comic situation. Instead, there
is only a parade of characters ("humours," in the old medical sense)
with names like Moses Merry and Mr. Medler, whose comments to
Sir Francis Freeman are meant to be wry judgments on the manners
of contemporary society. The plays were actually performed, not
only for the edification of Shaw's scholars but for the "entertainment
of the town and neighborhood at Christmastime." [29]

The allegorics or dialogues that Dissenters wrote for children may
also have been performed or at least read dramatically around a
circle. Often versified, these were produced more by sectarians than
by the more respectable branches of Dissent, preparing the way for
Bunyan's allegories. They began, quite inauspiciously, with the translation of an anonymous Dutch work, *A Spiritual Journey of a Young
Man, Toward the Land of Peace* (1659). This work labored to prove
that "the Bible is a dead letter without the Light within," so one
suspects a Quaker was behind its publication in England.[30] A Baptist
minister, Thomas Sherman, was the next to try this format in two
"dramatic poems," *Youth's Tragedy* (1671) and *Youth's Comedy* (1680).

They are extremely simple in their moralistic view of religion, as they try to raise some suspense over whether Youth will follow Vanity or Wisdom. The Devil, Death, and Time appear, much like the characters found in medieval morality plays or the sixteenth-century "interlude," but in this case written specifically for grammar school pupils.[31]

Benjamin Keach, the prolific Baptist poet, soon followed with several such allegories, beginning with *War with the Devil* (1673) and *The Glorious Lover* (1679). The protagonist of the first, Youth, represents the sensuality and pride of that short-sighted stage of life. Truth threatens and Conscience expostulates with him, only to be met with bravado:

> If you speak loud when I am all alone,
> I will rise up, and straightway will be gone
> To the brave Boyes, who toss the Pot about;
> And that's the way to wear your patience out.
> I'le go to Playes, and Games, and Dancings too,
> And e're a while, I shall be rid of you.[32]

The popularity of this tale of evangelical conversion required five editions before the appearance of *Pilgrim's Progress*, and five more had appeared by the end of the century. Such popularity is somewhat baffling given the lifeless plot and the stereotyped characters. Perhaps it is evidence of the hunger for anything resembling entertainment.

Keach reprobated stage plays at several points, as did other children's authors of all parties, but his various allegories were consciously intended to compete with them. While his plots are too static to be staged, they could have been read dramatically. Another Dissenting clergyman, Thomas Powell, produced *The Young Man's Conflict with and Victory over the Devil by Faith* (1675), which would have been easier to act. The central character, a young man named Paulus, is actually on his way to a play (within the play) when he meets Evangelus, a minister, who tries to dissuade the young man and is roundly denounced as a "phanatick." In the end, however, Paulus is prevented by a sudden paralysis from signing a compact with a polite "gentleman" (the Devil, of course) and is recovered for God's service.

The plots described above may seem to be without humor, and it is questionable whether they are even within the realm of entertainment. There were, to be sure, efforts made to introduce wit into the dialogues, for the nature of the dramatic medium demanded sharp exchanges. Unfortunately, the stakes in such confrontations were too high, since the Devil himself appears with such regularity. Had Powell employed Tempters instead, their efforts might have been treated more comically. It was John Bunyan's genius that introduced allegorical figures that finally took on a really human life and allowed for a more generous humor.

Pilgrim's Progress from This World to That Which Is to Come (1678) was not especially meant for children, but it was taken up by them almost at once.[33] This was partly because children had been prepared for such literature by the other works described above and partly, no doubt, because the book has moments of real humor. This is evident from the first page where Christian's family diagnoses his religious anxiety as brain fever and bundles him off to bed. The adoption of figures like Giant Despair from the folk tales of the time would have been refreshing to readers who were accustomed to a greater seriousness in treating religious themes.[34] Frequently the comic element has to do with the juxtaposition of antagonistic outlooks and the resulting misunderstandings. The first of the allegorical figures — Obstinate and Pliable — make just such a comedy team by virtue of a contradictory agreement. When Pliable decides to accompany Christian, the reader is aware that his eagerness is due to a misunderstanding and that he is about to take a sudden turn. And so it proves, when the pratfall into the Slough of Despond breaks the suspense.

Dissenters faced just such a divided society and culture during the Restoration. For children to see their neighbors' lack of comprehension treated as comic should have been reassuring, for the atmosphere of good humor would seem to include rather than exclude their antagonists. Readers soon lost touch with the theological abstractions involved, as the allegorical characters became social types and even rounded persons. They may be unsympathetic characters, and in Vanity Fair they even turn murderous, but by presenting the antagonism as a misunderstanding rather than as radical evil, Bunyan is showing that the principles on which the characters acted were not unreasonable. The citizens of Vanity Fair only wanted to preserve good order, commerce, and community solidarity. Whatever the deficiencies of this value system, it still produced worthwhile individuals. Thus, in the middle of the lynching party, "Some men in the fair that were more observing and less prejudiced than the rest began to check and blame the baser sort for their continual abuses done by them to the men."[35] Social conflict, then, was not as desperate as some young readers might have imagined.

As for the worldly reader, Bunyan realized that humor was sometimes a better tactic for making the reader face his false position than proof of his errors would be. Where social convention was the culprit rather than an inexplicable perversity, readers might respond to such caricatures as Mr. By-Ends (the representative of Ulterior Motives):

> CHRISTIAN: Pray who are your kindred there, if a man may be so bold?
>
> BY-ENDS: Almost the whole town; and in particular, my Lord Turn-about, my Lord Time-server, my Lord Fair-speech (from whose ancestors that town first took its name). Also Mr. Smooth-man, Mr. Facing-bothways, Mr. Anything, and the parson of our parish, Mr. Two-tongues, was my mother's own brother by father's side. And to tell you the truth, I am become a gentleman of good quality; yet my great-grandfather was but a waterman, looking one way, and rowing another; and I got most of my estate by the same occupation.
>
> CHRISTIAN: Are you a married man?
>
> BY-ENDS: Yes, and my wife is a very virtuous woman, the daughter of a virtuous woman. She was my Lady Feigning's daughter; therefore she came of a very honourable family, and is arrived to such a pitch of breeding that she knows how to carry it to all, even to prince and peasant. 'Tis true, we somewhat differ in religion from those of the stricter sort, yet but in two small points: first, we never strive against wind and tide. Secondly, we are always most zealous when religion goes in his silver slippers; we love much to walk with him in the street, if the sun shines and the people applaud it.[36]

Unmasking the timidity and hypocrisy of fashionable society reduced it to a scale that a beleaguered minority could find amusing, but it should be remembered that what we view as social satire was also directed inward, as symbolic of the struggles within each reader. How readers most commonly perceived or employed this is a moot question.

Some Dissenters wondered whether laughter was appropriate to such serious subjects. Bunyan's fellow Baptist, the minister Thomas Sherman, lamented an age that was so debauched that even religious apologists felt constrained to offer entertainment, specifically naming Richard Bernard's *The Isle of Man* (1626, with at least sixteen editions by 1683) and Clement Ellis's *The Gentile Sinner* (1660, seven editions by 1690). Sherman wrote a *Second Part of the Pilgrim's Progress* (1684) as a corrective to Bunyan's levity: "I have endeavoured to deliver the whole in such serious and spiritual phrases, that may prevent that lightness and laughter, which the reading some passages therein, occasion in some vain and frothy minds."[37] He achieved his goal of being unamusing but not that of challenging Bunyan's popularity.

The reaction of Dissenting writers and of book buyers demonstrates that Bunyan's approach was accepted much more widely than Sherman's. In the wake of the popularity of *Pilgrim's Progress* (fourteen editions in just five years), Benjamin Keach adopted the same theme of pilgrimage for *The Travels of True Godliness* (1683) and *The Progress of Sin* (1684). He also turned to prose and introduced a wider range of characters, representing the humours rather than his earlier theological abstractions. Keach felt the need to apologize: "I hope none will be offended, because *True Godliness* is here presented in an *Allegory*, sith the Holy Scriptures abound with them, and so fully justifie our practice herein."[38] Readers did not seem to mind; Keach's two works enjoyed ten editions by 1700, and Bunyan's saw another eight editions by that date.

In the 1690s an obscure Dissenting minister, Robert Russell, published a number of dialogues and allegories for small children. They were very poorly printed and are among the rarest of all early children's books, sometimes existing only in single, damaged copies. Judging from what has survived, it can be said that the loss is not great. The books appear to be sermon material that Russell endeavored to give a new and imaginative life, but unfortunately he lacked the charmed kiss which could accomplish this transformation. He was the sort who thought that the way to approach children was to tell them frankly that God does not like children who do not learn their catechism or say their prayers or who disobey their parents. At best, obedient children might go to heaven (early, it is hoped) where there are no whippings or hunger and there is nothing to frighten or hurt them.[39] Russell's debt is clearly more to James Janeway's *Token for Children* than to Bunyan. He recommends Janeway's work and pays him the compliment of lifting thoughts and even phrases from the book, as well as adopting the childish diction that Janeway had been the first to use. Bunyan's influence is limited to little more than the titles of *The Pilgrims Guide from His Cradle to his Death Bead* and *The Pearl of Great Price; or a Pilgrim, who, in his Pilgrimage to the New Hirusalem found a lump of Clay in the Dunghill of Mammon, afterwards a Pibble in the Field of Morality: and at last the Pearl, at his entrance in at the Straight Gate.* At least this testifies to the reputation of Bunyan's work among young readers and their parents, but it is a relief to find that Russell's works did not share the popularity of his models.

If Dissenters were so inclined, they had numerous occasions upon which to bring children together to read these allegories and dialogues. Many of the suspended, nonconforming clergy took in boarding scholars and needed to fill their time with edifying exercises. Calamy reports that some ejected ministers, who were forbidden by the Conventicle Act (1664) to discuss religion with groups of more than four persons outside their immediate families, made it a practice to invite "as many under sixteen years of age, as would come, they being too young to come under the Act."[40] Perhaps they intended to deliver the same kind of sermon they were accustomed to giving, but the preachers may also have found a use for the entertainment materials available. In addition to the dialogues and allegories, there was the Wordless Book, by the children's author Thomas White, for the very youngest children. As eventually used, it took the form of a booklet made up simply of unprinted leaves colored black, red, white, and gold, symbolizing the message of sin and judgment, Christ's atonement, the believer's purity, and heavenly glory.[41] There was also Richard Baxter's *The Mother's Catechism*, the first Bible-story book, in which a child asks questions and is answered with Bible stories in

a colloquial and dramatic form. All of this served as the background
for John Wesley's "children's sermon," which he limited to words of
one or two syllabus, and to his brother Charles's children's hymns.[42]

Last but not least among the entertainment materials is children's
verse, which, again, was produced more by the sectarian fringe than
by main-stream Dissent. Verse gives a kind of enjoyment similar
to humor in its management of surprise, and it met with some of
the same objections. The editor who introduced Keach's *War with
the Devil* acknowledged objections to the use of verse in religious
matters:

> Yet I dare say, how e're this scruple rose,
> Verse hath express'd as sacred things as Prose.
> Though some there be, that Poetry abuse,
> Must we therefore, not the same method use?
> Yea sure, for of conscience it is the best,
> And doth deserve, more Honour than the rest:
> For 'tis no Humane knowledge gain'd by Art,
> But rather 'tis inspir'd, into the Heart,
> By Divine means, for true Divinity,
> Hath with this Science, great Affinity.[43]

In short, poetry was considered, by Baptists and Quakers at least, to
be a charismatic gift.

The most gifted of these poets was the Baptist, Abraham Chear,
who has never been forgiven by historians of children's literature for
the famous lines in "Written to a Young Virgin":

> When by Spectators I am told,
> What Beauty doth adorn me:
> Or in a Glass, when I behold,
> How sweetly God did form me.
> Hath God such comliness display'd,
> and on me made to dwell
> 'Tis pitty, such a pretty Maid,
> as I should go to Hell.

The jolt of the last line is all the greater because the preceeding ones
contain such promise. Again, one wonders what a child of that era
would have made of such a verse. Hell was a familiar part of that

world, which may have been all but intolerable for more imaginative children,[44] but most would have come to terms with the idea in
order to go on with the business of living. For them, that last line
was only to be expected and not the bolt from the blue that it is to
us. If children needed to be preached at, it was better to make it a
game as Chear did:

> Doth Beauty such corruption Hide?
> is comliness a bait?
> Do costly Garments nourish pride?
> hath Treasure such deceit?
> Do Complements breed vanity?
> doth pleasure Grace expel?
> How little reason then have I
> for these to go to Hell?

One must note that Chear does not *expect* his little beauty to go
to hell, unless of course she should grow into a large and wanton
beauty in this heedless course.[45]

The true test of sympathy for the Puritans lies in whether one can
see this poem as an effort to amuse children rather than to terror-
ize them. Certainly, if it was meant to be entertaining, Chear had
chosen an awkward way of doing it, but equally, if terror was his goal,
there must have been easier ways than with versification. Even while
worrying over the rising generation, Chear's lines have a certain lilt:

> Young Isaacs, who lift up their eyes,
> And meditate in fields;
> Young Jacobs who the Blessing prize
> This Age but seldom yields.
> Few Samuels, leaving youthful plaies,
> To Temple-work resign'd;
> Few do as these, in youthful daies
> Their great Creator minde.
>
> . . . .
>
> What Children Pulse and Water chuse
> Continually to eat,
> Rather than Conscience should accuse
> For tasting Royal meat?
> Would you not bow, a King to please,

> Though tortures were behinde.
> Oh then in these your youthful daies
> Your great Creator minde.[46]

One young Baptist committed these lines to memory.[47]

While one should not be too apologetic about the Dissenters' efforts, part of the hard edge in their children's books is explained by their circumstances; Chear, Keach, and Bunyan all had the enforced leisure of prison in which to indulge the poetical impulse.

The last major effort at children's verse before Isaac Watts's century was, again, a book of religious poems—John Bunyan's *A Book for Boys and Girls: or, Country Rhimes for Children* (1686), sometimes called *Divine Emblems; or Temporal Things Spiritualized*. Again, whether or not the poems seem amusing, the very existence of such a work is significant. The child would have sensed that adults (not only the author but whoever gave him the book or read it to him) were trying to speak the child's language rather than making him speak theirs, and thus the medium became a message in itself. Children were being entertained and would have come to think of themselves as worthy of such treatment.

Bunyan realized that Puritan ministers had been heavy-handed in their earlier methods and that this had proved ineffective.

> Our Ministers, long time by Word and Pen,
> Dealt with them, counting them, not Boys but Men:
> *Thunder-bolts* they shot at them, and their Toys:
> But hit them not, 'cause they were Girls and Boys.
> The better Charge [powder], the wider still they shot,
> Or else so high, those *Dwarfs* they touched not.
> Instead of Men, they found them Girls and Boys,
> Addict to nothing as to childish Toys.
>
> . . . .
>
> While by their *Play-things*, I would them entice,
> To mount their Thoughts from what are childish Toys,
> To Heav'n, for that's prepar'd for Girls and Boys.[48]

One would have to count that last line as a comforting thought.

Bunyan was prepared for fellow ministers to disapprove of his verse as much as they had his allegories:

> I think the wiser sort my Rhimes may slight
> But what care I! The foolish will delight
> To read them, and the Foolish, God has chose,
> And doth by Foolish Things, their minds compose,
> And settle upon that which is Divine:
> Great Things, by little ones, are made to shine.

Thus, like Brookes and Peters before him, he agreed to some clowning:

> Wherefore good Reader, that I save them may,
> I now with them, the very Dottril play.
> And since at Gravity they make a Tush,
> My very Beard I cast behind the Bush,
> And like a Fool stand Fing'ring of their Toys;
> And all to shew them, they are Girls and Boys.
> Nor do I blush, although I think some may
> Call me a Baby, 'cause I with them play.

In a reference to 1 Corinthians 1:18–29 and 4:10, Bunyan remembered that "Paul seem'd to play the Fool, that he might gain / Those that were Fools indeed."[49]

In contrast with Brookes's earlier and more erudite generation, Bunyan understood children's attraction to the humbler of God's creatures. The exotic and even fabulous beings from Pliny and the ancient naturalists, which had served Christian authors for so long, give place to the mole, the bee, cuckoos and flies, the frog, snail, piss-ant, and swallow. In the dialogue between "The Sinner and the Spider," Bunyan makes the spider the more sympathetic of the two, which catches readers off balance, since they share the sinner's horrified reaction to that insect. Spider argues that he is only following his nature as the Creator made him; it is the sinner whose spiritual deformity should make him loathsome. But Bunyan sometimes uses the spider in the more accustomed role of tempter and entrapper, thereby creating an ambivalence in the dialogue. One cannot say whether he did a better job of making children feel good about spiders or bad about sin, but there is no doubt as to which of these goals was more surprising; Spider's sensible arguments and winning personality must have delighted children.

Several of the poems compliment children; "Of the Boy and Butter-Fly" concludes that grown men are even more foolish than children in the objects of their pursuit, and in "Of the Child with the Bird at the Bush," Bunyan makes the child (pictured in a smock) a Christ-like figure, caring for the bird he has rescued as the Savior cares for him.[50]

If the campaign in favor of humor and entertainment had not been entirely won in Dissenting circles, nine editions of this work by 1724 and the enormous popularity of Watts's *Divine and Moral Songs for Children* (1715) show that many readers outside Baptist circles were enlisting on Bunyan's side.

Quaker authors left the most evidence of children's devotion to verse, and several of the accounts of the sufferings of their children remark on the poetical inspiration that helped sustain them. Joseph Briggins had borne the scoffing of other boys with meekness and manliness, and the last words of this eleven-year-old were in verse, going on for over an hour in the following vein:

> That you may feel the virtue of his Grace,
> For mortal man is but to run his Race,
> And woe to them that shall not Obey his Grace,
> For such do not feel his Virtue, nor ere shall see his Face.[51]

Names and addresses of witnesses were given for the benefit of doubters.

To Quakers a poetical impulse was apparently taken as a sign of God's special blessing on injured innocence, and this association is found in the published lives of young Mary Whiting, Jonah Lawson, Samuel Mather, and William Fletcher.[52] Eight-year-old Sarah Camme had memorized a number of the difficult verses written by the Marian martyr Robert Smith to his wife and children. As she was dying of smallpox, she was heard to make sweet and melodious sounds, presumably another testimony to the innocence of life that the Quakers' principles protected.[53] In these circles, at least, poetry transcended mere diversion to foreshadow paradisiacal bliss.

In all of the emblem books, plays, dialogues, allegories, and poems, these Puritans and Dissenters attempted to relax some of the tension induced by a strenuous piety, but the quality of their efforts indicates that a playful atmosphere did not come naturally to them. They should get credit, however, for being the first to produce anything original as an alternative to the casual folklore of the chapbooks. It is odd to think of Puritans as pioneers in the field of humor or entertainment, but the understanding of comedy as a hint of transcending truth and the recognition of comic catharsis as something akin to mystical insight were not entirely beyond them. It remained a matter of debate between Bunyan and his coreligionists.

The fact that the more radical reformers—Baptists and Independents—were the most likely to accept the role of clowns can perhaps be attributed to their facing up to their pariah status more forthrightly. Presbyterians had greater hopes of some kind of accommodation within the Church of England and thus were more conscious of a need to maintain a semblance of dignity. They may well have been the main critics of "Martin," Brookes, Peters, Keach, and the rest. Whatever the identity of these critics, they cannot have been very successful; production figures for *Apples of Gold, War with the Devil,* and *Pilgrim's Progress* are out of all proportion to the number of Dissenting households in England. These were among the few dozen best-selling books in Restoration England, with total sales equivalent to bestsellers today in terms of the number of households. The absence of similar works by non-Puritans meant that religious conformists were also turning to Dissenting authors for edifying entertainment.[54] There is no indication that they ever admitted their debt to the Puritans. And yet, almost despite themselves, the Puritans had played a part in the development of English literary humor, as they were to do again in educational theory.

CHAPTER FIVE

Education
and Freedom

I f the Puritans and Dissenters could provide such a wealth of written advice on child-rearing to churches and to families, they were not likely to neglect schools, and a portion of what they published on education showed an originality of approach that might be termed revolutionary. Historians of early modern education have traced the addition of new subjects to make education more relevant, the reform of pedagogical methods to make teaching more effective, and the proliferation of schools to make education more accessible.[1] These historians have not been much occupied with the growing realization that education is something quite different from indoctrination. Indoctrination is the opposite of education, closing minds instead of opening them. The distinction is a critical one, indicating an awareness of the child as an individual whose freedom should be respected. One is surprised to find that this distinction originated within the Puritan tradition rather than in more liberal groups and, what is more, that it developed in a time of religious struggle.

The stakes in the religious conflict were so high that one would expect the methods of indoctrination to be especially heavy-handed and unapologetic. Yet it appears that religious groups recognized a difference precisely because of their new awareness of ideological conflict. More surprisingly, the distinction arose even in the context of religious catechizing, which is usually taken to epitomize the process of indoctrination. By the middle of the seventeenth century, none of the groups involved with catechizing — Anglicans, Catholics, Puritans, Quakers, Socinians — could expect to impose their respective views on all of England, and so, for the first time, a new approach to education appeared, one that combined ideological content with persuasion rather than with legal compulsion. By the end of that century, some Dissenters were even suggesting the possibility of truly reflective methods that would preserve the pupil's intellectual autonomy, an approach that most clearly merits the name education.

After Queen Elizabeth prevented Puritans from achieving a further purification of the church by political means, they turned to education. The founding of Emmanuel College, Cambridge, in 1584 is only the most prominent of their attempts to create educational institutions that would promote their program of renewal. Education of clergymen was, of course, the primary charge of such colleges, and this education would affect not only adult congregations but schooling as well, at a time when most teachers were clergymen. Initially, Puritans may have expected their educational efforts to impose an orthodoxy, but things were to work out rather differently.

The Puritans' educational efforts began with catechizing, the memorization of doctrinal terms and tenets that was meant to provide a check against error, to sharpen one's ear for wrong-sounding phrases. Memorization was required even of those who would later become fully literate and could easily have consulted doctrinal sources, because the purpose of this exercise was to make orthodoxy the child's second nature. To this end the catechism was not only learned but repeated, in devout homes at least, for years afterwards.[2] Traditionally, catechizing was viewed more as a precondition of education than as part of the schooling process itself. It bore a relation to religious instruction similar to that which grammatical drill bore to the study of literature or the multiplication tables to the study of mathematics.

Once in school, the pupil's religious training virtually ceased, if the complaints of numerous religious writers are to be believed. Of course, the grammar schools had been founded on a religious basis at a time when all intellectual culture was integrated by religious commitment, but it was precisely because religion permeated all intellectual endeavor that it had never become an explicit part of the education program. By the early modern period the religious aspect of grammar school training extended only to attending chapel and church and to the public reading of the Scriptures in English, Latin, or Greek as a test of the pupil's skill in those languages. Beyond that, it was expected that the schoolboys would be catechized on weekends, much as other children were.[3] Complaints that schoolmasters were not fulfilling even this minimal duty became a regular feature of pedagogical treatises.

Some writers, most notably Erasmus, had taken the view that a proper study of the classical authors would provide the knowledge for a good life, but others were not so sanguine about the incidental effects of the classics. So there was talk after 1560 of furnishing advanced catechisms in Latin that would have the effect of introducing religious instruction into the schools themselves.[4] Any such proliferation of catechisms would have the effect of loosening the connection of catechizing with a uniform and automatic religious response. Clearly, the earlier desire to consolidate the religious changes of the Reformation by rote memorization was now competing with the desire to reach higher levels of doctrinal sophistication. Accordingly, the first official English catechism (in the 1549 *Book of Common Prayer*) was supplemented by longer official ones (the "Small," "Large," and "Middle" catechisms), which by 1574 had been issued in Latin and Greek for use in grammar schools. These were primarily the work of Alexander Nowell, a leader of the Puritan party under Queen Elizabeth.[5]

Not satisfied even with this provision, Puritans insisted on producing scores or even hundreds of unofficial catechisms early in the next century. The popularity of some of them—most notably Stephen Egerton's *A Brief Method of Catechizing* (forty-fourth edition, 1644) and John Ball's *A Short Catechism; or, A Short Treatise Contayning all the Principall Grounds of Christian Religion* (fifty-fourth edition, 1688)—attests to the Puritan interest in catechizing. This activity was partly due to a sense of the doctrinal inadequacy of the Church Catechism. More importantly, though, it stemmed from the desire to achieve more appealing or logical presentations, a more complete view, or, on the contrary, a simpler understanding of the faith. In short, the Puritans were responding to a variety of truly educational impulses.

Anglicans, meanwhile, produced far fewer original catechisms, probably because the canons required them to teach the Church Catechism even if they used other catechisms as well. Unlike the ideas of the Puritan movement, the survival of Anglican views did not depend on their success in reaching children. The Anglicans lived within a world of traditions and habits that embodied their faith, whereas Puritans maintained their religious outlook on a relatively narrow basis of explicit belief. Formal education was therefore more crucial to the Puritan enterprise.

A proliferation of catechisms could only have an unsettling effect on religious indoctrination, quite the reverse of the original intention to create a community standard, and not all religious leaders accepted the practice. Some observed that Scripture's own way of teaching is through history rather than precept because history "is easily understood and retain'd and greatly affects."[6] Others rejected catechizing altogether as a "human invention," comparing it unfavorably with preaching, which appealed to the heart as well as the head. To them, a mere indoctrination might give an excessively intellectualistic notion of religion. Apologists pointed out that Christ himself submitted to something like catechetical instruction at age twelve and that St. Paul had enjoined the practice by his reference to "the form of sound words."[7]

Both the opponents and proponents of catechizing had, it seems, accepted as their goal the religious development rather than the religious stasis of the child. With many of the Puritan catechisms, one is immediately aware of the questions of educational technique that were arising in light of this goal. Some of the writers vied to produce the simplest and shortest catechisms; an Elizabethan Puritan referred to a one-penny catechism that started with questions any child could have answered — "Who made thee? God. What is God? He is almightie, etc. Wherefore did he make thee? To serve him."[8] Other authors thought that the best approach to children was to enlist their interest in narrative or nature; some of the "Little Child's Catechisms" introduced stories and became conversational. They were, in effect, the first Bible-story books.[9] Arthur Dent's *A pastime for parents; or, A Recreation, to pass away the time; containing the most principall grounds of Christian Religion*[10] was too erudite to be memorized and can hardly be considered entertaining, but it provides evidence that a few Puritans meant to make "catechizing" a more discursive, relaxed process. The association of catechizing with rote instruction was loosened even further by the appearance of John Paget's curious work on the wonders of creation. Starting with the various orders of the angels, the heavenly bodies, fire and lightning, winds, rainbow and rain, and progressing to man, children, insects, birds, elephants, beasts, trees, herbs, stones, metals, waters, fish, whales, and devils, he asked what each might teach about the glory and power of God and about the various commandments.[11] To compose this imaginative work as a catechism made little sense, but such works do show that writers recognized that their goal of enlarging the mind was better met by a programmed and progressive method than by simple statement.

A major step forward in educational technique was taken by Herbert Palmer, a Puritan advisor to the Westminster Assembly of Divines. His *An Endeavour of Making the Principles of Christian Religion . . . plaine and easie* (1640) came close to presenting a reflective method, drawing the truth from children rather than cramming it in. The plan was to present the main question and then, without waiting for an answer, to start suggesting possibilities that could be answered yes or no. Hearing these subsidiary questions would suggest the correct answer to the main question and even the proper wording of the answer:

Question 1, What is a man's greatest business in this world? Is it to follow the world, and live as hee list? No.
Or, Is it to glorifie God, and save his own soule? Yes.
[So, what is a man's greatest business in this world?]
A. A man's greatest business in this world is to glorifie God, and save his own soule.
2Q. How shall a man come to glorifie God and save his own soule?
Can they do so that are ignorant? No.
Or, They that do not believe in God? No.
Or, Do not serve him? No.
Or, must they not needs learn to know God? and believe in him and serve him? Yes.
[So how shall a man . . .]
2A. They that will glorifie God, and save their owne souls, must needs learn to know God, and believe in him and serve him.[12]

Presenting material in this way should have helped circumvent the resistance children might feel, giving them a sense of discovery and accomplishment during the process of doctrinal instruction.

Upon Palmer's death, the Puritan minister John Wallis used

Palmer's principles with the questions from the Assembly's Shorter Catechism, explaining that proper pedagogical technique exercised the judgment rather than simply the memory. With this method it should not be necessary to teach any answers at all, since hearing the subquestions would suggest the proper answers and even their wording.[13] In 1672 the Dissenting minister, Thomas Lye, followed with both an expansion and an abridgement of the Shorter Catechism along these same lines, offering children an abundance of wrong-sounding answers in order to sharpen their doctrinal discrimination. He acquired a wide reputation in Dissenting circles in London as others came to see the success of a method so well suited to the way children learn.[14]

Had Anglicans been so inclined, they could have followed a precedent of their own in this area, for the clergyman-poet George Herbert earlier had suggested the importance of a reflective method in catechizing. In *A Priest to the Temple* (written in 1632 but first published in 1652), he described how the catechist might ask subsidiary questions and offer analogies, pursuing the catechumen to make sure that he understood the logical necessity behind his answers. One might even suggest the very words of the proper response. Herbert acknowledged that one could not derive all the doctrines of revealed religion from nature, but catechizing was the closest thing to the Socratic method, he thought: "At Sermons and Prayers, men may sleep or wander; but when one is asked a question, he must discover what he is."[15]

After the Restoration, Palmer's method led to a number of true/false catechisms that tested primarily what the child had already picked up from his parents. These questions made it possible, at least, for catechists to spot areas of ignorance:

> Is the Eighth Commandment, Thou shalt not steal? Yes.
> Ought every man to have some lawful Calling? Yes.
> And to be careful and industrious therein? Yes.
> May such as have great Estates live in idleness? No.
>
> . . . .
>
> Is it sufficient for every man to look to himself, without regarding others? No.
> May he take Advantage of the Ignorance of another? No.

Or of the Poverty of another? No.

May a man commend beyond its worth what he is about to sell? No.[16]

By the turn of the century, this method was used in the Anglican charity schools, where both the Church Catechism and *The Whole Duty of Man* were adapted to the form of a quiz.[17] It was eventually realized, however, that the catechist only pursued wrong answers by the use of this technique and would not know whether the child had understood any of his correct answers.[18] Such a realization would never have occurred if the catechists had been satisfied with rote responses.

Another sign that catechizing was broadening into an educational method can be found in the graded series of catechisms that Puritans and later Dissenters produced. The Westminster Assembly offered Shorter and Longer Catechisms (1647), which were equally official. While they were engaged in this task, others of their camp were producing even more elementary catechisms such as Robert Abbot's *Milk for Babes; or, A Mothers Catechism for her children* (London, 1646) and John Cotton's *Milk for Babes* (London, 1646), known in New England as *Spiritual Milk for Boston Babes*. At the turn of the century the Dissenting leader Isaac Watts published *The Young Child's Catechism* (for ages three and four) and *The Child's Catechism* (for ages seven and eight), which were to be preparatory to Watts's later version of the Shorter Catechism.

One would think that such a staged approach would defeat the very purpose of catechetical method, for the child might well confuse the responses to various catechisms. Even more unsettling, catechists were now being advised to vary the words of each question a little each time so that children would not be dependent on a single expression of any truth.[19] The object was clearly a more thorough understanding of doctrine. Writers frequently claimed that they were accommodating children of various "capacities," a word which suggests containers of varying sizes, but they were obviously allowing for differences in memory, logic, and experience as well. The necessity of actually working with small children over their catechisms was forcing teachers to recognize children's abilities and limitations and to start from their own conceptual level.

More liberal minds were ready to carry some of these educational methods even farther than the Puritans and Dissenters had done after having been shown the way. The notorious *Racovian Catechism*, produced by Polish Unitarians and printed in English in 1652, was of the old and familiar type, meant as an exercise of the memory, but in 1687 there appeared an altogether remarkable work, *A Rational Catechism; Or, An instructive Conference between a Father and a Son*. It was the work of John Locke's friend, the liberal pamphleteer William Popple, and was meant to be a Socratic exercise in natural theology. Popple hoped that his reflective approach would help to heal the divisions caused by the partisan prejudice of Christians and the ignorance of atheistic scoffers, for he was determined to proceed only by such arguments as no reasonable man would deny.

The work begins as intimately as possible: "What is it that thou lovest best?" The son, obviously accustomed to religious hypocrisy, tries to think what his father would want him to say, but the latter encourages him: "No matter what I think, or what I doubt of." Eventually the child is surprised to hear himself say that he loves himself best. Other goods are then ranked in relation to the first principle of self-preservation: honor, power, pleasure, riches, knowledge. The son constantly shows a fear of self-exposure and has to be assured that the father will accept honest answers. Reflections on human nature then lead, in Cartesian fashion (Popple had lived in France), to general considerations of nature, to God as first cause, and to His attributes. A fundamentally naturalistic ethic is secured by the logical necessity of an afterlife.

The first mention of Scripture is made midway through the catechism. Popple suggests that revelation was given to incline unphilosophical minds to the truth, not to add to the truth, and he spends some time gaining assent to the historical trustworthiness of the Gospel accounts. Finally the father reaches the question of "the Perfection required from us," which in orthodox catechisms would have led to the doctrine of grace and salvation. Popple implicitly denies the ideas of atonement and imputed righteousness in favor of sincere efforts at obedience to moral law and charity to one's fellows. He holds that Jesus' simple teaching "consists wholly in Humility, Meekness, Moderation, and Benignity, and other such like Social

Virtues." He laments the perversion of this noble creed by priests and magistrates and by the inexplicable perversity of men, who love darkness rather than light.[20]

By the end of the catechism Popple becomes assertive and does not always wait for realizations to come spontaneously, but in the main, this is education in the classic sense of eliciting new realizations on the basis of previous experience. It is done with sufficient skill that one can imagine progressive parents actually leading their children through the questions.

Any contemporary would have recognized Popple's catechism as a Deist work, but many of the more orthodox catechisms of the Restoration had pointed in the same direction, in that they attempted to transcend the mid-century controversies by adopting a minimal statement of Christian doctrine. Lancelot Addison, the father of the essayist, identified the so-called Precepts of Noah (seven injunctions from Genesis 6–9) as "the Universal Catechism of all Mankind."[21] While various "Scripture Catechisms"—which limited answers to the very words of Scripture—were meant to avoid certain controversial formulations, others were obviously meant to insinuate liberal views by ruling out theological terminology. John Biddle, the Unitarian, and Robert Barclay, the Quaker, protected themselves by composing such "Scripture catechisms," and John Locke, who was not entirely orthodox, also favored this format.[22] Even the orthodox examples of the genre were meant to find a common ground where all parties might meet, leaving the individual's further doctrinal development to personal reflection. Reducing doctrine to essentials in this way would encourage the theological simplification and erosion that were apparent in earlier children's literature.

Naturally, the older ideas took some time to disappear. Early in the eighteenth century, Isaac Watts criticized those who still thought that it was sufficient to stuff children's memories at an early age and to hope that they would ruminate later. Watts felt that if children did not understand a point, they had not "learned" it. Such children would always remember their religious instruction in a sing-song manner that would make the very thought of religion ridiculous to them later, so he objected to making the process too easy. Requir-

ing only "yes" or "no" for an answer, without a reason or even a
Scripture to support the answer, did nothing to inform the child or
"improve the understanding."[23] The fact that Watts could assume
this as the goal of catechizing shows how far educators had come
from the original notion.

In the child's study of Scripture, seventeenth-century writers also
showed an awareness of the need to follow the developing child.
Puritans and Dissenters observed that young people did not respond
as well to precept and definition as to history and example. This
suggested that education should begin with the histories of the Old
Testament before moving on to Proverbs and Psalms, for "Nature
is pleased sooner with history than with precept." They could cite
St. Basil for his advice to start children with the histories, a method
that became traditional practice.[24] The Puritans and Dissenters did
not recommend that one simply read the Bible through in sequence.
Watts mentioned a young woman of his acquaintance who had done
that, as though the absurdity of the procedure were obvious.[25] Anglicans showed a greater wariness about using Scripture as an educational text, possibly feeling that those who had recently seized upon
literal prophecy had discredited religion in general.[26] Locke complained that the Bible was being read too "promiscuously" and voiced
the wish that young students would not read the books of the law,
the erotic Song of Solomon, or the prophetic books. He thought
children would enjoy the familiar stories of Joseph and David and
could profit from the books of moral instruction. He also hoped
that someone would produce "a good History of the Bible for young
People to read . . . [containing] every thing that is fit to be put into it,
being laid down in its due Order of Time, and several things omitted,
which were suited only to riper Age."[27] This prudery became typical
of eighteenth-century England; Baxter's *The Mother's Catechism* had
already retold these stories without bowdlerizing them.

In a rudimentary fashion, all of this advice implied that the religious education of each individual recapitulated that of the race.
Hence, one began with the experience of the patriarchs, then learned
the wisdom and praises of Israel before proceeding to the gospel and
the epistolary commentaries on it. Such a program seems to envision

education as a dialectical process, one in which children would develop through recognized stages of enlightenment, perhaps including the crisis of conversion. It does not appear, however, that contemporaries recognized such implications. The literature on catechizing suggests that religious development could be managed smoothly and without crisis, by a training that involved home, school, and church.

But how could this training be provided for the many children in England who were hardly touched by any of these institutions? From 1662 to 1720 the debate on this question would show indoctrination increasingly on the defensive.

At one time the state had expected to force the Anglican catechism on every child in the land. Henry VIII's first set of Royal Injunctions to his reformed church (1536) required parents and masters to teach children—"even from their infancy"—the paternoster, creed, and commandments, which comprised the elements in the earliest English catechism.[28] It remained the parents' responsibility to see that the Church Catechism of 1549 was learned, even though it was the clergy that was enjoined to teach it. Elizabeth's church established fines for parents whose children could not say the catechism by age eight, while allowance was made for the child who obviously lacked the mental capacity to learn it.[29] Even then there were complaints, especially by Puritans, that this duty was being neglected by parents and clergy and that many children lacked any knowledge of their faith.[30]

After 1662 conformists became concerned that Dissent was being institutionalized. In 1672 Archbishop Sheldon urged Parliament to establish statutory penalties for those clergy who failed to catechize every Sunday.[31] Perhaps the most ingenious effort to force compliance was that by John Parkhurst, Bishop of Norwich, who stipulated that no one in his diocese could be married until they could repeat the catechism, the justification being that only such parents could properly instruct their children. Although others tried to make the same demand, it never gained canonical force.[32] By the time of Locke's *A Letter Concerning Toleration* (1689, translated by William Popple), it was clear that compulsion had failed.

Accordingly, Dissenters and Anglicans turned to another means

of insuring that all of the nation's children were properly catechized, and this was with the charity schools, an educational philanthropy on a national scale under the direction of ideologically
committed trustees. Since the state was not immediately involved in
this effort, there was no question of compulsion, but the purpose of
these schools was clearly to extend religious training (originally catechetical) to all children if possible. The debate that grew up around
these schools, especially the accusation of Anglican partisanship and
"priestcraft," opened a public debate on indoctrination.

Up to this point in England's history, no embarrassment had been
expressed over the doctrinaire character of education. Every government from Henry VIII's time onwards had seen to it that educational institutions fell in line with the shifts in religious policy,
especially through the licensing of schoolmasters by ecclesiastical
authorities. In 1662 this licensing was restored (by the Act of Uniformity), along with the restoration of the Stuart dynasty and the
Church of England, as a matter of course, but licensing no longer
seemed stringent enough to enforce the old-style educational monopoly. So in 1665 the Five Mile Act specifically forbade any Dissenter from teaching, whether public or private. This law demonstrated a growing awareness of the threat of alternative instruction,
but it was widely evaded, and the presence of dozens of Dissenting
"academies" did not immediately become a national issue.

The founding of the first Catholic charity school, in 1685, was
a different matter. James II's approval of this Jesuit venture made
it seem especially sinister, and Anglicans and Dissenters immediately began to establish charity schools of their own to counteract
the threat.[33] The philanthropic rather than political nature of this
effort corresponded to a desire to use persuasion rather than force.
Since Anglicans were now in the novel position of opposing their
monarch, they could only refer obliquely to the obvious sectarian
character of their campaign. Only William III, in his invasion declaration of 1688, was in a position to express what was in their minds.
As one of the country's grievances, he listed the "colleges of Jesuits
in divers places, for corrupting of the youth." With the success of the
Revolution, the government imposed new restrictions on Catholic
education.[34]

As the Anglicans began to reimpose their educational monopoly, they found that Dissenters were assuming that the Toleration Act of 1689 had freed their schools as well as their chapels from the church's supervision. William III did not encourage Anglican partisanship, but when Queen Anne assumed the throne in 1702, churchmen began to appeal for her help in ending the Dissenters' freedom. In that year the clergy of Canterbury Province, and also the Earl of Rochester (Anne's uncle) in his dedication of Clarendon's *History of the Rebellion*, warned her of the dangers of Dissenting indoctrination.[35] Samuel Wesley, the father of the evangelists, took the opportunity to publish an attack on the Dissenting academies in which he himself had been educated as a schoolmate of authors Timothy Cruso, Daniel Defoe, and John Shower.

The debate that ensued developed an explicit distinction between education and indoctrination. Wesley, now an Anglican and a Tory, accused the Dissenters' schools of encouraging disloyalty and of being so poorly supervised as to allow the circulation of lewd books. He offered his pamphlet "to the Consideration of the Grand Committee of Parliament for Religion" and attracted the notice of the Reverend Henry Sacheverell, who for years would be the center of Anglican reaction. Sacheverell asserted that the Toleration Act did not extend to these "Academical Conventicles," which prejudiced their students toward republicanism and atheism.[36]

The Dissenters were not slow in answering Wesley's attacks. Daniel Defoe responded in *More Short-Ways with the Dissenters*; having attended the same Dissenting academy as Wesley, he was in a position to deny that subversive political ideas were taught to the children. A portion of the ensuing debate turned on strictly legal points. In 1703 Presbyterian Samuel Palmer argued that the Act of Uniformity had only restricted teachers in holy orders and not laymen, as Dissenting ministers were regarded by law. He reasoned that the Toleration Act must have implied a right to train ministers at least, since they would be needed to direct the worship of future generations.[37] In rebuttal, Wesley denied that the Toleration Act was meant for more than the generation then living and called on Parliament to make it clear that Dissent would not be allowed to perpetuate itself through indoctrination.[38]

A part of the debate transcended this legalism, however, and concentrated on the educational method used with Dissenting children. In answering Wesley's initial attack, Palmer asserted that the tutors at the academy he had attended (at Bethnal Green) did not attempt to influence students on controversial points, nor did they make reflections on the Church of England.[39] True or not, the statement obviously represented an ideal and a new ideal at that. In a later work, Palmer tried to shame the church with the accusation of obscurantism, asking whether the universities were monopolizing all instruction because they were afraid of the truth.[40] The implication was that education presupposes freedom and the challenge of intellectual diversity.

Sacheverell, in a 1704 sermon, made the very different assumption that all education took the form of mental conditioning: "The First Impressions that are made upon the Mind in the Tender State of Infancy, strike so strongly upon it, and sink so Deeply into it, that Nothing can, without much Force and Violence, Erase those Durable Characters."[41] In 1709, when he accused the Dissenting academies of openly teaching "Atheism, Deism, Tritheism, Socinianism, with all the Hellish Principles of Fanaticism, Regicide, and Anarchy," he was brought to court for his attacks on the Whig government that, among other things, countenanced such schools.[42] In one of England's most celebrated political trials, Sacheverell's defense reverted to the danger from these schools that "thro' the unhappy Prejudices of Education" had estranged so many young minds from the principles of the church.[43] The phrase suggested that all education was to be understood as the inculcation of prejudices and that a good education differed from a bad one primarily in that it prejudiced students in favor of the truth, not that it trained one to be discerning. John Wesley later recorded that his father Samuel claimed to have written Sacheverell's defense.[44]

Partly as a result of the uproar over that trial, the Tories emerged victorious in the election of 1710. Using Jonathan Swift's claim that the Whigs had been planning to take education out of the hands of the clergy, the Tories proposed the Schism Bill that would destroy Dissent as a cultural tradition and as a political threat.[45]

The resulting pamphlet debate treated this bill, however, as an educational rather than a political issue. Curiously enough, it was moderate Anglicans who offered the most telling arguments, developing the Dissenters' positions of ten years earlier. Journalist Richard Steele asked if the church party was admitting that it did not have "Reason" on its side in its educational restrictions. Like Samuel Palmer, Steele took his stand on the natural right of parents to educate their children, which the bill seemed to deny in its sweeping prohibition of all instruction in reading.

Steele carried the argument over education a step further when he justified the parents' right, not by the fact that they would be correct in what they taught their children, but by the fact that they would be sincere. He took it to be a Protestant principle that every man should be allowed to examine Scripture for himself, and pamphlets by Presbyterian Thomas Reynolds and an anonymous author likewise asserted that it was "a Principle avow'd by all Protestants, That every Man ought to judge for himself" in controverted matters.[46] Steele believed that being true to one's conscience was more important than being correct in every detail: "What allowance God will give Erroneous Consciences, it is not our Business to Enquire; but as an Erroneous may be a sincere Conscience, we should be Barbarous in pretending to Oppress or put Hardships upon it." He did not exactly say that sincerity was more important than truth, but he had introduced the relativity of thought into the debate on education. Education was an individual quest. Being left free in this quest was only part of the individual's natural right to a quiet life. It would be no more cruel, Steele thought, to eliminate Dissent by not allowing Dissenters to marry than to prohibit them from educating their children in their beliefs.[47]

Daniel Defoe developed a different line of argument. In his collusive *Letter to Mr Steele, Occasion'd by his Letter to a Member of Parliament* (supposedly the thoughts of a Tory squire), he worried over the economic consequences of the bill. But in the end, even he rested his case on the Christian principle that governments should not force conscience, since "whatever is not of Faith is Sin" (quoting Romans 14:23).[48]

As the House of Lords debated the Schism Bill, it was besieged by petitioners to allow exceptions for the teaching of reading and writing in English and of applied mathematics. Perhaps this met the embarrassing charge that parents were not being allowed to teach their own children. Although the bill passed, five bishops and twenty-eight peers registered their protest in the journal of the House of Lords, declaring that the law was impolitic and divisive.[49]

While the lords were debating the issue, the most penetrating discussion came from the Anglican lawyer, John Shute Barrington, in his *Letter from a Lay-Man in Communion with the Church of England, Tho' Dissenting from Her in some Points.* He expands on Steele's relativism: God gave man reason so that he could think for himself, and reason leads men to differing opinions. "Reason," to Barrington, meant not Truth but intelligence—something within man rather than above him. Dissent is therefore a matter of degree, since everyone's ideas are colored somewhat differently. For example, everyone has some objection to a particular religious establishment, but anyone who has his own opinions "thereby becomes a Party, and therefore cannot be a Judge." So even in the case of this present argument, everyone is in the position of partisan; there can be no impartial judges in matters of belief. A party or government that forces conscience usurps a power that God denies to Himself. Thus Barrington justifies what he took to be the essential principle of the Reformation, an assertion of the freedom of the individual conscience.[50] In short, whereas Sacheverell referred to the differing intellectual "complexions" of men to justify an educational monopoly that would bring social harmony, Barrington uses the idea to argue that government cannot hope for complete agreement and should seek only to restrain men from actually injuring others.[51] It seems that the shadow of Locke's works on epistemology, education, politics, and toleration was falling across this debate, although he was not specifically mentioned.

If one carried Barrington's reasoning to its limits, even parents would be restrained from trying to force their children's minds, at least on ultimate questions. And, indeed, several Dissenters took exactly that line. Barrington lamented the effect of the Schism Bill on parental authority, saying that parents would lose interest in their children if they were kept from directing their education,[52] and two anonymous tracts presented an even more advanced position. In arguing against the bill, one writer credited Dissenters with taking the greatest care not to influence their children unduly. He claimed that Dissenters had not turned their children against "any Body of Protestants in the Nation, nor Perplex'd [them] with matters of doubtful Disputation; we desire they may be left as Free and Un-byast as can be in such Things, until they are capable of forming a Judgment for themselves."[53] Children were instructed only in "the common Sentiments of Christianity," said the other, leaving "matters controvertible" for a time when they were of an age to make their own judgments.[54]

With these anonymous statements, we have finally reached the point at which the child's autonomy is asserted even against his parents and claimed as a settled principle of Dissenting education. As far back as 1646, the Presbyterian Thomas Edwards had alarmed his readers by asserting that some sectarians were teaching that "Parents are not to catechize their little children nor to set them to read the Scripture or to teach them to pray, but must let them alone for God to teach."[55] This view might have been dismissed as rumor in 1646, but now some Dissenters were acknowledging the principle openly.

Apparently this assertion of the child's freedom was more than a mere sentiment. In 1730 Isaac Watts complained that Dissenting parents were so fearful of indoctrinating their children that they allowed them to grow up without any religious instruction at all. These parents claimed that they wanted their children's choice in religion, in his words, to "be perfectly free, and not biased and influenced by the authority of parents, or the power of education." Watts was suspicious of this high-sounding principle, for these parents were not backward about teaching any lesson that they considered of practical importance. He could not believe that anyone with a firm faith would withhold it from his children, seeing that it was for their eternal good, and he warned that children would learn from others if not from parents.[56]

Very likely Watts was implying what Steele had openly stated about Dissenters—that many of them "connive at the Conformity of their Children" and are "secretly pleased" at it, though unable to bring themselves to conform.[57] Such parents were disguising their true motives in promoting the new and more liberal view of education. Whatever their true motives, a full awareness of the distinction between education and indoctrination was now evident. The first constituency for the views of Socrates and Popple can be found in this group of half-convinced Dissenters. Their respect for children's freedom extended even to, and perhaps especially to, their consideration of the ultimate questions of life.

There is some evidence that the Dissenting academies institutionalized this approach to education. Educational historian J. W. A. Smith has asserted that the practice in some academies of having students compare several Bible commentaries was the first use of any sort of comparative method in English education.[58] Of course the commentaries used would have represented a relatively narrow range of opinion, but the practice introduced a relativism into education which had once been reserved for the mature scholar. Several of the academies had a reputation for "freedom of inquiry," at least from the time of Thomas Rowe at Newington Green in the 1680s. By the 1750s, according to Joseph Priestley's recollection of Daventry Academy, that school was characterized by a spirit of free inquiry and discussion, of polite but serious disagreement over religious questions even among the faculty.[59]

As the day approached for the implementation of the Schism Act in 1714, Tories calculated that the country now took education so seriously that the Act would provoke Dissenters into actual rebellion. Lord Bolingbroke was plotting with French agents to use French troops to put down any such rising, hoping that their presence in England would then block the Hanoverian succession when Queen Anne died,[60] but apparently he misjudged the temper of the Dissenters. Their preachers were all too willing to see the bill's passage as divine judgment on themselves for laxity in educating their children, although they also prophesied God's judgment on the nation for this cruelty.[61] As matters transpired, Dissenting schools were providentially saved by the death of Queen Anne on the very day that the Act was to take effect.[62]

The notion of the child's autonomy still faced a struggle, however, against the traditional understanding of education as indoctrination. No sooner were the Whigs back in power than they tried to make education responsive to political pressures by creating elected lay vestries in each parish, which would choose the teachers of all charity schools. Their bill died in the House of Lords when the Whig bishop William Wake, who had signed the protest against the Tories' Schism Act in the previous year, spoke against it.[63] His impartiality showed that some individuals thought that such pressure had no place in education.

Thwarted at the legislative level, Whigs tested their power in the courts and thereby brought this struggle to a comic end. In 1718, at the height of a Jacobite (pro-Stuart) invasion scare, some charity scholars were in Chislehurst, Kent, for a charity sermon benefiting their school in London. At the service there was a fracas in which the local sheriff and justices of the peace attempted to stop the collection and then succeeded in seizing it. They boldly declared that they cared nothing for the fact that the Tory Bishop of Rochester had given permission for the affair. At the next assizes these officials claimed that the children of the charity schools were begging and should be treated as vagrants. They also boasted that they would serve all charity schools thus and pretended to suspect that the collection was to go to the Stuart pretender. The Whig judge was even more extreme, accusing the schools of working for the dreaded Cardinal Alberoni and of levying a tax without Parliament's permission—which was, of course, "the tenderest part of our constitution." The court was unable to decide whether to treat the episode as ridiculous, as when it snickered over the sermon and the hymns used in the money-raising effort, or to view it as a desperate rebellion against the Hanoverian dynasty.[64] Finally, the judge instructed the jury to find the children guilty of begging. When it did, he fined them six shillings eightpence each and gravely declared that collecting money under the shelter of the church's sanctuary was a danger to the realm.[65]

The comedy of the situation attracted Defoe, who had earlier defended the Dissenting schools when it had been the Tories who were overbearing. He lampooned the Whig prosecution, calculating whether the £3 collected, multiplied by all the parishes in England, would raise enough money to send James Stuart's entourage to Italy so that he could consummate his marriage with the Princess Sobieski and beget new pretenders. "In short," he concluded, the episode reminds us that "we cannot be too careful to preserve and transmit to Posterity, a Religion void of all Principle, of all Faith, of all Charity . . . a Religion that frees us from all Foreign Tribunals, especially that of the Day of Judgment." [66]

Establishing pedagogical methods that work to free the child's mind from social and personal prejudice will forever seem a new thought. Indeed, the public may always insist that its prejudices are being inculcated by the schools before it will give them full support. It is one of the ironies of history that the idea of education as a process of discovery should have grown out of a consideration of catechizing and primary education—and at a time when England was rent by doctrinal controversy. But it is, after all, a difficult lesson, and it took a group with the radicalizing perspective of Dissent to rediscover it.

Family Feeling
versus
Puritan Individualism

The Puritan discovery of childhood is only half of a story; the other half concerns the ways in which that discovery changed the Puritans. There is evidence that their reflection on childhood put pressure on their theology, their educational approach, and their families, and it is obvious that the failure of the movement and its hardening into sects soured relations between the generations. There is a further twist to the story—when the forces of the family reasserted its position against the individualism that was implied in a discovery of the child.

This part of the account comes from a later time and left only the faintest trace in the historical record. It was only in the 1790s that the radical heirs of the Dissenting tradition made clear what the child's autonomy meant for society and the family, which is a measure of the delayed effect ideas may have on their host movements. The historian can only infer an inarticulate resistance and argue from analogous cases. The other two cases sketched here, however, are not only analogous but related to our Puritans in a genealogical descent. Puritanism shows a parallel with the early Christian movement in its challenge to the family, and it passed that tradition down to the English "Jacobins."

The evidence of Puritan and Dissenting interest in childhood has been gratifyingly consistent, the available literary sources supporting one another. Since the present study has been organized by types of sources rather than by topic, one can be confident that the concerns expressed in those sources have not been neglected in favor of later interests. So it is apparent that these groups looked more closely at children than did other Englishmen and that they began to see children as individuals. In their concern over names, in their description of actual children, in creating a literature for them and their efforts to make it appealing, in an educational method that implied an intellectual and moral autonomy, they showed a new respect for the child.

The individualism implied in this concern for children is, however, a threat to family solidarity, and Puritan and Dissenting families reacted accordingly. The fact that Puritanism formed a movement certainly directed their attention to the presence of children, but their social basis remained in the family. Movements provide a subject for cultural history, to a large degree, whereas family is more properly a part of social history. Movements depend on a more conscious level of purposes and meanings and transcend the most basic determinants of life, whereas families are immersed in them. It is for this reason that the family has the greater resilience and will have the final say in any dispute between the two.

There are sure to be disputes, for families and movements represent the opposite poles of stability and movement. Any form of the family is, in certain respects, more conservative than any type of movement. While families and movements are notoriously diverse, all movements present a challenge to the family as well as to other institutions. Religious movements are like other movements in this respect. Because of their dynamics—and sometimes in spite of their intentions—they cannot help having an unsettling effect upon families.

First, by definition, movements promote social change, whereas "the family" is one of society's most traditional institutions—one, in other words, in which members regard each other with a particularistic, affective, and diffuse interest. In ordinary language, traditional groups value you for who you are and not for what you can do. "The family," in its various forms, exemplifies this attitude and, in fact, usually serves as the model of this kind of relationship. Its members are not recruited but have a right to the consideration and care of other family members. In movements, on the other hand, members are accepted to fill universalistic, instrumental, and specific roles and serve as workers toward some goal, with the individualizing tendency that is implied in this program. The family's "purpose" is just to be together, in the kind of comforting mutual regard just mentioned. So for a start, the value orientations of families and movements put them at odds.

Second, both movements and families tend to be exclusive, asking for a loyalty from their members which will override competing loyalties. Any movement must be concerned as to whether its members' enthusiasm can survive the need to maintain family bonds; and on the other hand, families worry about losing members to a "cause." Balance is hard to maintain. A movement may lose its original vision and come to serve those in control and their loved ones through nepotism, or it may succeed in using the family as a recruiting and training station. Such compromises will, of course, change both families and movements.

Third, there are modernizing movements such as Maoism that have attacked the family directly as the very bastion of traditional injustice. Here it is not only the dynamics of the movement that pose a threat to the family; family domination is the very essence of the inequality that is under attack. Such movements make their own organization, along universalistic and individualistic lines, the model for all social relations.[1]

Sociologists have largely ignored the importance of family loyalty in sapping the energy of a movement, perhaps because of their general neglect of the reasons that cause movements to fail.[2] Of course, some movements are thoroughly unrealistic, some are simply inept, and still others are torn apart by disagreement. A few are successful and disband when their goals are realized; others are accepted into the social system as parties, sects, or educational or welfare agencies. In considering hostility against movements or actual repression, one tends to think of the state and not the family. The state can mount concerted campaigns against a movement that it views as threatening, whereas the resistance that stems from family fears may be more subtle, even unconscious, and will probably leave no documentary evidence. Nevertheless, the following examples provide ample reason to suspect that the family's opposition is the more potent.

ONE CUSTOMARILY THINKS of the church as a champion of the family, but from the very beginning there was a tension between the Christian movement and the contemporary family. This unrest shows up in the New Testament writings themselves, which meant so much to our Puritans, and since so little Puritan testimony exists on this unacknowledged problem, it will help to trace a parallel case in some detail. In the Gospels it appears that Jesus had two great difficulties, both related to the Jewish family of his day. One was in establishing his authority as a prophet or a messianic Son of Man, even against the skepticism of his own brothers, and the other was in trying to overcome the religious pride of his contemporaries, who maintained their exclusive sense of divine favor. When his own family could not accept him, Jesus is recorded as having announced, "Whoever does the will of my Father in heaven is my brother, and sister, and mother,"[3] recognizing that no prophet could be honored in his own house or among his own kin.[4] This drew him all the closer to his Father in Heaven, whom he addressed endearingly as *abba* in all of his recorded prayers.[5] Such familiarity with God provides an interesting contrast with several records of near rudeness in addressing his mother.[6] The point is that he had to create some distance from his family in order to establish any sort of divine authority.

But Jesus ran a risk in resisting the familiarity of his own family. He encountered suspicions concerning his own legitimacy, such as those expressed by his critics in John 8, and in this dispute the second difficulty emerges, the family pride of Judaism. Jesus' accusers doubted that he was truly the son of Joseph, a shameful accusation, but he broadened this question to include the ethnic presumption of his accusers; he doubted that they were true children of Abraham, the source of their pride. Or, if they were in an obvious physical sense the children of Abraham, did that necessarily mean that they were spiritual children of God? Could righteousness be handed down through the family in this way? When it came to that, how righteous were their forebears? Had they not murdered the prophets?[7] Thus Jesus found himself in a contest with the "tribal" nationalism at the heart of Judaism. His followers would later recall his various warnings that they, too, must turn their backs on family ties and be "born again."[8]

Disciples were comforted by the favor Jesus promised to those who renounced family for his sake. Early spokesmen faced a growing opposition within Israel and reacted by developing Jesus' distinction between the children of Abraham by faith and those who trusted to natural descent.[9] Attachment to Israel's familial symbolism was considered by these preachers to be a major obstacle to the spread of the movement. Thus, the issue of family (or ethnic) loyalty was both a source of the movement's strength and a limit on its growth within Judaism; few could make the break with family but those who did were committed wholeheartedly. Undoubtedly, Jesus' challenge to religious nationalism was a comfort to Gentile converts who felt no family claim upon God. The new age was neatly symbolized by juxtaposing the twelve apostles, uprooted from family and nation, with the twelve patriarchs, the sons of Israel.[10]

From the very first, then, the church represented a threat to family solidarity, but the movement soon found itself accommodating the family by domesticating grace within the family. It was natural to assume that the children of members would have an easier entry into the Kingdom than children of nonmembers. Even though the church did adopt clerical celibacy, which preserved some of the charismatic quality of the original leadership, and gave its blessing to monasticism, which offered an alternative to the family as God's pattern for society, the church realized, as generations came and went, that it depended on the family.

The church's most fateful compromise with the family was in allowing infant baptism or, more properly, family baptism. This can hardly be called a decision, for there is no record of debate on the subject. The earliest Christian writers had said little of a practical nature on children, presumably because time seemed so short before the End.[11] They hardly expected children to have time to grow up, and this is apparently the reason that infants were baptized with their parents. As in Jewish proselyte baptism, forgiveness of sins was not the main issue; rather, the rite was primarily to mark off God's people from the doomed around them. There was no time to wait for adult repentance; God's people had to identify themselves by this rite before the judgment. So God's people were being counted by families from a very early date.[12]

Family baptism and the baptism of subsequent infants made a profound change in the movement. Just as with Dissent, it insured that the family would at least hold its own against the individualistic bias of the movement. It is a commonplace that the children of the committed are seldom committed to quite the same degree; birthright membership would keep the question of commitment from even coming up. Instead, filial piety became a main motive for adherence, as it had been in Judaism. In time, new members were not typically converts but had grown up thinking they belonged, accepting Christianity as they accepted the other traditions of their people. Thus, Christianity became traditional and ceased to offer a reformist challenge to its world.

By the time the church was accepted as an institution of Roman life in the fourth century, it had become the spokesman for the family. At the height of the Roman state's power, Church Father Lactantius could assert that the family was the more basic institution of the two. Specifically, he challenged the Roman notion of the family as "a creature of the state, deriving its constitution from law." Rather, he presented it as preeminently a natural association and therefore divinely ordained. Lactantius realized, as earlier emperors had not, that the family was not created by law and could not be revitalized by force. Far from using the state to strengthen a weakened family structure, he thought that only a stronger family could save the Roman state. Indeed, he looked forward to a withering away of the state, as the Christian family became the model of a new, classless, and noncoercive society that was bound together by love.[13]

Not only was the church becoming the family's spokesman, it was acting more and more as its servant. For example, to accommodate their unwanted children, the aristocratic families forced the monasteries to open their doors; in the tenth and eleventh centuries this may have been the main source of monastic recruitment.[14] It is ironic that the very monastic institutions that represented the objection against a domestic routinizing of religion should be pressed into the service of the family in this manner. The Mass itself was changed in line with the family's needs. By the fourteenth century the Mass had virtually ceased to be a community affair and had become a family matter, most Masses being said privately at the request of the family and for the sake of family members. Those Masses requested for the dead suggest something like a cult of living family members in the service of their ancestors.[15] Can one imagine a greater transformation of the original impulse of the Christian movement? Jesus had said to let the dead bury the dead,[16] but by now the church was primarily concerned with burying the family's dead.

It is only fair to point out that the church did not necessarily accept the family as it found it. Scholars have documented the church's attempt to mold the barbarian family into something more like the conjugal pattern, which seemed to be the pattern implicit in Scripture, but they have also recorded the compromises made by the church — allowing closer consanguinity than it approved, for the sake of family solidarity; breaking marriages in order to preserve the peace between clans or dynasties; allowing dowries despite its preference for community property and the more companionable relationship that the latter implied.[17] Much later, when the church came up against non-Western civilizations, it stopped making such compromises. Missionaries to India, for instance, led a direct attack on the family power represented by caste, infanticide, child sacrifice, child marriage, and the immolation of widows. In the context of alien societies, Christianity encouraged reform and challenged family authority, but generally speaking, the recovery of the early church's sense of individual commitment has depended upon the birth of new Christian movements.

PURITANISM was just such a movement, marking another cycle in the relation of religious individualism and the family. The Protestant Reformation rejected the domestication of the faith, drawing upon Christianity's legacy of spiritual individualism. The view that the Reformation revived the family as a spiritual institution does not carry analysis far enough, nor does it reveal the tension between family and ideology which was present in Protestantism from the beginning.[18] As a monk, Luther had utilized monastic asceticism to help him break with his family. He later came to think that this celibate elitism was wrong; the family was the real school of human character, not the convent. Family life was not second best; it was the natural environment for religious instruction and even for worship.[19] But there was another facet to Luther's teaching that placed limits on the family's authority; there was to be no second-hand religion in the new age. Each individual represented himself or herself before God, even if this meant defying parental influence.

The Puritans even seemed to suggest that each *child* represented itself before God, and this is where trouble started. Religious individualism had been well and good when it was a matter of freeing oneself from one's family, but what about one's children? Would they use their freedom wisely or recognize the truth and embrace it? The Puritans' relationship with children was on a new footing. Their concern over educational method shows that they knew they could not force belief but had to work with the child's mind rather than against it. The child's moral and ideological commitment had to be heartfelt and individual, and this interfered with the traditional exercise of parental authority.

As can be expected, the Puritans dealt with this issue theologically. Their response was to emphasize that the church was now God's people in a sense closely analogous to the position of ancient Israel, or, more properly, certain families were God's special concern. Covenant theologians emphasized those passages in the New Testament hinting that God still favored certain families and nations. They sensed the dangers in extreme religious individualism, for there was an anarchistic and "antinomian" tendency within Puritanism that threatened the family along with the rest of the social order.

A number of theologians sensed that tendency in John Milton's divorce tracts. Milton was one of those Puritans who was able to follow the movement's implications to their possible conclusions, and his series of pamphlets on divorce pursued its implicit individualism. Certainly he did not speak for all Puritans on this subject, but he was developing a tradition that stretched back through a century of Puritan writings. Even the protestations against his views suggest that it worried his fellow Puritans to think that divorce because of incompatibility was a logical tendency of their spiritualization of family relations. Since several writers had made mutual comfort the primary end of marriage, even above procreation, it followed (for Milton) that the lack of mutual comfort was grounds for divorce. This meant that the rights of the parents to their individual happiness were central to marriage, rather than the rights of the children to a stable family.[20] This challenge did not shake the family of Milton's day, but the idea was to continue to ferment within religious radicalism.

In America there was a clear decision concerning the demands of the family as opposed to a religious individualism. The founders of Massachusetts Bay became concerned about children who had grown up without owning the covenant for themselves, and they adopted a "Half-Way Covenant" in 1662. It would save a seat in church (and a vote) for those children of godly parents whose conversions had somehow been delayed. In effect, protecting the family interest had overridden the demand for a regenerate membership. Historian Edmund Morgan has suggested that this "Puritan tribalism" — a concentration on their own families — drained the energies that might have been employed in evangelizing later arrivals to the colony.[21] In America, Puritanism ceased to be a movement when it lost sight of society as a whole and began to concentrate on its own children.

In England, the end of the Puritan movement was obviously caused by the mid-century failure to translate its ineffable goals into political reality, but Christopher Durston has argued that fears for the traditional family also played a part in the nation's rejection of the Puritan Revolution.[22] As the movement decomposed into sects, it became apparent that survival would depend upon loyalty to family traditions of nonconformity. One example of these sects, the Quakers, shows the compromises that the family demanded in return for this service. Richard Vann has demonstrated that the Quaker movement was originally bound up with generational revolt. In the early years it was typical for only one member of a family to be converted to Quakerism, and this was almost never the family's heir. In short, the Society of Friends (not Brothers) was a group of the dispossessed.[23] Their simple refusal to doff their hats was an affront to parents who were accustomed to having children stand or kneel in their presence until bidden to sit down. When the Quaker convert addressed those parents as "thee" or "thou," it would have seemed shockingly familiar.

Things soon changed, however. When the converts had children of their own, and when recruitment from outside had slowed to a trickle, the family seemed important once again. Joining the Society was no longer an act of rebellion; quite the opposite, it became a matter of filial piety. After little more than one generation, it came to be assumed that children of members had a birthright membership in the meeting.[24] Conversion, which had once been an intense experience, was now largely a matter of adopting the religious outlook, speech, and dress of the founders. Children of members could pick these up, of course, far more easily than was possible for the converts. Converts might have proved a continuing source of enthusiasm for the movement; instead they felt at a disadvantage in relation to the children whose very silence bespoke their superiority.[25] Nothing could have been farther from the intention of the founders than to establish a new set of manners as a mark of one's righteousness. Once again, devotion to the family had turned a movement around.

PURITAN DISCUSSION of childhood may or may not have brought changes in the actual treatment of children, beyond the changes in attitudes expressed toward them, but it is apparent that the new literature on the child was sometimes apologetic concerning the traditional methods of dominance. Such ideas were not forgotten just because they were inconvenient or because the religious impulse behind the Puritan movement faded. Eventually they were adopted by those English radicals who attacked the very notion of the family during the time of the French Revolution. The foremost of these radicals came directly from the Puritan tradition.

In revolutionary France the conflict over family authority involved truly secular thinkers. Family loyalty seemed a major obstacle to reform and to the broader "fraternal" spirit that the revolutionaries promoted.[26] But English "Jacobin" radicalism came out of a fundamentally religious tradition. Although it was a small movement, it involved some of the most famous names of that time—Thomas Paine, William Godwin, William Blake, and Samuel Taylor Coleridge—and the fact that many of these revolutionaries came from Dissenting backgrounds did not go unnoticed at the time. Joseph Priestley (the scientist), Richard Price (the philosopher), Paine, and Godwin had all been Dissenting ministers. With them, it is uncertain where Puritan millenarianism leaves off and political radicalism begins. Their millenarian rhetoric is often mistaken for proto-Marxism,[27] but their hope for an entirely spiritualized family was the culmination of the Puritan tendencies described earlier.

The story of the radicalism of the 1790s has always been told in political terms, as though the state were the main target and the primary instrument of suppression. The family was also a target, however, and loyalty to the family may well have played a more important role in radicalism's defeat.

In 1792 Paine published Part Two of *The Rights of Man*, appending some practical suggestions for social reform, which included his famous scheme for a progressive tax on landed income. The rate of this tax was to reach 100 percent of all income from land over £23,000. This was meant, Paine states, to encourage the division of large estates and hence the reduction of the great families. The idea of the stem family would have to be dropped if the family members were to avoid confiscatory tax rates. Paine's point in trying to break the power of the aristocratic family was to create bonds of human sympathy, because under primogeniture children were turned against each other. The stem family was a system for creating princes and paupers from the same blood line, and it deserved to be destroyed. Paine also proposed other taxes on inheritance that increased as the kinship relation became more remote, thus encouraging less subservience to relatives.

What the state took away in these taxes, it was to return as national benefactor. Paine wanted to help children of the working classes to become independent of their parents. He proposed that every marrying couple would receive a wedding benefit of one pound from the state and that every individual would receive a grant of fifteen pounds upon reaching the age of twenty-one. Newlyweds over that age would thus begin married life with a guarantee of thirty-one pounds—a capital sum in those days. Parental authority would count for just that much less. The state's new bounty would also provide a maternity benefit of one pound per child and four pounds per annum until the child reached fourteen.[28] To say that this well-meaning program was destructive to the family may seem perverse, but it encouraged weaker, nuclear families in which the economic bond was not primary. Paine did not see any loss in this; his earliest literary efforts, in the *Pennsylvania Magazine*, had been directed against the family as he had experienced it. As with Milton, the breakup of his own marriage had suggested arguments for what he termed "rational" marriage and divorce.[29]

When *The Rights of Man* appeared, Paine's friend Thomas Holcroft wrote to William Godwin in ecstasy over the work's reception. It seemed to Holcroft that a new age, which he jocularly termed the New Jerusalem,[30] had dawned. Godwin became the prophet of this new era in the following year, 1793, when his *Enquiry Concerning Political Justice* replaced Paine's works in importance, at least among more educated readers.

William Godwin was typical of these radicals in being recently emancipated from a Dissenting background. He had been stimulated by Janeway's *Token for Children* to achieve an individual eminence and indeed to publish several children's books.[31] Though he had begun his ministry as an extreme Calvinist, he soon came under the Unitarian influence of Joseph Priestley. One biographer has termed his later humanism "a product of Protestant theology in its last agonies."[32]

The most sensational aspect of Godwin's notorious anarchism was his unequivocal attack on the family, his objections to that institution stemming from his moral as much as his psychological doctrines. Godwin observed that the more violent passions burn themselves out in time, so that marriage, as an effort to preserve a passion, was based on an erroneous morality and mistaken view of happiness. He thought that a more intelligent assessment of pleasure would put universal empathy above particular affections; gratitude to parents, concern for one's children, fidelity to one's spouse, all of these stood in the way of wider moral sympathies.[33] Accordingly, Godwin's foremost disciples, authors Maria Williams and John Hurford Stone, both from Dissenting backgrounds, began living together in Paris where they had gone to observe the Revolution.

If some advanced Dissenters were taken in by his logic, others were not. Significantly, the literary attacks on this work focused not on his

political anarchism but on his advocacy of free love — "universal benevolence" to use Godwin's phrase.[34] Critics found new irony in the
phrase, "the seductions of philosophy." A portion of this reaction was
a response to any form of radicalism at a time when French invasion
seemed imminent, but it also represented a fear greater than that of
class revolt. The destruction of the family would mean an even more
sweeping social revolution than class war. Fears of promiscuity, after
all, are born from the experience of family life, and this emphasis
of his critics indicates the source of the reaction against Godwin's
proposals.

The experience of Godwin's former disciples suggests the personal
and emotional reasons that favored the family's side in this contest.
Poets Coleridge and Robert Southey, one-time Unitarians, were on
their way to found a Godwinian utopia in America in 1795 when they
were waylaid by domestic affections. Their project never set sail, for
in Bristol they met the Fricker sisters and were undone by matrimony. Their friend Wordsworth, who had fathered a child in France
during the Revolution, wrote *The Borderers* (in 1795–96) to disavow
his earlier attachment to Godwin's principles. James Mackintosh announced a similar deconversion in a series of lectures called "The
Law of Nature and Nations" (1799), in which he argued that his
earlier theorizing had not recognized the importance of the family in
the necessary order of things. Far from thinking that a happier future
depended upon destroying the institutions of family and property,
Mackintosh now argued that "the Progressive Civilization of mankind" depended upon maintaining them. Even Dissenting spokesmen
expressed the same thought, though in a religious idiom. One Dissenter worried that "the Salvation of the World" depended on the
proper performance of domestic duties that were increasingly being
left to servants.[35] To Mackintosh it now seemed that the family was
on the side of progress rather than pitted against it. Far from standing in the way of universal benevolence, he now thought that the
family was the very "school of the kind affections."[36]

Even William Blake, who had admired Godwin's thought if not
his person, became part of the reaction against his ideas. "A Little
Girl Lost" and others of his *Songs of Experience* (1794) had given

readers the idea that extreme (sexual) individualism was part of his early creed.[37] Blake appeared to be wrestling with Milton's legacy, the notion of a union of souls that could not be institutionalized. In *The Marriage of Heaven and Hell* (1790), Blake had presented what he took to be the true meaning of *Paradise Lost*, frankly accepting the moral antinomianism that had both attracted and repelled the Puritans.[38] In 1799 or 1800, however, Blake had something of a religious reconversion and a renewal of his own marriage, bringing into his writing certain themes associated with social conservatism. Humility, forgiveness, and self-giving love began to displace his older emphasis on liberty and energy. He even broke off work on a major poem (*Vala*) to write one called *Milton*, in which he and Milton recant their error in the presence of Milton's wives and daughters.[39]

The most striking change of all came over Godwin himself. In 1797, at the age of forty-one, having long scorned marriage, he decided to try it. Mary Wollstonecraft and he had been living together only a short time when they decided to marry. Even though Mary had never expressed herself against marriage per se, she and Godwin felt it necessary to apologize to their friends for this step. The pair continued, rather ostentatiously, to accept separate invitations.[40] To Godwin's surprise he found that marriage agreed with him, so much so that when Mary died, giving birth to the future Mary Shelley, Godwin soon considered marrying again. He had abandoned completely his earlier notion of a severely impartial benevolence and was now saying that men would do more general good by devoting themselves to their wives and children.[41]

Godwin's children spoke for the society of their day when they also rebuked him for his heroic originality. After a liaison with Lord Byron, his stepdaughter, Jane Clairmont, converted to the Catholic church and considered writing a book against free love, in hopes of turning her experience to some good.[42] When Mary Shelley was looking for a school for her boy, someone suggested that it should be one in which he would be free to think for himself: "To think for himself," she exclaimed, "Oh my God, teach him to think like other people!"[43] These words could stand as an epitaph on a Puritan individualism gone to seed.

It is probably fruitless as well as unnecessary to look for the usual sorts of documentation in reference to the family's reaction to radical individualism. If a movement had been organized on the family's behalf, it would have kept records, the newspapers would have noticed it, and there would be the usual kinds of evidence. Movements to save the family are not unheard of, but one would expect such a movement to develop the same kind of tensions with the family that other movements have demonstrated. Its ideology would be bound to assume certain family patterns as normative and end by attacking deviant families. When the reaction takes a more inchoate form and is less self-conscious, as seems to have been the case in 1800, the damage to existing families may be less.

There are various hints in the literature as to what more conventional Dissenters thought of the rather disreputable radicals who were pushing their individualistic principles to a conclusion. By 1770 Joseph Priestley was noticing "a new species of Dissenters that I was sensible had been for some time springing up among us . . . who have as little of the spirit as they have of the external appearance of the old Puritans." He was dismayed that the fashionable young gentlemen at some of the Dissenting Academies were learning the "politeness" of conventional society and becoming theologically flabby. Samuel Palmer, the eighteenth-century editor of Edmund Calamy's biographical collections, also complained of Dissenters who dined so late and so well with their families that they missed Sunday afternoon services.[44]

Given such an atmosphere of devotion to convention and to family, one need hardly invoke political repression to account for the radicals' retreat. Hackney Academy, founded in 1786 to maintain the intellectual freedom that Priestley thought was being smothered in conformity, proved too much for the main body of Dissenters. It closed in 1796 after "one mad enthusiastic day" when the college entertained Tom Paine for dinner.[45] The Dissenting establishment was again in step with society, at a time when royalty itself lost a round to public opinion by violating family proprieties. When the Prince Regent openly flouted his marriage, the press and the people took the ridiculous Queen Caroline to their hearts for no other reason than to show their disapproval of George's philandering. When he had the gall to have her tried for adultery in 1820, even the remaining radicals supported the humbug of her defense just for the pleasure of ridiculing him. Whatever radicals now thought of the institution of the family, they knew which way the wind was blowing.

It is tempting to take any and all expressions of social reaction as evidence of loyalty to the family, but the real question is whether one is justified in doing so. Surely the objection to sexual license is best understood in the context of family feeling and directs our attention there rather than to the state's opposition. Sexual identity and inhibitions are formed within the family, for the most part. Likewise, the public's objections to state regulation of inheritance, legitimacy, and even education are best understood within the context of family ambition. In fact, loyalty to church and state was in direct proportion to their guarantee of the family's position in the world.

Dissenters had more reason than other groups to depend on the family. Faced with ostracism and stigmatized as radicals, they would have been dependent on their children as potential converts and even as companions. On the other hand, the spiritual vitality of Dissent would be lost if it were to become a respecter of persons. Naturally, the Dissenters tried to have it both ways, and their reputation as consistent reformers suffers as a consequence. Covenant Theology does not seem to be a necessary development of Calvinism, except for the understandable desire to justify a special status for one's children. Nor was "dry baptism" necessary to the Baptists, to say nothing of the Americans' Half-Way Covenant. These were all part of an irresistible tendency toward Birthright Membership, which helped change a movement into sects.

It seems a very unequal struggle. Movements must be taken up by the state or by the families of some subcultural enclave if they are to survive. The family does not rest on the state, nor does it rest on the enthusiasm that sparks a movement. If anything can be called natural in human relations, it would be some form of the family. This has been variously understood as reflecting reproductive needs or the necessary organization of material and economic life, but one can just as easily think of family companionship as a primary social goal.

It might be more realistic to see economic life as organized for the sake of family values—like a family meal—than to see the family as a strategy for the production of goods. Today's society credits itself with such motives, and Puritan parents were not that much different. They had hoped to organize family relations around the proper worship of God; in the end, their piety was valued for its contribution to family solidarity.

NOTES

Introduction. Children, Historians, and Movements

1. Jay Mechling, "Advice to Historians on Advice to Mothers," *Journal of Social History* 9 (1975): 44–63.

2. E.g., Luke Demaitre, "The Idea of Childhood and Child Care in Medical Writings of the Middle Ages," *Journal of Psychohistory* 4 (1977): 461–90; Jerome Kroll, "The Concept of Childhood in the Middle Ages," *Journal of the History of the Behavioral Sciences* 13 (1977): 384–93.

3. E.g., Barbara Hanawalt, "Childbearing among the Lower Classes of Late Medieval England," *Journal of Interdisciplinary History* 8 (1977): 1–22; Stephen Wilson, "The Myth of Motherhood a Myth: The Historical View of European Child-Rearing," *Social History* 9 (1984): 181–98.

4. Lawrence Stone, *The Family, Sex and Marriage in England, 1500–1800* (London, 1977), 13; Elizabeth Godfrey (Jessie Bedford), *English Children in the Olden Time* (London, 1907), xv.

5. Philippe Ariès, *Centuries of Childhood: A Social History of Family Life* (New York, 1962), 9–10, 43, 405–15. In general agreement, see Jean-Louis Flandrin, *Families in Former Times: Kinship, Household, and Society* (New York, 1979).

6. Gordon Rattray Taylor, *The Angel Makers: A Study in the Psychological Origins of Historical Change, 1750–1850*, rev. ed. (New York, 1974), 29, 155–56, 338. See also Boyd Berry, "The First English Pediatricians and Tudor Attitudes Toward Childhood," *Journal of the History of Ideas* 35 (1974): 561–77, and John McLeish, *Evangelical Religion and Popular Education: A Modern Interpretation* (London, 1969).

7. Taylor, *Angel Makers*, 159–61, 173–74.

8. Ibid., 314.

9. Ibid., 336; Lloyd deMause, ed., *The History of Childhood* (New York, 1974).

10. Stone, *Family, Sex and Marriage*, 4.

11. Ibid., 175; see also John Demos, *A Little Commonwealth: Family Life in Plymouth Colony* (New York, 1970), 102.

12. Stone, *Family, Sex and Marriage*, 194.

13. Ibid., 410.

14. Ibid., 123, 151, 216, 226–29, 406, 515.

15. Philip Greven, *The Protestant Temperament: Patterns of Child-Rearing, Religious Experience, and the Self in Early America* (New York, 1977), 17.

16. Keith Wrightson, *English Society, 1580–1680* (New Brunswick, N.J., 1982), 104–18.

17. Linda A. Pollock, *Forgotten Children: Parent-Child Relations from 1500 to 1900* (Cambridge, 1983), 269.

18. Margo Todd, *Christian Humanism and the Puritan Social Order* (Cambridge, 1987).

19. John Wilson, *Introduction to Social Movements* (New York, 1973), 8.

20. Nicholas Tyacke, "Puritanism, Arminianism and Counter-Revolution," in *The Origins of the English Civil War*, ed. Conrad Russell (New York, 1973), 139; Patrick Collinson, *The Religion of Protestants: The Church in English Society, 1559–1625* (Oxford, 1982); Jerald C. Brauer, "Reflections on the Nature of English Puritanism," *Church History* 23 (1954): 100.

21. Alan Simpson, *Puritanism in Old and New England* (Chicago, 1961), 2.

22. Peter Lake, *Moderate Puritans and the Elizabethan Church* (Cambridge, 1982), 1–15, 282. See also, Patrick Collinson, "A Comment: Concerning the Name Puritan," *Journal of Ecclesiastical History* 31 (1980): 483–88, and Christopher Hill, *God's Englishman: Oliver Cromwell and the English Revolution* (London, 1970), chapter 9.

23. Wilson, *Introduction to Social Movements*, 3–88.

24. Benjamin Brook, *The Lives of the Puritans* (London, 1813), 1:v–x.

25. The ecclesiastical census of 1676 has now been studied in some depth in Anne Whiteman, ed., *The Compton Census of 1676: A Critical Edition* (London, 1986). Despite the wish of the authorities to minimize the number of nonconformists, some of the census figures have been generally confirmed by local studies. See S. A. Peyton, "The Religious Census of 1676," *English Historical Review* 48 (1933): 99–104, and W. M. Wigfield, "Religious Statistics Concerning Recusants of the Stuart Period," *Theology* 41 (1940): 99–103.

26. G. R. Cragg, *Puritanism in the Period of the Great Persecution, 1660–1688* (Cambridge, 1957), 38, 49.

27. Edmund Calamy, *The Non-Conformist's Memorial*, ed. Samuel Palmer, 2d ed. (London, 1802–3), 2:131.

28. E. P. Thompson, *The Making of the English Working Class* (New York, 1963), 345–46; Taylor, *Angel Makers*, 305.

29. Pollock, *Forgotten Children*, 184–85, 197.

30. William Sloane, *Children's Books in England and America in the Seventeenth Century* (New York, 1955), 47; Monica Kiefer, *American Children through Their Books, 1700–1835* (Philadelphia, 1948), 29; David Stannard, "Death and the Puritan Child," *American Quarterly* 26 (1974): 473–75.

31. See C. John Sommerville, "Anglican, Puritan, and Sectarian in Empirical Perspective," *Social Science History* 13 (1989): 109–35, for further discussion of the measurable differences between these theological positions.

Chapter One. The Puritan Preoccupation with Children

1. Charles W. Bardsley, *Curiosities of Puritan Nomenclature*, new ed. (London, 1897), 118, 127, 39, 30.

2. Ibid., 156. See also Nicholas Tyacke, "Popular Puritan Mentality in Late Elizabethan England," in *The English Commonwealth, 1547–1640: Essays in Politics and Society*, ed. Peter Clark et al. (New York, 1979), 77–92.

3. Robert Cleaver, *A godly form of household government* (London, 1598), 247; Dorothy Leigh, *The Mothers Blessing*, 7th ed. (London, 1621), 27–46.

4. William Sloane, *Children's Books in England and America in the Seventeenth Century* (New York, 1955). Sloane's bibliography, the most comprehensive for this period, need not be exhaustive for our comparative purposes. His principle of selection was only that the books be written exclusively for children (121).

5. Biographical data comes from the *Dictionary of National Biography* (London, 1921–22); Edmund Calamy, *The Non-Conformist's Memorial*, ed. Samuel Palmer, 2d ed. (London, 1802–3); John Venn, *Alumni Cantabrigienses* (Cambridge, 1922–27); and Joseph Foster, *Alumni Oxonienses* (Oxford, 1891–92), unless otherwise noted.

6. Louis B. Wright, *Middle-Class Culture in Elizabethan England* (Chapel Hill, 1935).

7. Roger Ascham, *The Scholemaster* (1570; reprint: London, 1903), 31, 46.

8. Leah Sinanoglou Marcus, *Childhood and Cultural Despair* (Pittsburgh, 1978), 43.

9. M. G. Jones, *The Charity School Movement* (Cambridge, 1938), 165–66.

10. Taking the first ones on Sloane's list, Francis Seager's *Schoole of Vertue* was always attributed to a Puritan: Anthony a Wood, *Athenea Oxonienses* (London, 1691), 1:544. Robert Smith was a Marian martyr, James Can-

celler was aptly identified as a Puritan by Sloane from internal evidence, and Henry Smith was a famous Puritan preacher. These works are discussed in Chapter 3.

11. John E. Mason, *Gentlefolk in the Making* (Philadelphia, 1935), 291.

12. Edward Burton, *The Father's Legacy*, (London, 1649), 1–10, 79–86.

13. Michael Jermin, *The Fathers Institution of his Childe: Directing the Conversation of his whole life* (London, 1658).

14. E.g., Henry Hesketh, *The Importance of Religion to Young Persons* (London, 1683), 1–7; William Smythies, *Advice to Apprentices, and Other Young Persons, To beware of Evil Courses: and Particularly of Theft* (London, 1687), 1–8.

15. Samuel Peck, *The Best Way to Mend the World, and to Prevent the Growth of Popery* (London, 1680), sigs. A2v–A5v. See also John Strype, *Lessons Moral and Christian, for Youth and Old Age* (London, 1699), 2–3; Samuel Brewster, *The Christian Scholar*, 5th ed. (London, 1710), 32–33.

16. Sloane, *Children's Books*, 214.

17. E.g., Thomas Vincent, *The Principles of the Doctrine of Christ, or A Catechism* (London, 1691), 1–51, "A Catechism of Conscience"; John Paget, *A Primer of Christian Religion, or a forme of catechising, drawne from the beholding of God's works in the creation of the world* (London, 1601).

18. Samuel Shaw, *Words made Visible* (London, 1679), and *The Different Humours of Men* (London, 1692).

19. See Chapter 4.

20. William Jole, *The Father's Blessing Penn'd for the Instruction of his Children* (London, 1674); William Ronksley, *The Child's Weeks-work* (London, 1702).

21. Daniel Williams, *The Vanity of Childhood and Youth*, 5th ed. (London, 1758), sig. A3v, 2, 8.

22. F. J. Harvey Darton, *Children's Books in England*, 2d ed. (Cambridge, 1966), 45; Samuel F. Pickering, Jr., *John Locke and Children's Books in Eighteenth-Century England* (Knoxville, 1981), 116.

23. Of those I have seen, only Thomas White, *A Little Book for Little Children* (London, 1674); Robert Abbot, *The young-mans warning-peece* (London, 1636); and anon., *The Apprentices Warning-Piece* (London, 1641), made more than passing reference to punishment either by providence or the state.

24. Thomas Becon, *A New Catechism* (Cambridge, 1844), 358; Cleaver, *Godly form of household government*, 349; Thomas Cobbett, *A Fruitfull Discourse Touching the Honour due from Children to Parents, and the duty of Parents towards their Children* (London, 1656), 15; Richard Baxter, *The Catechising of*

Families, in *The Practical Works of Richard Baxter* (London, 1854), 4:131–32; Josias Nichols, *A Order of Household Instruction* (London, 1596), sigs. B5–B5v.

25. Alan Macfarlane's *The Family Life of Ralph Josselin: A Seventeenth-Century Clergyman* (Cambridge, 1970), 15, 90, 100, 120. Macfarlane concludes, "If Josselin is typical, Puritan Fathers were less austere and less able to exert control of their children than some historians would have us believe" (125).

26. Joseph Waite, *The Parents Primer and the Mothers Looking-Glasse* (London, 1681), 43; Owen Stockton, *A Treatise of Family Instruction* (London, 1672), 325–31; Samuel Slater, *An Ernest Call to Family-Religion* (London, 1694), 136–37; Simon Ford, *A Sermon of Catechizing* (London, 1655), 29; (Joseph Bennet), *The Address of some Ministers of Christ* (London, 1658), 16.

27. See Chapter 3.

28. Edmund Morgan, *The Puritan Family*, 2d ed. (New York, 1966), 78; Robert H. Bremner et al., *Childhood and Youth in America: A Documentary History* (Cambridge, Mass., 1970), 1:28, 37–39.

29. Anon., *A Brief Relation of the Life and Death of Elizabeth Braythwaite* (n.p., n.d.).

30. Peck, *Best Way*, 10–12, John Chishull, *Two Treatises* (London, 1658), 89–90; John Maynard, *A Memento to Young and Old* (London, 1669), sig. A3v; Joseph Stennett, *Advice to the Young* (London, 1695), 56–57; John Shower, *An Exhortation to Youth to Prepare for Judgment* (London, 1681), sig. a1v; Matthew Mead, *The Young Man's Remembrancer, and Youth's Best Choice*, 3d ed. (London, 1701), 87–88.

31. James Fischer, *The Wise Virgin*, 5th ed. (London, 1664), explicitly suggests this possibility (158).

32. A possible exception would be those published by Benjamin Harris (see Sloane, *Children's Books*, 229).

33. For a discussion of the priority of instrumental over psychological explanations in history, see Gerald Izenberg, "Psychohistory and Intellectual History," *History and Theory* 14 (1975): 139–55. I do not mean to deny that Puritan ideology and even rationality itself have psychodynamic roots. The point is that, at some level, ideas transcend their original impulses, otherwise even debates on the history of childhood would remain at the level of rationalizations.

34. For the relationships between these writers—Richard Greenham, Henry Smith, John Dod, Robert Cleaver, William Gouge, and Stephen Egerton—see William Haller, *The Rise of Puritanism* (New York, 1957), 5–10, 25–28, 53–56, 66–69, 80–82, 120–22.

35. Vincent was assistant pastor of Thomas Doolittle's congregation in London. Doolittle had been converted under the ministry of Richard Baxter, and both of these men wrote treatises for youth and parents. Vincent's brother Nathaniel, who published two catechisms, preached the funeral sermons of Janeway and Edward Lawrence, another children's author. Vincent's and Doolittle's funerals were preached by Samuel Slater and Daniel Williams, respectively. Both of them wrote for youth and on family worship. Other children's authors, Christopher Ness, Robert Franklin, Thomas Lye, and John Ryther were associated with this circle, as evidenced in Christopher Ness's *Complete History and mystery of the Old and New Testament* (London, 1696), and [Richard Alleinc], *A Murderer Punished and Pardoned* (London, 1668).

36. Thomas Vincent, *The Good Work Begun in the Day of Grace* (London, 1673), 30, and *Words of Advice to Young Men* (London, 1668).

37. Matthew Mead, *The Good of Early Obedience* (London, 1683), and *Young Man's Remembrancer*.

38. J. Paul Hunter, *The Reluctant Pilgrim* (Baltimore, 1966), 47–48, 31–32.

39. The standard biographical sketches of John Shower, Timothy and John Rogers, Philip Taverner, John Howe, and Francis Fuller point out these personal and professional connections.

40. John Shower, *Family Religion* (London, 1694), 4; George Hamond, *A Discourse of Family-Worship Undertaken Upon the Request of the United Ministers in and about London* (London, 1694).

41. Shower, *Exhortation to Youth*, 13, and *Seasonable Advice to Youth* (London, 1692), 8–9; Henry Downes, *A Sermon Preach'd in the Parish Church of St. Warbrough, Dublin* (Dublin, 1721), 7. The phrase "the teens" appears in Samuel Pomfret, *A Sermon Preached to Young People* (London, 1698), 48.

42. Pomfret, *Sermon Preached*, 8. See Steven R. Smith, "Religion and the Conception of Youth in Seventeenth-Century England," *History of Childhood Quarterly* 2 (1975): 493–516, for a discussion that comes to similar conclusions.

43. Maynard, *A Memento to Young and Old*, 85–91, sig. A4; Thomas Gouge, *The young man's guide, through the wilderness of this world to the heavenly Canaan* (Boston, 1742), 87–126; Edward Lawrence, *Parents Groans over their Wicked Children* (London, 1681), sig. A6; Oliver Heywood, *Youth's Monitor*, in *The Whole Works of the Rev. Oliver Heywood* (London, 1826), 5:559, 566; Williams, *Vanity of Childhood*, 14–72; Joseph Porter, *A Caution Against Youthful Lusts* (London, 1708), 20; Shower, *Seasonable Advice*, 5–10; Samuel Pomfret, *A Directory for Youth* (London, 1693), 7–45.

44. Leonard T. Grant, "Puritan Catechising," *Journal of Presbyterian History* 46 (1968): 111–19.

45. *Dictionary of National Biography* (London, 1921–22), 15:131.

46. Anon., *A Plain and Easie Way of Catechising Such as are of Weakest Memories and of the meanest Capacities* (London, 1680); R. M., *The Church-Catechism Enlarg'd and Explain'd, in an Easie and Familiar Method* (London, 1697).

47. Jones, *Charity School Movement*, 266–89, 110.

48. David Owen, *English Philanthropy, 1660–1960* (Cambridge, Mass., 1964), 13. Michael Sanderson, "Literacy and Social Mobility in the Industrial Revolution in England," *Past and Present* 56 (1972): 72–104, disputes recent denials that this activity amounted to a general movement, on the basis of local studies. See also Dudley Bahlman, *The Moral Revolution of 1688* (New Haven, 1957). D. H. Webster, "A Charity School Movement? The Lincolnshire Evidence," *Lincolnshire History and Archaeology* 15 (1980): 39–46, questions the involvement of the Society for Promoting Christian Knowledge but helps demonstrate the movement's organized character.

49. For the earlier Puritan interest, see W. A. L. Vincent, *The State and School Education, 1640–1660* (London, 1950), and Richard L. Greaves, *The Puritan Revolution and Educational Thought* (New Brunswick, N.J., 1969).

50. See above, note 47.

51. Calamy, *Non-Conformist's Memorial*, 2:234–39.

52. Foster, *Alumni Oxonienses*, 4:1677; 3:1135; Venn, *Alumni Cantabrigienses*, 3:333.

53. White Kennett, *The Charity of Schools for Poor Children Recommended* (London, 1706), 8; Robert Moss, *The Providential Division of Men into Rich and Poor* (London, 1708), 22, 26; William Hendley, *A Defence of the Charity-Schools* (London, 1725), 12; Samuel Clarke, *A Sermon Preach'd Upon Occasion of erecting a charity school as a House of Education for Women-Servants*, in *The Works of Samuel Clarke* (London, 1738), 4:511–12.

54. James Talbott, *The Christian School-Master* (London, 1707), 19, 91–99; Daniel Waterland, *Religious Education of Children* (1723), in *Twenty-Five Sermons preached at the Anniversary Meetings of the Children Educated in the Charity-Schools* (London, 1729), 441; anon., *An Account of Charity Schools lately erected in England, Wales and Ireland* (London, 1706), 2–3.

55. Bernard Mandeville, *The Fable of the Bees*, ed. F. B. Kaye (Oxford, 1924), 1:276–311.

56. John Trenchard, *Cato's Letters*, 5th ed. (London, 1748), 238–44.

57. See Isaac Watts, *An Essay Toward the Encouragement of Charity Schools*

(London, 1728), 21, 14. Jones, *Charity School Movement*, 87–88, explained the schools' difficulty here.

58. John A. Passmore, "The Malleability of Man in Eighteenth-Century Thought," in *Aspects of the Eighteenth Century*, ed. Earl R. Wasserman (Baltimore, 1965), 35.

59. J. W. Adamson, *Pioneers of Modern Education in the Seventeenth Century* (Cambridge, 1905), 16–17; Francis Osborne, *Advice to a Son*, ed. Louis B. Wright (Ithaca, N.Y., 1962), 42–43; Henry Home, Lord Kames, *Sketches of the History of Man* (Edinburgh, 1774), 2:50–51.

60. Edward Eyre, ed., *European Civilization* (London, 1937), 6:970–77; H. R. Fox Bourne, *The Life of John Locke* (New York, 1876), 2:383–86; James A. Leith, "Modernization, Mass Education and Social Mobility in French Thought, 1750–1789," in *Studies in the Eighteenth Century*, ed. R. F. Brissenden (Toronto, 1973), 223–38.

61. Adamson, *Pioneers of Modern Education*, 60–142, 197–204, 222–49.

62. Philippe Ariès, *Centuries of Childhood: A Social History of Family Life* (New York, 1962), 27, 43, 108–27, 310–12, 389, 412.

63. Robert Folkenflik, "Child and Adult: Historical Perspective in Gibbon's Memoirs," *Studies in Burke and his Time* 15 (1973): 37–38.

64. Caroline Robbins, *The Eighteenth-Century Commonwealthman* (New York, 1968), mentions champions of more widespread education, and they are figures who are more religiously inclined (97, 204, 363).

Chapter Two. Puritan Realism in Picturing Children

1. Lotte B. Graeffe, "The Child in Medieval English Literature from 1200 to 1400" (Ph.D. dissertation, University of Florida, 1965).

2. The categories include, respectively: SS. Agnes, Agatha, Margaret, and the daughters of St. Sophia; SS. Benedict, Martin, Peter Martyr, Vitus; SS. Dominic, Bernard, Ambrose, John the Baptist. *The Golden Legend of Jacobus de Voragine*, trans. Granger Ryan and Helmut Ripperger (London, 1941). See also the lives of SS. Pancratius, Nazarius, Mary, and Elizabeth.

3. Helen C. White, *Tudor Books of Saints and Martyrs* (Madison, Wisc., 1963), 54–55.

4. Leah Sinanoglou Marcus, *Childhood and Cultural Despair: A Theme and Variations in Seventeenth-Century Literature* (Pittsburgh, 1978), 24–26.

5. V. Norskov Olsen, *John Foxe and the Elizabethan Church* (Berkeley, 1973), 3–19; see also, J. F. Mozley, *John Foxe and His Book* (New York, 1970),

111–12; and Patrick Collinson, *The Elizabethan Puritan Movement* (London, 1967), 121.

6. John Foxe, *The Acts and Monuments of John Foxe*, ed. George Townsend (New York, 1965), 5:697–703; 6:350–52.

7. Ibid., 6:384, 416–22.

8. Ibid., 4:123, 231, 235–36, 245; 6:740.

9. Izaak Walton, *Lives*, ed. George Saintsbury (London, 1936), 162–63, 350–51, 262.

10. James Heath, *A New Book of Loyal English Martyrs and Confessors* (London, 1663); William Winstanley, *The Loyall Martyrology* (London, 1665).

11. Clement Barksdale, *Memorials of Worthy Persons: Two Decads* (London, 1661), 201; Clement Cotton, *The Mirror of Martyrs* (London, 1613); Anthony a Wood, *Athenae Oxonienses* (London, 1813–20); William Winstanley, *England's Worthies* (London, 1684). Winstanley includes examples of extreme precocity (90, 264–65, 348, 426, 560, 650). Henry Holland's *History of the Modern Protestant Divines* (London, 1637), occasionally comments on the early years of its subjects. Holland may best be classified as a Puritan; he was in trouble with Archbishop Laud and served in the Parliamentary army.

12. Thomas Fuller, *History of the Worthies of England* (London, 1840).

13. David Lloyd, *Memoires of the Lives, Actions, Sufferings & Deaths of those Noble, Reverend, and Excellent Personages, That Suffered by Death, Sequestration, Decimation, or otherwise, for the Protestant Religion, and the great Principles thereof, Allegiance to their Soveraigne, in our late Intestine Wars, From the Year 1637, to the Year 1660* (London, 1668), 447, 53, 290.

14. Ibid., 353, 225, 308, 170.

15. Keith Thomas, *Religion and the Decline of Magic* (New York, 1971), 423.

16. Lloyd, *Memoires*, 138.

17. Ibid., 157, 341. Among Anglicans only John Aubrey's notes show a similar interest in such stories, though we cannot know how many of them he would have published. See John Aubrey's *Brief Lives*, ed. Oliver Lawson Dick (London, 1950), 45, 56, 148–49, 162, 237, 242, 285, 300.

18. Richard Challoner, *Britannia Sancta* (London, 1745), 2:4.

19. Ibid., 1:87, 95.

20. Ibid., 2:323–26.

21. Richard Challoner, *Memoirs of Missionary Priests* (n.p., 1741–42), 2:20; 1:262–63.

22. Ibid., 2:27, 123, 172, 278.

23. John Bryan, *The Vertuous Daughter* (London, 1640).

24. Charles Croke, *A sad memoriall of Henry Curwen esquire* (Oxford, 1638).

25. Robert Abbot, *The young-mans warning-peece* (London, 1636). Rogers's story also appeared in a ballad, *Youth's warning-peice*, published in the same year. See William Sloane, *Children's Books in England and America in the Seventeenth Century* (New York, 1955), 144–45.

26. Anon., *The apprentices warning-piece; Being a confession of Peter Moore* (London, 1641).

27. (Richard Alleine), *A Murderer Punished and Pardoned* (London, 1668). See Sloane, *Children's Books*, 228–29.

28. John Batchiler, *The Virgins Pattern: in the exemplary life, and lamented death of Mrs. Susanna Perwich* (London, 1661).

29. John Vernon, *The Compleat Scholler; or, A Relation of the Life, and latter-end especially, of Caleb Vernon* (London, 1666).

30. Henry Jessey, *A Looking-Glass for Children*, comp. H. P. (London, 1672).

31. James Fisher, *The wise virgin* (London, 1653).

32. The debate on the relation of Puritanism and empiricism is surveyed in R. L. Greaves, "Puritanism and Science: The Anatomy of a Controversy," *Journal of the History of Ideas* 30 (1969): 353–68.

33. John Eliot and Thomas Mayhew, *Tears of Repentance; Or, A further Narrative of the Progress of the Gospel Amongst the Indians in New-England* (London, 1653), 46–47.

34. (Samuel Acton), *The virgin saint: or, a brief narrative of the holy life, and Christian death of Mary Wilson* (London, 1673), offers nothing new to this pattern, except the best anagrams — "Your nam' liv's" and "In warm Soyl."

35. James Janeway, *A Token for Children: Being An Exact Account of the Conversion, Holy and Examplary Lives and Joyful Deaths of several Young Children* (Boston, 1700).

36. Ibid., 14–19.

37. Elton and Esther Smith, *William Godwin* (New York, 1965), 122.

38. Cotton Mather, *A Token for the Children of New-England* (Boston, 1700), 3. Mather had published some of these lives earlier, in *Early piety, exemplified in the life and death of Mr. Nathanael Mather* (1689), *Early religion* (1694), and *A good man making a good end* (1698).

39. This work is not to be confused with one by T. W., *A Little Book for Little Children, Wherein are set down, in a plain and pleasant way, Directions for Spelling*. See F. J. Harvey Darton, *Children's Books in England*, 2d ed. (Cambridge, 1966), 59–61.

40. Samuel Clarke, *The Marrow of Ecclesiastical Historie* (London, 1650), 228, 308.

41. Ibid., 414, 420, 461.

42. Fuller, *Worthies of England*, 1:78–81.

43. Samuel Clarke, *The Lives of Thirty-Two English Divines* (London, 1677), 22, 168, 218.

44. Ibid., 377, 160, 184.

45. Ibid., 234, 264, 279, 391, 414.

46. Samuel Clarke, *Lives of Sundry Eminent Persons* (London, 1683), 3–4, 168–69, 182.

47. Ibid., 177, 154, 81, 125–26.

48. Ibid., 135–36, 152, 95, 102, 106, 138.

49. Ibid., 90.

50. Ibid., 197–200.

51. Edmund Calamy, *Non-Conformist's Memorial*, ed., Samuel Palmer, 2d ed. (London, 1802–3), 2:164; 1:124, 110, 165, 191, 271.

52. Ibid., 1:331; 2:159.

53. Ibid., 3:393; 1:322, 222.

54. Ibid., 1:343; 2:449; 3:258–59.

55. Ibid., 2:340, 290–91.

56. Ibid., 3:31; 2:133–35.

57. Christopher Ness, *A Spiritual Legacy* (London, 1684), 93, 115–16.

58. Anon., *Living Words of a Dying Child* (n.p., 1675); John Whiting, *Early Piety Exemplified, in the Life and Death of Mary Whiting* (n.p., [1681]).

59. Thomas Lawson, *A Serious Remembrancer to Live Well* (London, 1684); Thomas and Anne Camme, *The Admirable and Glorious Appearance of the Eternal God, in his Glorious Power, in and through a Child* (London, 1684).

60. Anon., *A Brief Relation of the Life and Death of Elizabeth Braythwaite* (n.p., n.d.). Richard Manliffe made an exception to the rule of unbroken innocence among the children described in Quaker works, having left the Society briefly before his repentance: anon., *A seasonable account of the Christian and Dying-Words of some Young-Men* (Philadelphia, 1700, originally published in London, 1697).

61. Christopher and Frances Taylor, *A Testimony to the Lord's Power and Blessed Appearance In and Amongst Children* (n.p., 1679), 49, 66–67. In the same year four different tracts reported the appearance of a Wunderkind, Charles Bennet, who was brought to London in June to exhibit his phenomenal knowledge of Hebrew, Greek, Latin, and knotty "Scriptural Questions." Many gentry and clergy and the king himself were said to have come to the

Bear Inn in West Smithfield to see him. The authors never suggested an apocalyptic significance in this episode but only that such a marvel should be proof of a Deity to those "unwilling to believe any other Deity than Nature." *The Wonderful Child*, ed. William E. A. Axon, in *Chetham Miscellanies*, new series, 1 (1902): 1–21. The tone of these tracts would suggest that they were part of the Dissenting tradition.

62. Pierre Jurieu, *The Reflections of the Reverend and Learned Monsieur Jurieu, upon the Strange and Miraculous Exstasies of Isabel Vincent* (London, 1689).

63. Anon., *A Relation of Several Hundreds of Children & Others That Prophesie and Preach in Their Sleep, etc.* (London, 1689), 27.

64. (Francois-Maximilien Misson), *A Cry from the Desart; or, Testimonials of the Miraculous Things Lately come to pass in the Cevennes*, 2d ed. (London, 1707); Hillel Schwartz, *Knaves, Fools, Madmen and That Subtile Effluvium: A Study of the Opposition to the French Prophets in England, 1706–1710* (Gainesville, Fla., 1978).

65. Anon., *Praise out of the Mouth of Babes* (London, 1708); Sir Richard Bulkeley, *An Answer to Several Treatises Lately publish'd on the Subject of the Prophets* (London, 1708), 116–18.

66. William Erasmus Arends, *Early Piety Recommended in the Life and Death of Christlieb Leberecht Von-Exter* (London, [1709?]).

67. Anon., *Daily Conversation with God* (London, 1710).

68. Anon., *A Short Account of the Conversion of Three Jewish Children to Christianity*, 2d ed. (London, 1717), reprinted in John Gillies, *Historical Collections Relating to Remarkable Periods of the Success of the Gospel* (Glasgow, 1754–61), 3:232–43.

69. Josiah Woodward, *The Young-Man's Monitor* (London, 1706), sig. A3. Woodward showed that he knew of the Waltham Abbey episode and also of the Silesian children when he questioned the "excesses" of the "French prophets" and their children: *Remarks on the Modern Prophets* (London, 1708), 8, 24, and *An Answer to the Letter of John Lacy, Esq.* (London, 1708), 26. Woodward died in 1712, which may explain the lapse of these publications at about this time.

70. William Matthews, "Seventeenth-Century Autobiography," in *Autobiography, Biography, and the Novel: Clark Library Papers, May 13, 1972* (Los Angeles, 1973), 16–18, 25.

71. Paul Delany, *British Autobiography in the Seventeenth Century* (London, 1969), 169.

72. Owen Watkins, *The Puritan Experience* (New York, 1972), 54.

Chapter Three. Childhood in Theory

1. T. L. Underwood, "Child Dedication Services among British Baptists in the Seventeenth Century," *The Baptist Quarterly* 23 (1969): 168–69.

2. John Calvin, *Institutes of the Christian Religion*, 2 vols., trans. Ford Lewis Battles and John T. McNeill (Philadelphia, 1960), II, viii, 21; IV, xvi, 5. See C. John Sommerville, "Conversion versus the Early Puritan Covenant of Grace," *Journal of Presbyterian History* 44 (1966): 178–97.

3. Calvin, *Institutes*, IV, xvi, 7–10, quoting Matt. 19:14.

4. Ibid., IV, xvi, 17, quoting Luke 1:15.

5. Ibid., IV, xvi, 18–20.

6. Ibid., IV, xvi, 21 (my italics).

7. Zacharias Ursinus, *The Summe of Christian Religion* (Oxford, 1587), 727–28, and *Certain learned and excellent Discourses* (London, 1613), 66, 15–16, 27–29, 287–88, 24; Calvin, *Institutes*, III, xiii, 5; IV, ii, 10; xvi, 24.

8. Dudley Fenner, *Certain Godly and Learned Treatises* (Edinburgh, 1592), 138, 123, 101, 132, 148.

9. William Perkins, *An Exposition of the Symbole or Creede of the Apostles* (Cambridge, 1600), 196, and *Treatise Tending Unto a Declaration Whether a Man be in the Estate of Damnation, or in the Estate of Grace* (n.p., 1600), 581.

10. William Ames, *The Marrow of Sacred Divinity* (London, 1642), 182–83.

11. Richard Sibbes, *The Faithful Covenanter*, in *Complete Works of Richard Sibbes, D.D.* (Edinburgh, 1863), 6:22.

12. Christopher Blackwood, *The Storming of Antichrist* ([London], 1644), 34; Thomas Blake, *The Birth-Privilege or Covenant-Holiness of Beleevers and their Issue* (n.p., 1644), 18.

13. Thomas Cobbett, *A Just Vindication of the Covenant and Church-Estate of Children of Church-Members* (London, 1648), 294–95, 94–95, 47–48, 17, 20, 36.

14. Ibid., 106, 150.

15. John Cotton, *The Grounds and Ends of the Baptisme of the Children of the Faithfull* (London, 1647), 12, 77, 70, 43, and *A Treatise of the Covenant of Grace* (London, 1659), 222–27.

16. Thomas Hooker, *Covenant of Grace Opened* (London, 1649), 20, 9–10, 15–16, 27, and *The Faithful Covenanter* (London, 1644), 19–20.

17. Joseph Haroutunian, *Piety Versus Moralism: The Passing of the New England Theology* (New York, 1970); Perry Miller, *The New England Mind: From Colony to Province* (Boston, 1961), chapter 2.

18. Anthony a Wood, *Athenae Oxonienses* (New York, 1967), 1:544.

19. William Sloane, *Children's Books in England and New England in the Seventeenth Century* (New York, 1955); Robert Smith, *The Exhortation that a Father Gave to His Children*, in *The Complaynt of veritie, made by John Bradford* (n.p., 1559); James Canceller, *The Alphabet of Prayers* (London, 1564), preface.

20. Henry Smith, *The Young Mans Taske*, in *The Sermons of Maister Henrie Smith* (London, 1593), 450, 470, 474, 454, 464.

21. William Cecil, *Certain Precepts for the Well Ordering of a Man's Life*, in *Advice to a Son*, ed. Louis B. Wright (Ithaca, 1962), 10–11.

22. Walter Raleigh, "Instruction to His Son and to Posterity," in *Advice To a Son*, ed. Louis B. Wright (Ithaca, 1962), 19–22.

23. Of the thirty authors of courtesy books listed by Sloane, only William Martyn, William Tipping, and William Higford may have been Puritans. Elizabeth Joceline was reared in a bishop's household but exhibited such Puritan biases that later Anglican editors changed the Puritan citations in her work to more approved Anglican authors. Sloane's characterization of Leigh as "puritanic" is confirmed in her comments on Jacobean society.

24. Dorothy Leigh, *The Mothers Blessing*, 7th ed. (London, 1621), 30–31; Elizabeth Joceline, *The Mother's Legacy to her Unborn Child* (London, 1624), sigs. B5v–B6.

25. Charles W. Camp, *The Artisan in Elizabethan Literature* (New York, 1924), 7, 115; Robert E. Moore, *Hogarth's Literary Relationships* (Minneapolis, 1948), 58–60. The etchings appeared in 1747 and in turn inspired a play.

26. John Wilson, *A Song or Story for the Lasting Remembrance of Divers Famous Works, which God hath done in Our Time* (London, 1626). For Foxe's popularity among children, see James Janeway, *A Token for Children: Being An Exact Account of the Conversion, Holy and Exemplary Lives and Joyful Deaths of several Young Children* (Boston, 1700), 35, 64; Edmund Calamy, *The Non-Conformist's Memorial*, ed. Samuel Palmer, 2d ed. (London, 1802–3), 2:191; Thomas and Anne Camme, *The Admirable and Glorious Appearance of the Eternal God, in his Glorious Power, in and through a Child* (London, 1684), 7.

27. Robert Abbot, *Young-mans warning-peece* (London, 1657), sigs. A3v–A5, 58–60; "Youth's Warning-Peice" (1636), in *Roxburghe Ballads*, ed. William Chappell (Hertford, 1880), 3:1–5; cf. "A Warning to Youth" in *Roxburghe Ballads*, 3:35–41.

28. Thomas Brookes, *Apples of Gold for Young Men and Women* (New York, 1825), 68–78.

29. Ibid., 46–47.

30. John Chishull, *Two Treatises* (London, 1658), 89–90, 9, 100, 86, 102, 110.

31. John Maynard, *Memento to Young and Old* (London, 1669), sigs. A3v–A4, A7v–A8, 85–91, 51–64.

32. Thomas Vincent, *Words of Advice to Young Men* (London, 1668), sig. A2v, 22–24. See C. F. Allison, *The Rise of Moralism* (London, 1966), on semi-Pelagianism.

33. Janeway, *Token for Children*, sig. A3; Thomas White, *A Little Book for Little Children*, 12th ed. (London, 1702), 7.

34. John Ryther, *The Morning Seeker* (London, 1673), sigs. A3v, a3–a3v.

35. Samuel Pomfret, *A Directory for Youth* (London, 1693), 11.

36. Samuel Pomfret, *A Sermon Preach'd to Young People* (London, 1698), 14; Timothy Cruso, *The Necessity and Advantage of an Early Victory over Satan* (London, 1693), 16–17; Thomas Gouge, *The Young Man's Guide* (Boston, 1742), 125–26.

37. Oliver Heywood, *Youth's Monitor*, in *The Whole Works of the Rev. Oliver Heywood* (London, 1826), 5:566; Edward Lawrence, *Parents Groans over their Wicked Children* (London, 1681), 58. On Lawrence's disappointment over his own children, see Calamy, *Non-Conformist's Memorial*, 2:140

38. Joseph Porter, *A Caution Against Youthful Lusts* (London, 1708), 9.

39. Matthew Mead, *The Good of Early Obedience* (London, 1683), 115; Gouge, *Young Man's Guide*, 164.

40. From Job 11:12. Lawrence, *Parents Groans*, 3; Porter, *Caution Against Youthful Lusts*, 4; Mead, *Good of Early Obedience*, 116, 228; Heywood, *Youth's Monitor*, 5:564, 570.

41. Daniel Williams, *The Vanity of Childhood and Youth*, 5th ed. (London, 1758), sig. A3v, 116, 22, 118.

42. Gouge, *Young Man's Guide*, 117.

43. See John Shower, *An Exhortation to Youth to Prepare for Judgment* (London, 1681), 26–28; Timothy Rogers, *Early Religion* (London, 1683), 40–43; Porter, *Caution Against Youthful Lusts*, 42.

44. Williams, *Vanity of Childhood*, 119–24, sig. A7. See also Philip Taverner, *A Grand-Father's Advice* (London, 1681), 8–19, 32; Rogers, *Early Religion*, 29–30.

45. Pomfret, *Directory for Youth*, 32–36.

46. Gouge, *Young Man's Guide*, 3–6; Matthew Mead, *The Young Man's Remembrancer, and Youth's Best Choice*, 3d ed. (London, 1701), 16–17, 87–88; Cruso, *Necessity and Advantage of an Early Victory*, sig. A1v; Heywood, *Youth's Monitor*, 5:554–57.

47. Shower, *Exhortation to Youth*, sig. a2; Williams, *Vanity of Childhood*, 114; Gouge, *Young Man's Guide*, 9–13.

48. Joseph Stennet, *Advice to the Young* (London, 1695), 80–89; Mead, *Young Man's Remembrancer*, 122; Timothy Cruso, *God, the Guide of Youth* (London, 1695), 25.

49. Robert Russell, *Of the Accepted Time, and Day of Salvation* (London, n.d.), 13; Mead, *Good of Early Obedience*, 127–36.

50. Williams, *Vanity of Childhood*, 91. John Morgan, *Godly Learning; Puritan Attitudes towards Reason, Learning, and Education, 1560–1640* (Cambridge, 1986), 28–30, 186, alludes to the mitigation of predestinarian doctrine in the context of education.

51. Robert Russell, *A Little Book for Children and Youth* (London, n.d.), sigs. A7–B1; White, *Little Book for Little Children*, 10, 16.

52. Cruso, *God, the Guide of Youth*, 30; Lawrence, *Parents Groans*, sig. A2v; Heywood, *Youth's Monitor*, 5:582–84; Mead, *Young Man's Remembrancer*, sigs. A2v–3; Rogers, *Early Religion*, sig. a2v.

53. Williams, *Vanity of Childhood*, 2; Mead, *Good of Early Obedience*, 227.

54. E. A. Wrigley and R. S. Schofield, *The Population History of England, 1541–1871: A Reconstruction* (Cambridge, Mass., 1981), 528.

55. Samuel Peck, *The Best Way to Mend the World, and to Prevent the Growth of Popery* (London, 1680), sig. A2v; John Strype, *Lessons Moral and Christian for Youth and Old Age* (London, 1699), 2–3; (Samuel Brewster), *The Christian Scholar* (London, 1700), 32.

56. Thomas Willis, *The Key of Knowledge* (London, 1682), sigs. A2v–A3; (Josiah Woodward), *Pastoral Advice to Young Persons* (London, 1708), 5–10.

57. Thomas Ken, *A Manual of Prayers For the Use of the Scholars of Winchester Colledge* (London, 1675), 2.

58. Simon Patrick, *A Book for Beginners* (1679), in *The Works of Symon Patrick, D.D.*, ed. Alexander Taylor (Oxford, 1858), 1:629.

59. Richard Kidder, *The Benefit of Early Piety* (London, 1684), 157–59; Richard Kidder, *The Young Man's Duty*, 6th ed. (London, 1690), 22–37.

60. Henry Hesketh, *The Importance of Religion to Young Persons* (London, 1683), 6–7; John Norris, *Treatises Upon Several Subjects* (London, 1697), 494.

61. Ken, *Manual of Prayers*, 7–8; Norris, *Treatises*, 502.

62. Josiah Woodward, *The Young-Man's Monitor* (London, 1706), 14–88.

63. William Smythies, *Benefit of Early Piety*, 45, 75–76. For this Anglican emphasis, see C. John Sommerville, "The Anti-Puritan Work Ethic," *Journal of British Studies* 20 (1981): 70–81.

64. Norris, *Treatises*, 462; Ken, *Manual of Prayers*, 60, 17, 9, 5, 23, 63–64; Patrick, *Book for Beginners*, 1:616.

65. William Bayly, *Some Words of Warning and Exhortation unto all Young-People and Children throughout the Whole World* (1664), in *A Collection of the Several Wrightings* (n.p., 1676), 531. J. William Frost, *The Quaker Family in Colonial America* (New York, 1973), 66–67, indicates the Quakers' ambiguity in the matter of childhood innocence.

66. Anon., *A short testimony from some of those that are come to the Obedience of the Gospel, Against all false Liberty in Youth* (n.p., 1677), 3–4; Bayly, *Words of Warning*, 536–37; John Gibson, *A Faithfull Testimony for the Lord* (London, 1663), 5; John Pennyman, *Instructions to his Children* (London, 1674), 4–5.

67. Anthony Tomkins and Richard Needham, *A Few Words of Counsel and Advice to all the Sons and Daughters of Men* (London, 1687), 1; Pennyman, *Instructions to his Children*, 3, 6; William Penn, *Fruits of a Father's Love*, 6th ed. (Philadelphia, 1776), 4.

68. Ibid., 20–22, 32–34.

69. Bartholomew Batty, *The Christian Mans Closet* (London, 1581), 10–11, 7–8, 14, 23–26, 45–49. To show how historians can read matters differently, Lawrence Stone thought Batty's name perfectly appropriate for this work, and the one thing he remembered particularly was Batty's theory that God had designed the buttocks so they could be "severely beaten" without lasting damage: *The Family, Sex and Marriage in England, 1500–1800* (London, 1977), 170.

70. Thomas Becon, *A New Catechism* (Cambridge, 1844), 358, 383–85, 347–49, 354; see Ecclesiasticus 7:23–25 and 30:1–13.

71. Richard Greenham, *Of the Good Education of Children* (1584), in *The Works of the Reverend and Faithful Servant of Iesus Christ, M. Richard Greenham*, 4th ed. (London, 1605), 446–48, 314.

72. Linda Pollock, *Forgotten Children: Parent-Child Relations from 1500 to 1900* (Cambridge, 1983), 103, 116, 156.

73. Thomas Elyot, *The Book named the Governour* (London, 1962), 16–29.

74. Sir Thomas More, *Utopia* (New Haven, 1964), 75–80, 109.

75. Robert Cleaver, *A godly form of household government* (London, 1598), 50–56, 294.

76. Ibid., 292–96; John Bryan, *The Vertuous Daughter* (London, 1640), 19.

77. Cleaver, *Godly form of household government*, 157, 301.

78. Ibid., 235, 253, 277–82, 333, 320–21, 351, 349. Morgan, *Godly Learning*, noticed a Puritan concern over manners, 186, 302.

79. Cleaver, *Godly form of household government*, 310, 305.

80. William Gouge, *Of Domesticall Duties* (London, 1622), 507–17, 153–55.

81. Owen Stockton, *A Treatise of Family Instruction* (London, 1672), 315–

31; Thomas Cobbett, *A Fruitfull Discourse Touching the Honour due from Children to Parents* (London, 1656), 135.

82. Philip Goodwin, *Religio Domestica Rediviva* (London, 1655), 227; William Gouge, *Of Domesticall Duties*, 499–504.

83. Gouge, *Of Domesticall Duties*, 558; Richard Baxter, *The Catechising of Families*, in *The Practical Works of Richard Baxter* (London, 1854), 4:132; Stockton, *Family Instruction*, 123; Robert Abbott, *A Christian Family Builded by God* (London, 1652), 51; Samuel Slater, *An Earnest Call to Family-Religion* (London, 1694), 125–27.

84. Joseph Waite, *The Parents Primer and the Mothers Looking-Glasse* (London, 1681), 56–79.

85. Williams, *Vanity of Childhood*, 105.

86. Edmund S. Morgan, *The Puritan Family: Religion and Domestic Relations in Seventeenth-Century New England*, 2d ed. (New York, 1966), 78. There is doubt that those under sixteen fell under this penalty: James Axtell, *The School Upon a Hill* (New Haven, 1974), 156–59.

87. Baxter, *Catechising of Families*, 4:134–35, and *The Church Book of Bunyan Meeting. 1650–1821*, intro. G. B. Harrison (London, 1928), 28, 106, 54.

88. Goodwin, *Religio Domestica*, 380; Thomas Gataker, *Davids Instructer* (London, 1620), 20–21; Heywood, *Youth's Monitor*, 5:559.

89. Thomas Lye, in Thomas Doolittle, *The Young Man's Instructer* (London, 1673), sig. A6v. See also Edward Burghall, *The Great Benefit of the Christian Education of Children* (London, [1663]), 11; John Bunyan, *A Book for Boys and Girls* (1686), in *John Bunyan: The Poems*, ed. Graham Midgley (Oxford, 1980), 267; Caleb Trenchfield, *A Cap of Gray Hairs for a Green Head*, 5th ed. (London, 1710), 35.

90. Stockton, *Family Instruction*, 23.

91. Richard Baxter, *The Poor Man's Family Book*, in *The Practical Works of Richard Baxter* (London, 1854), 4:235; Waite, *Parents Primer*, 65, 123; Stockton, *Family Instruction*, 33–39; Shower, *Family Religion* (London, 1694), 71–72; Cobbett, *Fruitfull Discourse*, 17; Kenneth Charlton, "'Not publicke only but also private and domesticall': Mothers and familial education in pre-industrial England," *History of Education* 17 (1988): 2.

92. See references to Becon and Cleaver, notes 70 and 78, and also Josias Nichols, *An order of household instruction* (London, 1596), sigs. B5–B5v; Baxter, *Catechising of Families*, 4:131–32; Cobbett, *Fruitfull Discourse*, 15.

93. Cobbett, *Fruitfull Discourse*, 119.

94. Greenham, *Good Education of Children*, 88; Stockton, *Family Instruction*, 135–36; Slater, *Family-Religion*, 274–75, 287; Matthew Henry, *Christ's Favour to Little Children* (London, 1713), 26.

95. Jeremy Taylor, *Holy Living*, in *The Whole Works of Jeremy Taylor*, ed. Reginald Heber and Charles Page Eden (London, 1855–65), 3:107–8.

96. Richard Kidder, *A Discourse Concerning the Education of Youth in Religion* (London, 1672), 4; William Payne, *Learning and Knowledge Recommended to the Scholars of Brentwood School* (London, 1682), 11.

97. (Richard Allestree), *The Whole Duty of Man* (London, 1677), 310.

98. John Locke, *Some Thoughts Concerning Education* (London, 1693), sig. #A3, 34–35, 51–54, 99, 85–86.

99. Ibid., 163–64.

100. Ibid., 33–34, 37, 83–85, 117–18.

101. Ibid., 123–25, 134, 107, 152; Paul Sangster, *Pity My Simplicity: The Evangelical Revival and the Religious Education of Children, 1738–1800* (London, 1963), 29–32.

102. J. A. Passmore, "The Malleability of Man in Eighteenth-Century Thought," in *Aspects of the Eighteenth Century*, ed. Earl R. Wasserman (Baltimore, 1965), 22–24, 33–42; Locke, *Concerning Education*, 75, 149–51, 178.

103. Locke, *Concerning Education*, 130–32.

104. Charles Wareing Bardsley, *Curiosities of Puritan Nomenclature*, new ed. (London, 1897), 228–29; Locke, *Concerning Education*, 171.

105. Cleaver, *Godly form of household government*, 59.

106. Erik Erikson, *Childhood and Society*, 2d ed. (New York, 1963).

107. Elizabeth Godfrey (Jessie Bedford), *English Children in the Olden Time* (London, 1907), 232–33.

108. (Joseph Bennet?), *Address of Some Ministers of Christ* (London, 1658), 17.

109. John Evelyn, *Miscellaneous Writings of John Evelyn*, ed. William Upcott (London, 1825), 106–10.

110. Daniel Defoe, *The Family Instructor* (1715), in *The Novels and Miscellaneous Works of Daniel DeFoe* (Oxford, 1841), 15: 106–7.

111. Maldwyn Edwards, *Family Circle: A Study of the Epworth Household in Relation to John and Charles Wesley* (London, 1949), 59; Samuel Annesley, ed., *A Continuation of Morning-Exercise Questions and Cases of Conscience, Practically Resolved* (London, 1683), 160.

112. See Samuel Wesley, *Poems on Several Occasions* (Cambridge, 1743), 41–42, 53–54, 88, 167–68.

113. Sangster, *Pity My Simplicity*, 93–104, 178, 29.

Chapter Four. Puritan Humor and Entertainment for Children

1. Stuart M. Tave, *The Amiable Humorist* (Chicago, 1960), 12–24, 164–65, 94–100, 118.

2. Ibid., 91–94.

3. Raymond A. Anselment, *"Betwixt Jest and Earnest": Marprelate, Milton, Marvell, Swift, and the Decorum of Religious Ridicule* (Toronto, 1979).

4. Anon., *Theses Martinianae* (n.p., [1589]), sig. D4.

5. Norman N. Holland, *Laughing; A Psychology of Humor* (Ithaca, 1982), 37–38; Harvey Cox, *The Feast of Fools* (New York, 1969).

6. Holland, *Laughing*, 47–53; Sigmund Freud, *Jokes and Their Relation to the Unconscious*, trans. James Strachey (New York, 1960), 234.

7. Keith Thomas, "The Place of Laughter in Tudor and Stuart England," *Times Literary Supplement*, Jan. 21, 1977, 77ff.

8. Lewis Bayly, *The Practice of Piety*, 38th ed. (London, 1637), 253.

9. Quoted in Anselment, *"Betwixt Jest and Earnest,"* 14.

10. Thomas Brookes, *Apples of Gold for Young Men and Women* (New York, 1825). At 3,000 copies in each of the 16 reprintings (by 1693), the total of nearly 50,000 would relate to the 1,360,000 English families (calculated by Gregory King), as 3,162,000 relates to the 86,000,000 American households in the 1980 census—one copy per 27.2 families. See C. John Sommerville, "On the Distribution of Religious and Occult Literature in Seventeenth-Century England," *The Library* 29 (1974): 221–25. At almost 5 percent of the population in 1676, Dissenting households numbered about 65,000, including the illiterate.

11. (Samuel Acton), *The Virgin Saint; or, A Brief Narrative of the Holy Life, and Christian Death of Mary Wilson* (London, 1673), 21, 28, 41, 47.

12. Holland, *Laughing*, 30.

13. Brookes, *Apples of Gold*, 144.

14. Ibid., 142–43, 55.

15. Ibid., 141, 45.

16. Ibid., 152, 155, 128, 189.

17. Ibid., 165, 169.

18. Edmund Calamy, *The Non-Conformist's Memorial*, ed. Samuel Palmer, 2d ed. (London, 1802–3), 1:150.

19. Brookes, *Apples of Gold*, 42, 93.

20. Raymond Phineas Stearns, *The Strenuous Puritan: Hugh Peters, 1598–1660* (Urbana, 1954), 140–43; Anon., *The Tales and Jests of Mr. Hugh Peters* (London, 1660), and anon., *Hugh Peters his Figaries* (n.p., 1660).

21. Anon., *Tales and Jests*, 11–12; for another version of this story, see Stearns, *Strenuous Puritan*, 216.

22. Anon., *Tales and Jests*, 27, 13, 25.

23. Ibid., 27, 16.

24. Ibid., 17–18; Stearns, *Strenuous Puritan*, 216, 365–66.

25. Antonia Fraser, *Cromwell: The Lord Protector* (New York, 1973), 643–44.

26. Stearns, *Strenuous Puritan*, 140–143.

27. Calamy, *Non-Conformist's Memorial*, 1:116, 168, 203–4, 211; 2:53, 89–90, 176, 200, 265; 3:18, 26, 44, 45, 67, 305, 450.

28. Ibid., 2:409, 406; Samuel Shaw, *Words made Visible; or, Grammar and Rhetoric accommodated to the Lives and Manners of Men* (London, 1679), sig. A1.

29. Samuel Shaw, *The Different Humours of Men represented at an Interlude in a Country School* (London, 1692).

30. Joseph Smith, *A Descriptive Catalogue of Friends Books* (London, 1867), 1:36.

31. William Sloane, *Children's Books in England and America in the Seventeenth Century* (New York, 1955), 168, 172.

32. Benjamin Keach, *War with the Devil*, 4th ed. (London, 1676), 11.

33. Young John Draper read it as soon as it appeared; see Christopher Ness, *A Spiritual Legacy* (London, 1684), 115, and see the works of Keach and Russell which followed Bunyan's lead.

34. Harold Golder, "Bunyan's Giant Despair," *Journal of English and Germanic Philology*, 30 (1931), 361–78.

35. John Bunyan, *The Pilgrim's Progress*, ed. F. R. Leavis (New York, 1964), 87.

36. Ibid., 93.

37. T. S., *Second Part of The Pilgrim's Progress*, (London, 1684), sigs. A7–A7v. Bernard was a Puritan. James Blanton Wharey describes Bernard's work as "not without wit," meaning, of course, that it was very nearly so: *A Study of the Sources of Bunyan's Allegories* (New York, 1968) 89. Sherman's work saw three editions by 1700 plus another two in Scotland, which reflects badly on Scottish humor.

38. Benjamin Keach, *The Travels of True Godliness*, 3d ed. (London, 1684), sig. A2v.

39. Robert Russell, *The Little Book for Children and Youth* (London, n.d.), sigs. A4–7.

40. *Non-Conformist's Memorial*, 1:352, 394; 2:141.

41. Thomas White, *A Little Book for Little Children*, 12th ed. (London,

1702), 18. This is not to be confused with a book with the same title by "T. W.", described in F. J. Harvey Darton, *Children's Books in England*, 2d ed. (Cambridge, 1966), 60; Richard Baxter, *The Mother's Catechism*, in *The Practical Works of Richard Baxter* (London, 1854), 4:34–64.

42. Leslie Church, *The Early Methodist People* (London, 1948), 237–41.

43. Keach, *War with the Devil*, sig. A3v, E. B.'s "Epistle to the Reader."

44. Lawrence Stone, *The Family, Sex and Marriage in England, 1500–1800* (London, 1977), 174, recounts an example of a child's hysteria associated with the threat of damnation.

45. Chear's verses appear in John Vernon, *The Compleat Scholler; or, A Relation of the Life, and latter-end especially, of Caleb Vernon*, 2d ed. (London, 1666), 24–26.

46. Ibid., 61–62, corrected by H. P., comp., *A Looking-Glass for Children*, 3d ed. (London, 1673), 23–24.

47. Vernon, *Compleat Scholler*, 61.

48. *John Bunyan: The Poems*, ed. Graham Midgley (Oxford, 1980), 60.

49. Ibid., 190–92.

50. Ibid., 202–3, 214–24, 234–35.

51. Anon., *The Living Words of a Dying Child* (n.p., 1677), 4, sig. A3.

52. John Whiting, *Early Piety Exemplified in the Life and Death of Mary Whiting, A Faithful Handmaid of the Lord* (n.p., n.d.), 9; Thomas Lawson, *A Serious Remembrancer To Live Well* (London, 1684), 30–32; William Mather, *The Young Man's Companion* (London, 1681); anon., *A Seasonable account of the Christian and Dying-Words of some Young Men* (Philadelphia, 1700), 7.

53. Thomas and Anne Camme, *The Admirable and Glorious Appearance of the Eternal God, in his Glorious Power in and through a Child* (London, 1684), 7.

54. Of the books listed in Sloane's *Children's Books*, only William Jole's *The Father's Blessing Penn'd for the Instruction of his Children* (London, 1674), and William Ronksley, *The Child's Weeks-work* (London, 1712), may have been "Anglican" attempts to produce entertainment for children.

Chapter Five. Education and Freedom

1. See Kenneth Charlton, *Education in Renaissance England* (London, 1965); Norman Wood, *The Reformation and English Education* (London, 1931); Foster Watson, *The English Grammar Schools to 1660: Their curriculum and practice* (Cambridge, 1908); and *The Beginnings of the Teaching of Modern Subjects in England* (London, 1909); Joan Simon, *Education and Society*

in Tudor England (Cambridge, 1966); Nicholas Hans, *New Trends in Education in the Eighteenth Century* (London, 1951); W. A. L. Vincent, *The State and School Education, 1640–1660, in England and Wales* (London, 1950), and Richard L. Greaves, *The Puritan Revolution and Educational Thought* (New Brunswick, N.J., 1969).

2. See directions in Thomas Lye, *A Plain and Familiar Method of Instructing the Younger Sort* (London, 1672), 1–12; Thomas Vincent, *Words of Advice to Young Men* (London, 1668), 58; Thomas Gouge, *The Young Man's Guide, through the wilderness of this world to the heavenly Canaan* (Boston, 1742), 45.

3. W. A. L. Vincent, *The Grammar Schools: Their Continuing Tradition, 1660–1714* (London, 1969), 86–90.

4. T. W. Baldwin, *William Shakspere's Small Latine and Less Greeke* (Urbana, Ill., 1944), 1:80, and *William Shakspere's Petty School* (Urbana, Ill., 1943), 79–82; Joe William Ashley Smith, *The Birth of Modern Education: The Contribution of the Dissenting Academies, 1660–1800* (London, 1954), 259–60; R. R., *To all Magistrates, Teachers, Schoolmasters, and People in Christendom Who Teach your Children the way of the Heathen out of their Books* (London, 1660), 1–6.

5. *Dictionary of National Biography* (London, 1921–22), 14:688–94; also Patrick Collinson, *The Elizabethan Puritan Movement* (London, 1967), 66, 74.

6. Anon., *Principles of the Doctrine of Christ, Delivered in the Assemblies Shorter Catechism, Made plainer to Babes in Knowledge* (London, 1701), preface.

7. Zachary Crofton, *Catechizing Gods Ordinance* (London, 1656), sig. a4, 25, quoting 2 Tim. 1:13; Simon Ford, *A Sermon of Catechizing* (London, 1655), preface.

8. Josias Nichols, *An Order of Household Instruction* (London, 1596), sig. C1. From a later period, see the brief catechisms by John Mason, *A Little Catechism, with Little Verses, and Little Sayings for Little Children* (London, 1692), and Robert Russell, *A Little Book for Children and Youth* (London, [c. 1693]).

9. Benjamin Keach, *Instructions for Children; or, the Child's and Youth's Delight* (New York, 1695), 1–6; Richard Baxter, *The Mother's Catechism,* in *The Practical Works of Richard Baxter* (London, 1854), 4:34–64.

10. Arthur Dent, *A pastime for parents; or, A Recreation, to pass away the time; containing the most principall grounds of Christian Religion* (London, 1609).

11. John Paget, *A primer of Christian Religion, or a forme of catechising, drawne from the beholding of God's works in the creation of the world* (London, 1601).

12. Herbert Palmer, *An Endeavour of Making the Principles of Christian*

Religion, namely the Creed, the ten Commandments, the Lords Prayer, and the Sacraments, plaine and easie, 3d ed. (London, 1644), 1.

13. John Wallis, *A Brief and Easie Explanation of the Shorter Catechism,* 8th ed. (London, 1662), "To the Reader"; Palmer, *Endeavour,* sigs. A3–A3v.

14. Thomas Lye, *A Plain and Familiar Method of Instructing the Younger Sort* (London, 1672); Edmund Calamy, *The Non-Conformist's Memorial,* ed. Samuel Palmer, 2d ed. (London, 1802–3), 1:84.

15. George Herbert, *The Works of George Herbert* (Oxford, 1941), 256–57. I owe this reference to Professor Stanley Fish.

16. Anon., *A Plaine and Easie Way of Cathechising Such as are of weakest Memories and of the meanest Capacities* (London, 1680), 42. See also Thomas Doolittle, *A Plain Method of Catechizing* (London, 1698); and anon., *The Church-Catechism Enlarg'd and Explain'd, in an Easie and Familiar Method* (London, 1697).

17. Anon., *Church-Catechism*; anon., *The Art of Catechizing, or The Compleat Catechist* (London, 1691); Robert Nelson, *The Whole Duty of a Christian, by Way of Question and Answer* (London, 1704); James Talbott, *The Christian School-Master* (London, 1707), 82.

18. Isaac Watts, *A Discourse on the Way of Instruction by Catechisms* (1730), in *The Works of the Reverend and Learned Isaac Watts* (London, 1810), 3:224.

19. Nichols, *Order of Household Instruction,* sigs. C2–C2v.

20. (William Popple), *Two Treatises of Rational Religion* (London, 1692), sig. A6, 2–30, 114–29.

21. Lancelot Addison, *The Primitive Institution; or, A Seasonable Discourse of Catechising,* 2d ed. (London, 1690), 12–15.

22. John Locke, *Some Thoughts Concerning Education* (London, 1693), 188.

23. Watts, *Discourse on the Way of Instruction,* 3:210–15, 224.

24. William Gouge, *Of Domesticall Duties* (London, 1622), 540; the quotation is from Richard Baxter, *The Poor Man's Family Book* (1672), in *The Practical Works of Richard Baxter* (London, 1854), 4:233.

25. Watts, *Discourse on the Way of Instruction,* 205–6.

26. Thomas Ken, *A Manual of Prayers For the Use of the Scholars of Winchester Colledge* (London, 1675), 11–12; Symon Patrick, *A Book for Beginners; or, An Help to young Communicants* (1679), in *The Works of Symon Patrick, D.D.* (Oxford, 1858), 1:625–28.

27. Locke, *Some Thoughts Concerning Education,* 186–89, 226.

28. Walter Howard Frere and William M. Kennedy, eds., *Visitation Articles of the Period of the Reformation* (London: Alcuin Club Collections, 1910), 15:6–8; Philippa Tudor, "Religious Instruction for Children and Ado-

lescents in the Early English Reformation," *Journal of Ecclesiastical History* 35 (1984): 391–413.

29. Edward Cardwell, ed., *Synodalia: A Collection of Articles of Religion, Canons, and Proceedings of Convocations* (Oxford, 1842), 2:510–11.

30. Claude Jenkins, ed., *Collectanea II: Act Book of the Archdeaconry of Taunton* ([London], 1928), 43:11–13; W. P. M. Kennedy, *Elizabethan Episcopal Administration* (London, 1924), 27:151.

31. Edward Cardwell, ed., *Documentary Annals of the Reformed Church of England* (Oxford, 1844), 2:337–38.

32. Frere and Kennedy, *Visitation Articles*, 16:98, 259–60, 277; Kennedy, *Elizabethan Episcopal Administration*, 27:71, 94, 130, 144, 224, 271; Ford, *Sermon of Catechizing*, 20; Jeremy Taylor, *A Discourse of Confirmation* (1663), in *The Whole Works of the Right Reverend Jeremy Taylor* (London, 1855–65), 5:666.

33. M. G. Jones, *The Charity School Movement* (Cambridge, 1938), 266–89, 110.

34. E. Neville Williams, ed., *The Eighteenth-Century Constitution* (Cambridge, 1970), 12. The new laws were 1 Will. & Mary, c.8; 7&8 Will. III, c.27; and 11 Will. III, c.4. Older acts sometimes invoked against Dissenters were 23 Eliz., c.1; 1 Jac. I, c.4; 14 Car. II, c.4.

35. Cardwell, *Synodalia*, 2:712–13, 718; Edward Hyde, Earl of Clarendon, *The History of the Rebellion and Civil Wars* (Oxford, 1826), 1:38.

36. (Samuel Wesley), *A Letter From a Country Divine to his Friend in London Concerning the Education of the Dissenters in their Private Academies* (London, 1703); Henry Sacheverell, *The Nature and Mischief of Prejudice and Partiality* (London, 1704), 54–57.

37. Samuel Palmer, *A Vindication of the Learning, Loyalty, Morals, and Most Christian Behavior of the Dissenters Toward the Church of England* (London, 1705), 8. For the same argument, see anon., *A Defence of the private Academies and Schools of the Protestant Dissenters* (London, 1714), 2. This tract was originally part of James Owen's *Moderation Still a Virtue* (London, 1704).

38. Samuel Wesley, *A Reply to Mr. Palmer's Vindication of the Learning, Loyalty, Morals, and Most Christian Behavior of the Dissenters towards the Church of England* (London, 1707), 14–16.

39. (Samuel Palmer), *A Defence of the Dissenters Education in their Private Academies: In Answer to Mr. W——y's Disingenuous and Unchristian Reflections upon 'em* (London, 1703), 6.

40. Palmer, *Vindication of the Learning*, 10–11.

41. Sacheverell, *Nature and Mischief of Prejudice*, 17–18.

42. Henry Sacheverell, *The Perils of false brethren, both in Church and State* (London, 1709), 15.

43. Henry Sacheverell, *The Speech of Henry Sacheverell, D. D., Made in Westminster-Hall, on Tuesday, March 7, 1709–10* (London, 1710), 5.

44. Luke Tyerman, *The Life and Times of Rev. Samuel Wesley* (London, 1866), 339, 274–89.

45. Jonathan Swift, *The Examiner*, 26 (25 January, 1711).

46. Thomas Reynolds, *A Discourse preach'd at Little St. Helen's* (London, 1714), 30; anon., *A Collection of all the Papers that have been Giv'n to the Lords and Commons, in Relation to the Bill to Prevent Schism* (London, 1714), 22.

47. Richard Steele, *A Letter to a Member of Parliament Concerning the Bill for Preventing the Growth of Schism* (London, 1714), 11–15.

48. (Daniel Defoe), *A Letter to Mr. Steele, Occasion'd by his Letter to a Member of Parliament, concerning the Bill for preventing the Growth of Schism* (London, 1714), 20.

49. *Historical Manuscripts Commission: House of Lords Manuscripts*, new series, 10:334–47; *Debates and Speeches*, 14–18.

50. John Shute Barrington, *Letter from a Lay-Man in Communion with the Church of England, Tho' Dissenting from Her in some Points* 2d ed. (London, 1714), 5–8, 12–14.

51. Ibid., 7.

52. Ibid., 21.

53. Anon., *A Letter to a Member of Parliament, Relating to the Bill for preventing the Growth of Schism* (London, 1714), 11. This tract appended some specifically Quaker objections and might be the "Considerations on the Schism Bill" by John Bellars, which we know only from an advertisement in his *An Epistle to the Quarterly-Meeting of London and Middlesex* (n.p., 1718). Bellars frequently wrote on educational matters.

54. Anon., *Collection of all the Papers*, 28.

55. Quoted in Christopher Durston, *The Family in the English Revolution* (Oxford, 1989), 134, 13.

56. Watts, *Discourse on the Way of Instruction*, 203–4.

57. Steele, *Letter to a Member of Parliament*, 17.

58. Smith, *Birth of Modern Education*, 257.

59. Michael R. Watts, *The Dissenters; From the Reformation to the French Revolution* (Oxford, 1978), 370–71; Irene Parker, *Dissenting Academies in England* (Cambridge, 1914), 103.

60. G. M. Trevelyan, *England Under Queen Anne* (London, 1965), 3:302.

61. Reynolds, *Discourse*, 16–17; Josias Maultby, *God the Hope, and the Saviour of his People* (London, 1714), 4, 23, 27; Nathaniel Weld, *A Sermon*

Preach'd at Dublin (London, 1714), 11–22; John Cumming, *The General Corruption and Defection of the Present Times, as to Matters of Religion* (London, 1714), 30–31.

62. Trevelyan, *England Under Queen Anne*, 3:302.

63. Sidney Webb and Beatrice Webb, *English Local Government* (London, 1906–29), 1:252–56.

64. Daniel Defoe, *Charity still a Christian Virtue; or, An Impartial Account of the Tryal and Conviction of the Reverend Mr. Hendley, For Preaching a Charity-Sermon at Chisselhurst* (London, 1719), 29–40, 59.

65. Thomas B. Howell, *A Complete Collection of State Trials* (London, 1809–28), 15:1407–22.

66. Defoe, *Charity still a Christian Virtue*, 59–60.

Epilogue. Family Feeling versus Puritan Individualism

1. William J. Goode, *World Revolution and Family Patterns* (New York, 1963), 312–13; C. K. Yang, *The Chinese Family in the Communist Revolution* (Cambridge, Mass., 1959), 3 21.

2. Cf. John Wilson, *Introduction to Social Movements* (New York, 1973), 131–32, 317–19.

3. Mark 3:31–35 and parallels.

4. Mark 6:1–14 and parallels; Luke 4:22–24; John 6:42 and 7:1–10.

5. Joachim Jeremias, *New Testament Theology: The Proclamation of Jesus* (New York, 1971), 36, 62–67.

6. John 2:3–4; Luke, 2·49 and 11:27–28; Mark 3:31–35.

7. Luke 6:22–26, 11:47–48 and parallels.

8. Luke 12:51–53 and parallels, 14:26, 9:59–62 and parallels; Mark 10:29–30 and parallels; John 3:3.

9. Acts 13:12–26 and 7:2–53. Paul, who reportedly heard Stephen's sermon, used the contrast in Acts 13:16–41, Gal. 3:6–8, and Rom. 4:1–18.

10. See Rev. 4:4, where the two groups are associated.

11. 1 Cor. 7:8–9, 26–31.

12. Joachim Jeremias, *Infant Baptism in the First Four Centuries* (London, 1960), and *The Origin of Infant Baptism* (Naperville, Ill., 1963).

13. Charles N. Cochrane, *Christianity and Classical Culture* (New York, 1957), 194–98.

14. Mary M. McLaughlin, "Survivors and Surrogates," in *The History of Childhood*, ed. Lloyd deMause (New York, 1974), 129.

15. John Bossy, "Blood and Baptism: Kinship, Community and Chris-

tianity in Western Europe from the Fourteenth to the Seventeenth Centuries," in *Sanctity and Secularity: The Church and the World*, ed. Derek Baker (New York, 1973), 129–43; Natalie Z. Davis, "Some Tasks and Themes in the Study of Popular Religion," in *The Pursuit of Holiness in Late Medieval and Renaissance Religion*, eds. Charles Trinkhaus and Heiko Oberman (Leiden, 1974), 327–29.

16. Matt. 8:22 and parallels.

17. Mark 10:8 and parallels, and Eph. 5:31, in which both Jesus and Paul quote Gen. 2:24 concerning men leaving their parents to join their wives—the essence of a conjugal relationship. Carle Zimmerman, *Family and Civilization* (New York, 1947), 466–71, 482–89.

18. Cf. Christopher Hill, *Society and Puritanism in Pre-Revolutionary England* (New York, 1967), 443–81.

19. Roland Bainton, *Here I Stand* (New York, 1955), chapter 17.

20. Chilton Latham Powell, *English Domestic Relations, 1487–1653* (New York, 1917), 93–98. William Haller, *Liberty and Reformation in the Puritan Revolution* (New York, 1955), 78–99; John M. Perlette, "Milton, Ascham, and the Rhetoric of the Divorce Controversy," *Milton Studies* 10 (1977): 202, 207; John Halkett, *Milton and the Idea of Matrimony* (New Haven, 1970), 27.

21. Edmund S. Morgan, *The Puritan Family*, revised ed. (New York, 1966), 161–86.

22. Christopher Durston, *The Family in the English Revolution* (Oxford, 1989), 173–74.

23. Richard T. Vann, "Nurture and Conversion in the Early Quaker Family," *Journal of Marriage and the Family* 31 (1969): 639–43.

24. J. William Frost, *The Quaker Family in Colonial America* (New York, 1973), 68, says the principle was widely accepted by 1700 but without much discussion. Richard Vann, *The Social Development of English Quakerism, 1655–1755* (Cambridge, Mass., 1969), 203, notes that the famous ruling of 1737 on birthright membership only established where one's membership was recognized and not whether it was recognized.

25. Vann, "Nurture and Conversion."

26. Fred Weinstein and Gerald M. Platt, *The Wish to be Free: Society, Psyche, and Value Change* (Berkeley, 1969), 60. See also S. Maccoby, *English Radicalism, 1786–1832: From Paine to Cobbett* (London, 1955), 463.

27. E.g., Rosalie Glynn Grylls, *William Godwin and His World* (London, 1953), 37. See also Clarke Garrett, *Respectable Folly* (Baltimore, 1975); J. F. C. Harrison, *The Second Coming: Popular Millenarianism, 1780–1850* (New Brunswick, N.J., 1979); Jack Fruchtman, Jr., *The Apocalyptic Politics of Richard*

Price and Joseph Priestley (Philadelphia, 1983).

28. Thomas Paine, *The Rights of Man* (Garden City, N.Y., 1961), 493, 477–85; Maccoby, *English Radicalism*, 466–67.

29. H. N. Brailsford, *Shelley, Godwin, and Their Circle* (New York, 1913), 59.

30. Ibid., 65.

31. Elton Smith and Esther Smith, *William Godwin* (New York, 1965), 122–23.

32. Brailsford, *Shelley, Godwin, and Their Circle*, 80; Grylls, *William Godwin and His World*, 181.

33. William Godwin, *Enquiry Concerning Political Justice*, ed. F. E. L. Priestley (London, 1946), 3:219.

34. B. S. Allen, "The Reaction Against William Godwin," *Modern Philology* 16 (1918): 225–43.

35. Clement Dukes, *The Model Woman* (London, 1850), 92–95.

36. James Mackintosh, "A Discourse on the Law of Nature and Nations," in *The Miscellaneous Works of the Right Honourable Sir James Mackintosh* (Boston, 1857), 36–37.

37. Peter Coveney, *The Image of Childhood* (Baltimore, 1967), 62; E. P. Thompson, *The Making of the English Working Class* (New York, 1963), 162.

38. G. R. Sabri-Tabrizi, *The "Heaven" and "Hell" of William Blake* (London, 1973), 193; J. G. Davies, *The Theology of William Blake* (Oxford, 1948), 57.

39. H. N. Margoliouth, *William Blake* (London, 1961), 121–26; *Cambridge History of English Literature*, ed. A. N. Ward and A. R. Waller (Cambridge, 1907–27), 11:216–18; John Beer, *Blake's Humanism* (Manchester, 1968), 141–46, 173, 189–90, 194–96.

40. Grylls, *William Godwin and His World*, 62, 112; Brailsford, *Shelley, Godwin, and Their Circle*, 151–52; Eleanor Flexner, *Mary Wollstonecraft* (New York, 1972), 238–39.

41. Brailsford, *Shelley, Godwin, and Their Circle*, 159–62; David Fleischer, *William Godwin: A Study in Liberalism* (London, 1951), 34–38, 138.

42. *Dictionary of National Biography* (London, 1921–22), 4:370.

43. Smith and Smith, *William Godwin*, 121.

44. Anthony Lincoln, *Some Political and Social Ideas of English Dissent, 1763–1800* (New York, 1971), 54.

45. Ibid., 95–97.

INDEX

Abbot, Robert, 50–51, 81–82, 141
Addison, Lancelot, 143
Adolescence, 34, 82–83, 87
Advice to parents, 22–23, 29, 32–33, 92–106
Allegories, 27, 121–26
Allestree, Richard, 5, 101, 141
America, 4, 6–7, 13–14, 30, 33, 55, 57, 76–77, 99, 166, 172
Ames, William, 75
Anagrams, 52–53, 184 (n. 34)
Anglicans, 10, 16–17, 22–27, 34–37, 46–48, 50, 55, 58–59, 64–67, 84, 89, 91, 93, 101–6, 132, 135, 137, 140–41, 144–50
Annesley, Samuel, 60, 106
Apprentices, 15, 33, 51, 81, 85, 91
Ariès, Philippe, 4, 38
Aristocracy, 95, 101–2, 104, 124, 162, 166
Aristotle, 99
Arminians, 26, 103
Ascham, Roger, 24
Astrology, 47
Atheism, 25, 27, 35, 57, 61, 85, 87, 89, 142, 147–48
Aubrey, John, 48
Augustinianism, 29, 88
Autobiographies, 66–67

Autonomy of the child, 93, 104–5, 107, 135, 151–54, 157

Bacon, Francis, 38
Ball, John, 137
Ballads. See Verses
Baptism, 52, 71–77, 161
Baptists, 25, 52–53, 71–72, 74–77, 112, 114, 121–22, 125, 127, 131–32, 172
Barclay, Robert, 143
Barrington, John Shute, 150
Batty, Bartholomew, 93
Baxter, Richard, 5, 61, 99, 126, 144
Bayly, Lewis, 114
Becon, Thomas, 93–94
Bedford, Jessie, 105
Bernard, Richard, 125
Bible, 22, 52–53, 56, 61, 74, 83, 89, 93, 97–101, 121, 125, 136, 138, 142–44, 149, 151, 159, 163; Geneva version, 21, 114; commentaries, 152
Bible-story books, 27, 126, 138, 144
Biddle, John, 143
Biographies, 16, 27, 43–68
Blackwood, Christopher, 76
Blake, Thomas, 76
Blake, William, 166, 169–70

Book popularity, 81, 96, 194 (n. 10), 122, 125–26, 131–32
Breaking the will, 94, 96, 106
Brooke, Humphrey, 25
Brookes, Thomas, 28, 82–84, 115–18, 130
Bryan, John, 49–50
Bunyan, John, 27, 66–67, 121–26, 129–32
Burton, Edward, 25

Calamy, Edmund, 14, 60, 62, 66, 118, 120, 126, 171
Calvinism, 5, 11, 24, 26, 55, 58, 60, 71–74, 77–79, 83, 87–89, 91, 105, 107, 168, 172
Canceller, James, 79
Catechisms, 27, 34–35, 56, 59, 105, 126, 135–46
Catholics, 22, 26, 35, 45, 48–49, 58, 75, 87, 117, 135, 146, 153, 170
Cautionary tales, 28, 49–51, 81, 85, 118
Caxton, William, 44
Cecil, William (Earl of Burghley), 80
Challoner, Richard, 48–49
Chapbooks, 28, 50–51, 79, 82, 85, 87, 115–16, 118, 132
Chapman, George, 81
Charity schools, 22, 27, 35–39, 64–65, 141, 146–54
Charlton, Kenneth, 100
Chear, Abraham, 127–29
Childhood: defined, 15, 36, 82, 104
Child-rearing manuals. See Advice to parents
Children's books, 23, 25, 32–34, 36, 78–92

Chishull, John, 83
Church Catechism, 137, 141, 145
Clairmont, Jane, 170
Clarke, Samuel, 58–60
Cleaver, Robert, 96–98
Clown, 111–12, 118, 130, 132
Cobbett, Thomas, 76–77
Coleridge, Samuel Taylor, 166, 169
Collinson, Patrick, 10
Comenius, John Amos, 38
Conversion, 11, 26, 28, 48–49, 52, 55–62, 66–71, 74–75, 77, 83–84, 87, 90, 100, 105, 107, 145, 162, 165–66, 170
Cotton, John, 59, 77, 141
Courtesy literature, 25, 27, 31, 35, 79–81, 86, 92
Covenant theology, 11, 30, 71–78, 164–65, 172
Croke, Charles, 50
Cromwell, Oliver, 13, 68, 118–20
Crossman, Samuel, 35
Crowley, Robert, 79
Cruso, Timothy, 33, 89, 147

Death, 28, 31–32, 45–46, 49–50, 52–57, 61, 63–64, 67, 74, 87, 89, 101, 105, 116, 122, 131
Defoe, Daniel, 33, 105, 147, 149, 153–54
Deists, 143
Delany, Paul, 67
DeMause, Lloyd, 6
Demography, 4, 32
Demos, John, 6
Dent, Arthur, 138
Depravity. See Original sin
Despair, 28, 61–62, 68, 82
Discipline, 29, 93–106

Dissenters, 10–15, 17, 22, 25, 27,
    30–31, 33, 35, 37, 39, 50, 55–62,
    66–68, 76, 85–87, 91–92, 105–6,
    118, 125, 141, 145–54, 157, 161,
    166, 168–72
Downing, Joseph, 64–65
Durston, Christopher, 165

Education, 23–24, 34, 36–40, 85,
    100, 102, 105, 120, 126, 135–54,
    171
Edward VI, 45, 67
Edwards, Jonathan, 76
Edwards, Thomas, 151
Egerton, Stephen, 137
Election. *See* Predestination
Eliot, John, 55
Ellis, Clement, 125
Elyot, Thomas, 95, 104
Emblems, 116
Enlightenment, 39
Erasmus, 45, 136
Evangelicals, 59, 75, 77, 88, 100,
    102
Evelyn, John, 7, 105
Execution, 51, 85

Family authority, 9, 13, 17–18, 22,
    29, 46, 92–93, 95, 97, 100, 126,
    157–73
Fenner, Dudley, 74–75
Fifth-Monarchists, 114
Foxe, John, 45, 67, 81
France, 4, 22, 38, 58, 63–65, 142,
    152, 166, 169
Franklin, Benjamin, 56
Freud, Sigmund, 113
Fuller, Thomas, 46, 58

Gay, John, 38
Gibbon, Edward, 39
Girls, 16, 44, 46, 50–55, 59–60, 63–
    64, 80–82, 97, 103, 115, 118,
    127–31
Godwin, William, 56, 166, 168–70
Golden Legend, The, 44, 49
Gouge, Thomas, 35
Gouge, William, 32, 35, 98
Granger, Thomas, 114
Greenham, Richard, 32, 94–95
Greven, Philip, 7–8
Grey, Lady Jane, 45, 67

Hagiography, 44, 48–49, 51, 53, 68
Hamond, George, 33
Hanmer, Jonathan, 33
Haroutunian, Joseph, 78
Harris, Benjamin, 57
Hell, 14, 82, 84, 88–89, 106, 115,
    119, 127–28
Herbert, George, 140
Heywood, Oliver, 89
Heywood, Thomas, 81
Hobbes, Thomas, 38
Hogarth, William, 81
Holland, Norman, 116
Home, Henry (Lord Kames), 38
Hooker, Thomas, 77
Humanists, 24–25, 38, 44–46, 58,
    79–80, 83, 93–98, 101, 104, 137
Hume, David, 38
Humor, 17, 27, 111–32; opposition
    to, 118–19, 122, 125, 127,
    129–30, 132

Independents, 112, 115, 118, 132
Individualism, 68, 71–74, 78, 111,

Individualism (*continued*)
  157–59, 161, 164–65, 168,
  170–71
Infant depravity. *See* Original sin
Innocence, 26, 30, 32, 36, 40, 48–
  49, 55, 62–63, 91–92, 101, 107,
  131

Jacobins. *See* Radicals
Jail, 31, 51, 63, 129
Janeway, James, 5, 31, 51, 55–57,
  62, 84, 101, 126, 168
Jansenists, 39
Jermin, Michael, 26
Jessey, Henry, 53
Jesuits, 39, 146
Jesus, 91–92, 142, 159–61, 163
Jews, 64–65, 72, 117, 160–62
Joceline, Elizabeth, 80–81
Jole, William, 27
Jonson, Ben, 21, 81
Josselin, Ralph, 29

Keach, Benjamin, 122, 125, 127,
  129
Ken, Thomas, 90
Kidder, Richard, 35, 90

La Chalotais, Louis René de
  Caradeuc de, 38
Lactantius, 162
Lawrence, Edward, 85, 89
Leigh, Dorothy, 80
Lloyd, David, 47–48
Locke, John, 32, 38, 96, 100–104,
  107, 142–45, 150
London, 33, 35, 120, 153
Love. *See* Sympathy for children
Lusts. *See* Sin

Luther, 163
Lye, Thomas, 140

Macfarlane, Alan, 6, 29
Mackintosh, James, 169
Mandeville, Bernard, 37–38
Manners, 25, 80, 94, 97, 104, 166
Marcus, Leah, 24
Marprelate, Martin, 112, 114
Marston, John, 81
Martyrdom. *See* Persecution
Mather, Cotton, 57
Matthews, William, 66–67
Maynard, John, 83
Mead, Matthew, 33, 36, 89
Methodists, 5, 39, 59
Millenarianism, 54–55, 63–64, 167
Milton, John, 164, 168, 170
Moralism, 71, 78, 81, 88, 90–91,
  122, 142
More, Thomas, 95
Morgan, Edmund, 165
Mothers, 100
Movements, 9–13, 16–18, 22, 24–
  25, 29, 181 (n. 48), 37, 39, 58,
  61–62, 64, 86, 88, 96, 107, 112,
  157–66, 171–72

Naming, 21–23, 104
New England Primer, 79
Nowell, Alexander, 137
Nursing, 93, 97–98

Obedience. *See* Family authority
Original sin, 7, 12, 28–30, 32, 43,
  78, 83–85, 101
Osborne, Francis, 25, 38

Paget, John, 138
Paine, Thomas, 39, 166–68, 171
Palmer, Herbert, 34–35, 59, 139
Palmer, Samuel, 147–49
Patrick, Simon, 35, 90
Peck, Samuel, 36
Penn, William, 92
Perkins, William, 58, 75
Persecution, 45–46, 49, 53, 62–63, 79
Peters, Hugh, 118–20, 130
Pietism, 38, 64
Play, 56, 61, 63, 65, 93–94, 100–101, 103, 105–6, 129–30
Plays, 27, 52, 81, 106, 120–22
Pollock, Linda, 8, 14
Popple, William, 142–43, 145, 152
Powell, Thomas, 122–23
Prayer, 54–56, 59–60, 126
Precocity, 31, 183 (n. 11), 48, 52, 57, 60, 64
Predestination, 11–12, 51–52, 73, 75–76, 78–79, 87–88, 97
Premonitions. *See* Prophecy
Presbyterians, 23–24, 49, 132, 147, 149, 151
Priestley, Joseph, 152, 166, 168, 171
Profanity, 56, 61–62, 82, 106
Prophecy, 44, 47–48, 54, 58, 63–64, 152
Psychological interpretations, 6, 28–33, 179 (n. 33), 39–43, 53, 64, 73, 78, 83, 96, 107, 113, 172
Punishment. *See* Discipline
Puritanism: defined, 9, 11–12

Quakers, 14, 25, 31, 39, 54–55, 62–63, 91–92, 121, 127, 131, 135, 143, 165

Radicals, 16–17, 22, 37–39, 56, 157, 165–72
Raleigh, Walter, 25, 47, 80
Ranters, 114
Realism, 43, 49, 51, 53–54, 57–58, 60, 62, 67–68, 81, 107
Rebellion, 29, 84–85, 96, 99, 102, 107
Reformation, 5, 24, 67, 81, 150, 163
Rejection of children, 28, 32
Repression of children, 26, 30, 68, 80, 90–92
Restoration of 1660, 10, 14, 26, 31, 52, 55, 76, 113, 115, 120, 123, 132, 140, 146
Revelations, 53–54, 63
Revolution of 1688, 14, 27, 146–47
Reyner, Edward, 114
Reynolds, Thomas, 149
Romantics, 39
Ronksley, William, 27
Rousseau, Jean-Jacques, 38, 104
Rowe, Thomas, 152
Russell, Robert, 27, 88, 125–26
Ryther, John, 84

Sabbath, 55–56, 61, 88, 93, 106
Sacheverell, Henry, 147–48, 150
Sadism, 5, 12, 14–15, 29–31, 98. *See also* Psychological interpretations
Salmon, Nathaniel, 66
Salvation, 26, 50, 71, 76, 85, 142
Satan, 54, 116, 118, 122–23, 139
Savage, Thomas, 51
Savile, George (Marquis of Halifax), 25, 27
Schism Bill, 148–53
Scotland, 23–24
Seager, Francis, 79

Sectarianism, 10, 13, 25, 39, 91, 112, 121, 127, 151, 157, 165, 172
Secularization, 16, 22, 38–39, 66–67, 166
Semi-Pelagians, 26, 84, 88, 90, 101
Sentimentality, 30, 84, 101
Sermons, 27, 33, 49, 61, 73, 87–88, 118–19, 125–27, 153
Shakespeare, William, 9, 45, 80
Shaw, Samuel, 27, 120–21
Shelley, Mary, 170
Sherman, Thomas, 121, 125
Shower, John, 147
Sibbes, Richard, 75
Sin, 25–29, 34, 50, 58–59, 61, 66, 68, 84–87, 90–91, 104, 122
Sloane, William, 23, 25–27, 49–51, 79
Smith, Henry, 80
Smith, J. A. W., 152
Smith, Robert, 79, 131
Southey, Robert, 169
Steele, Richard, 149–51
Smythies, William, 90–91
Societies for the Reformation of Manners, 16, 65
Society for Promoting Christian Knowledge, 16, 66
Society for the Propagation of the Gospel, 16
Socinians. *See* Unitarians
Spoiling children, 58, 93, 97, 101–3
Stanhope, Philip (Earl of Chesterfield), 27, 39
Stone, Lawrence, 6–7, 191 (n. 69)
Swaddling, 93, 98
Swift, Jonathan, 148
Sympathy for children, 30, 72–73, 76–77, 82, 94, 96–99, 101

Tabula rasa, 83, 99–101
Talbot, James, 36
Tave, Stuart, 111, 115
Taylor, Gordon Rattray, 5–6, 14
Taylor, Jeremy, 5, 101
Thomas, Keith, 47, 114
Thompson, E. P., 14
Tillotson, John, 35
Todd, Margo, 9
Toilet-training, 29
Tombes, John, 76
Traditionalism, 9, 158–59, 162, 164–65
Trenchard, John, 37–38
Trenchfield, Caleb, 28

Unitarians, 135, 142–43, 148, 168–69
Ursinus, Zacharias, 74–75

Vann, Richard, 165
Vernon, John, 52
Verses, 25, 27, 81–82, 87, 127–31
Victorians, 15, 30, 32, 62, 101
Vincent, Thomas, 33, 83
Visions. *See* Revelations
Voltaire, 38

Wake, William, 153
Walker, John, 66
Wallis, John, 139–40
Walton, Izaak, 46
Watkins, Owen, 67
Watts, Isaac, 129, 131, 141, 143–44, 151
Weeping, 50, 54, 56, 63, 84
Wesley, Charles, 127
Wesley, John, 60, 106, 127, 148
Wesley, Samuel, 107, 147–48

Wesley, Susannah, 103, 106
Westminster Catechisms, 34,
    139–41
White, Thomas, 28, 57, 84, 88, 126
Williams, Daniel, 28, 86–88, 99
Wilson, John, 81

Wollstonecraft, Mary, 170
Woodward, Josiah, 35–36, 65–66,
    91
Wordsworth, William, 169
Wright, Louis, 23
Wrightson, Keith, 8